More praise for

THE HUNT FOR HISTORY

"In another life, I want to be Nathan Raab, living with our most celebrated heroes of the past. In *The Hunt for History*, we get a firsthand look at a time traveler, document detective, and historical harvester as he mines for—and often procures—lost treasures. Raab describes the intriguing business side of the deals, but he's also a historian with a passion for his subjects and a true appreciation of their context."

—Dan Abrams, coauthor of *Lincoln's Last Trial* and *Theodore Roosevelt for the Defense*

"Like a combination short-story collection by Agatha Christie and reminiscence by Robert Caro, this leading autograph dealer's memoir boasts a trove of mystery leavened with a good deal of illuminating history. . . . Like John Hancock writing in large, bold letters, I would mark this book: 'Highly recommended.' "

—Harold Holzer, author of *Lincoln at Cooper Union*

"Chasing down historical documents is always fascinating. It's doubly fascinating when keen-eyed prospectors like Nathan Raab find the rare gleaming diamonds of our common past. This is a book of captivating adventures. It's great fun to read."

—Richard Rhodes, author of *The Making of the Atomic Bomb*

"An absorbing narration of Raab's adventures as a rare documents dealer. His account underscores the richness of our heritage, adding intriguing footnotes to the history we thought we knew."

—Susan Eisenhower, president of
the Eisenhower Group and author
of *Breaking Free* and *Mrs. Ike*

"*The Hunt for History* fascinates with its stories of tracking down rare artifacts from America's past. Over the years, Raab's discoveries of personal belongings and documents associated with Lincoln, Edison, JFK, and Churchill have made international news. His track record as an antiquarian, restorer, curator, and field researcher is extraordinary. This book is highly recommended!"

—Douglas Brinkley, professor of history at
Rice University and author of *American Moonshot:*
John F. Kennedy and the Great Space Race

"For those who collect—or just care about—the artifacts of history, Nathan Raab offers a compelling account of his wide-ranging adventures: absorbing journeys into the past that teach valuable lessons. A terrific feat of storytelling, *The Hunt for History* will forever change the way you think about the events that have shaped our current reality."

—Daniel Weiss, president and CEO
of The Metropolitan Museum of Art

THE HUNT *for* HISTORY

On the Trail of the World's Lost Treasures—from the Letters of Lincoln, Churchill, and Einstein to the Secret Recordings Onboard JFK's Air Force One

---

NATHAN RAAB

WITH LUKE BARR

SCRIBNER

New York London Toronto Sydney New Delhi

Scribner
An Imprint of Simon & Schuster, Inc.
1230 Avenue of the Americas
New York, NY 10020

First Scribner hardcover edition March 2020

SCRIBNER and design are registered trademarks of The Gale Group, Inc., used under license by Simon & Schuster, Inc., the publisher of this work.

For information about special discounts for bulk purchases, please contact Simon & Schuster Special Sales at 1-866-506-1949 or business@simonandschuster.com.

The Simon & Schuster Speakers Bureau can bring authors to your live event. For more information or to book an event, contact the Simon & Schuster Speakers Bureau at 1-866-248-3049 or visit our website at www.simonspeakers.com.

Interior design by Kyle Kabel

Manufactured in the United States of America

1 3 5 7 9 10 8 6 4 2

Library of Congress Control Number: 2019024822

ISBN 978-1-5011-9890-8
ISBN 978-1-5011-9892-2 (ebook)

INSERT PHOTOGRAPH CREDITS:

p. 3: Ernest Hemingway, © CORBIS/Corbis via Getty Images; p. 3: Ronald Reagan and Patti Davis, Everett Collection Inc/Alamy Stock Photo; p. 4: George Washington, Everett Collection Historical/Alamy Stock Photo; p. 5: Winston Churchill, Time Life Pictures/Mansell/The LIFE Picture Collection via Getty Images; p. 6: young inventor Thomas Edison, Bettmann Archive via Getty Images; p. 7: Amelia Earhart, Bettmann Archive via Getty Images; p. 7: John F. Kennedy, photo by Art Rickerby/The LIFE Picture Collection via Getty Images; p. 8: Martin Luther King Jr., Associated Press

For Karen and Elizabeth

Contents

Preface

In 1849, my great-great-grandfather Charles Vaughn Houston boarded a ship in Boston, an ambitious young man bound for the California gold rush. He rounded the Horn at Tierra del Fuego and landed in San Francisco. He traveled to the gold fields and worked them until 1855, when he took the gold he'd found by ship to Panama, and from there began a hazardous, yellow-fever-periled land trip across the isthmus. A vessel brought him back to Maine, where he married his sweetheart, Sophronia Ann Potter. It took him years to accumulate that gold, a product of his own growing expertise, his efforts, and a lot of luck.

I've often thought of how many times he must have struck ground in failure, searching a rugged landscape, panning in riverbeds, looking for treasure, seeing a speck and wondering what lay below it, what more was hidden. His "white whale" would have been to tap into some dazzling vein of gold that wound deep into the earth. I don't know if he ever found such a thing, but I do know he came back from the gold fields well-to-do. One artifact is left in the family from this period: a gold nugget that Houston found in California. Maybe it was his first find.

I'm on a different kind of hunt. I'm searching for history, for relics of the past, for historical documents and artifacts, for the significant, even the priceless—priceless in the sense of importance, not merely value. Then I do my best to acquire these items for our firm, the Raab Collection, and offer them for sale to the public.

PREFACE

A newly found box in a Maine attic with twenty letters written by Alexander Hamilton; a handwritten address given by George Washington; the pilot's landing certificate form filled out and signed by Amelia Earhart when she became the first woman to fly the Atlantic; an American flag carried to the moon and back by Neil Armstrong; an unpublished letter written by Albert Einstein discussing the theory of relativity.

Each day, people from all over the world contact us looking to understand what they have, what it might be worth, and how to sell it. Every day, I sift through dozens of historical documents and artifacts, looking for a few gems. Some are valuable, but many aren't. Some are authentic, some aren't. In the former cases, I am the bearer of good tidings; in the latter cases, I am the wrecker of dreams. No, unfortunately, that Abraham Lincoln letter you bought online is not real. No, the book personally inscribed by Mahatma Gandhi in the early 1970s is also not real. He died in 1948.

I'm searching for those elusive remnants of past lives, forever looking to some undiscovered horizon. In that sense, I'm a seeker of people, of the great characters that shaped history. The moment of discovery, when it comes, is sublime and causes everything else to fade into insignificance. The English Romantic poet John Keats captured the feeling in the sonnet "On First Looking into Chapman's Homer": "Then felt I like some watcher of the skies / When a new planet swims into his ken; / Or like stout Cortez when with eagle eyes / He star'd at the Pacific—and all his men / Look'd at each other with a wild surmise— / Silent, upon a peak in Darien."

I have come to know that feeling. That moment when all of history comes rushing forward into the present.

Each day brings new hope, a renewed thrill of discovery; it's the reason we're in this business in the first place. It never gets old. The contours of discovery are always changing, and each day the texture of discovery—the rarity and significance of the artifacts, the size and origin of the collection—varies. An original survey of land in Concord, Massachusetts, drawn up by Henry David Thoreau; a letter from

Gandhi saying he believes in Jesus; a George Washington letter from the winter encampment of Valley Forge; a letter from Churchill from his underground war rooms thanking the Americans for helping the British in their fight against Hitler. My great-great-grandfather had to sift and sift and sift before finding a single nugget of gold, and we do the same, in the hopes of finding historical treasures.

In my fifteen years in this business, first as apprentice and now running the daily operations, I have found many. I've also been met with disappointment: forgeries, great collections that the owner wouldn't sell, stolen artifacts. I once had to tell Gerald Ford's nephew that his signed photograph of his uncle was a reproduction. That was weird, made no less so by the man's uncanny resemblance to the former president.

But when you find the real deal, the excitement is palpable. And just as my ancestor Houston must have dreamed of tapping into a deep vein of gold, hitting the mother lode, so do we. I dream of some large historical find, something no one else has seen in eons, a vast trove of significant documents, letters, or objects—a find that changes our view of history itself. Perhaps a single family has held on to such a collection for generations and only discovered it now, hidden away in a basement, a stunning legacy handed down from early America.

Late in the day a couple of years ago—one of those perfect spring afternoons that can tempt you into sneaking out of the office early—I was looking at my watch and thinking about heading home and taking my bike out for a spin when the phone rang.

A soft-spoken man with a gentle southern accent, let's call him Bill Crawford, was on the line, calling from Mississippi. Bill claimed—without pomp, without flair, without even changing the subdued inflection in his voice—to own some letters and other pieces passed down from William H. Crawford, his great-great-great-great-grandfather.

Crawford may be one of the more important individuals in American history that few people have ever heard of. He may be *the* most important: James Madison's minister to France during the rule of Napoléon and King Louis XVIII, then Madison's secretary of war and Monroe's secretary of the treasury, friend and adviser to various presidents going back to Jefferson, US senator from Georgia, and a plausible presidential candidate in 1824. He was one of the first major political figures with roots in the Deep South. James Madison turned to Crawford to head up his European diplomatic corps during the negotiations to end the War of 1812, a continents-wide conflict that tested America's global presence for the first time. Crawford's national rise was cut short by a stroke that sidelined him, but no account of the era can be written without him. He was a central figure.

All thoughts of my late-afternoon bike ride evaporated in an instant.

Was this guy for real? We entertain a lot of claims about documents that have little or no chance of being valid. Prime example: I've lost track of how often people have offered me a previously unknown copy of the Gettysburg Address in the president's own hand, *not*—the claim goes—a facsimile. The five known copies of this document include the two Lincoln wrote around the time of the speech and three others afterward, for various purposes. What are the chances that the next claim will actually deliver a sixth and unknown draft? The same thing happens with the Declaration of Independence and the US Constitution. I don't even ask to see a copy of these alleged treasures. Normally, the people who have copies, forgeries, or second-rate material are the most vociferous in claiming authenticity and importance.

"I will find out where you live and come to your house. That's what you deserve," one man recently threatened. He couldn't believe that his John Hancock document was worth $4,000 and not $1 million.

The finest historical discoveries enter a room with a whisper; rarely do they come heralded by choirs of angels. That is what makes the hunt such an all-encompassing endeavor. The more claims of authenticity, the more certificates of authenticity, the more sleight of hand might be at play.

Now, this gentleman in Mississippi, whose voice required full volume on my phone to be heard, wasn't alleging that he had such priceless material, but he was making a major claim indeed.

"I really like this Jefferson letter about the War of 1812," he told me.

He read me one line: "'It may be thought that useless blood was spilt at New Orleans, after the treaty of peace had been actually signed and ratified. I think it had many valuable uses. It proved . . . that New Orleans can be defended both by land and water; that the Western country will fly to its relief . . . that our militia are heroes when they have heroes to lead them on.'"

Nice letter.

"I have others," he said. And he listed names: Jefferson, Madison, Monroe, Lafayette, Clay, the Duke of Wellington, John Marshall, and many more.

"How many pieces do you have?" I asked.

"Oh, I'd say a few hundred."

A collection that big, and held in one family, and never before seen all these many years: it was a potential gold mine. In the nineteenth century, such large family accumulations were "discovered" with some frequency. In the late twentieth century and now in the twenty-first, they almost never surface. I was deeply skeptical, but if he had even half of what he said he did, this trove would be one of the greatest American historical treasures to come to light in at least a generation. It could be worth millions.

A spring thunderstorm roiled the skies—far enough away for our plane to dodge, close enough to be beautiful—as my father, my wife, Karen, and I approached the small regional airport closest to Crawford's rural home. We were headed to a conference room in a local bank to meet him.

He'd sent us an inventory of the supposed collection, and seven primitive photocopies of specific documents. Skepticism serves us well in this business, but we decided that he might have something special. Indeed, I was excited, on edge, filled with a sense of nervous anticipation. We might well encounter a pile of photocopies, Bill could be mistaken, but I was convinced he was sincere, so we'd rolled the dice and boarded a plane.

The following morning, Bill was waiting in the lobby of the bank, wearing khaki pants and a button-down shirt. We shook hands and exchanged pleasantries as we assessed one another. He led us upstairs to a conference room, where his wife, let's call her Jane, was seated at the circular wooden table that took up half the room. Jane rose and we shook hands; another round of pleasantries and assessments. My own: this nice couple was straight out of a Norman Rockwell painting, totally well-meaning.

We poured ourselves coffee. They both put on pairs of white gloves. Ugh. To us, this is something of a red flag, a tactic used by unscrupulous dealers to get unsophisticated buyers to pay more for minor documents. The image of such gloves—white, of course—as the vaunted protectors of our historical legacy is deeply ingrained in the collective imagination. The white-glove-wearing expert appears in movies and books all the time, most recently (at least for me) in an episode of *Pawn Stars* during which a trained archivist carefully removed a centuries-old historical document from its resting place and gently handed it to a celebrity to examine. They both wore what they assumed to be the all-important white gloves. The reality is that, with paper documents, gloves inhibit the dexterity required when handling the old paper. You're more likely to rip the document or bend it while wearing gloves of any sort. White cotton gloves are also more likely to sop up sweat and other oils that can then be *transferred to* the document. And small fibers from the gloves can be left behind and filed away with the document. So no gloves, please. They're counterproductive. Washing gets the oil off the hands, drying dries them.

The gloves came off.

What lay before us was a mystery, but we were about to find out if Bill had anything of value and, if so, how deep the vein ran.

Bill had arrived early and removed whatever he had from the large vault in the basement of the bank and transferred the material to a locked cabinet in the conference room. He took the bank's silver key from in front of us and walked over to the cabinet.

This man had either conned us big-time, was not smart enough to know that what he had was fake, or was sitting on a historical treasure trove the likes of which hadn't reached the market since before my father was born.

These moments of anticipation can be the harbinger of true discovery or of dejection, where you stand on the precipice of something new and unknown. You look over the edge at what lies below.

He turned the key to the right a half tick, the lock opened, and he swung the cabinet open.

PART I

APPRENTICE

CHAPTER 1

Early Days: Babe Ruth and Teddy Roosevelt

My dad was born a collector. He collected baseball cards, he collected old newspapers, he owned a suitcase used by Abraham Lincoln's vice president Hannibal Hamlin. My dad loved to tell me about that suitcase, and how he received it from his uncle who'd known Hamlin's son. But most of all we bonded over baseball. He loved baseball, and so did I. The game itself, of course—the Philadelphia Phillies—and all the ephemera surrounding the game too.

He would take me to the local baseball-card store—Mike's Collectibles, now long gone—and to the baseball-card shows that came through town every so often. These would inevitably take place in a windowless local hotel ballroom or in a vast, charmless event space filled with a frenzy of collectors, dealers, and baseball stars signing memorabilia piled up on folding tables. Nothing about any of it was glamorous, and I loved it all. The shows were exciting, and going to them with my dad, just the two of us, made them even more special.

I met my heroes, the sports celebrities I idolized. Even if it was only for a few seconds: you shake their hand, you give them your name, they sign a baseball or a photo or a baseball card or whatever you have with you. It was thrilling. I remember Pete Rose, who was nice, and Von Hayes, who couldn't have cared less that I was his biggest fan ever—and the Phillies needed fans. He was just rude. I met

Sandy Koufax. I'm pretty sure Mark McGwire's was the first autograph I ever got. I still have all those baseball cards and autographs.

And all around us, at those shows, the dealers sold other things as well, older material—signed photos of Lou Gehrig or Babe Ruth, for example. Behind one table hung a photo of the Bambino, signed at the bottom. This dealer had two display cases that spanned his folding tables and a board behind him that allowed for items to be hung. I went looking for baseball cards in his glass case. Then I turned and looked up to witness a hushed conversation between my father and the seller. My father seemed fixated on the photograph. He bought me a card I wanted, I don't remember which, and he also bought the signed photograph of Babe Ruth.

"Don't tell Mom what I spent on this," he said as he tucked the photo into his briefcase.

"Okay." I smiled.

That was the first autograph I saw my dad buy. I was about eight. I think it cost $300.

This was the late 1980s. I had no real interest in the hobby, broadly speaking. My father was a lawyer, not an autograph dealer, and I was trying to make it through school. But I just loved being part of it with him, going to the shows.

For him, unbeknownst to me, what began as an impulsive purchase at a baseball-card show would sprout roots. His mind strayed more and more often from his legal business; he looked at his legal papers with one eye on the latest dealer catalog. And what had started with baseball soon encompassed his true passion: history.

My father would pick me up after school, and he'd have the latest Topps box set of baseball cards, and I'd sit and go through them and pick out the cards I liked. He'd also buy me baseball-card guides, which we would go through to see what the cards we had were worth.

Looking back, it was through those baseball-card shows and the world of sports collectibles that my father nurtured his budding activity. He learned that historical things could be bought and sold too, just like sports memorabilia.

For me, the two worlds of sports and history continued to blend into one pot. One of the first books I read was called *The Glory of Their Times*, by Lawrence Ritter. This recounted the stories of the first professional baseball players, in their own words: early twentieth-century baseball—pre–Babe Ruth—and what that was like. I read the autobiography of Nolan Ryan, the great pitcher. I think the first bet I ever made was with my dad: I won $6 when the Mets beat the Red Sox in the World Series in 1986, which was the year of Billy Buckner. I was losing that bet until the very end.

We had season tickets to the Phillies; my dad was proud of that. He would bring autograph catalogs and read them during the games. By now he was collecting autographs and documents related to American political and military history. He didn't know it yet, but those Phillies games—including one in which we saw Doug Drabek come within one pitch of a no-hitter only to give up a single to Sil Campusano—were his proving ground, his training. I imagine he thought of that reading as a pleasant diversion from stressful legal work. But really he was in his own minor leagues.

A grandson of immigrants from Eastern Europe, my father grew up in Bradley Beach, near Asbury Park, New Jersey. He was a beach brat. His interest in history was long-standing: his father bought him things like antique rifles and other trinkets when the family could afford them, which wasn't often. When my father had the chance to pass this love on to his kids, he did so wholeheartedly, or attempted to. Our bedtime stories were tales from ancient Sparta and Rome. My dad wore the full Union officer's uniform for Halloween (and, embarrassingly for us, at other times). In the closet—but also frequently atop his head—was an iconic tricornered hat from the Revolutionary War. We visited Churchill's underground war rooms in London. That same trip, we brought home pieces of Lord Nelson's vessel, the HMS *Victory*. On July 4, when the other kids went to the Jersey shore, our family motored west to Gettysburg, equipped with maps and guides. We made this trip often, along with visits to other historical sites such as Old Sturbridge Village in Massachusetts, where he once promised to give me $5 if I could memorize the first ten Roman emperors, which I did. This might have been the first time I made money with my historical knowledge.

He didn't just want us to be present. He wanted us to get into it, to feel it. He was passionate, and he wanted to pass that passion along.

Nowhere else was this attempt to light our fires on display as vividly as at Gettysburg. We'd pile in the car and then cram into a single hotel room once we got there. During the days, we'd re-create the war on foot. My dad would pace the fields where Confederate general George Pickett's men marched to obliteration against Union general George Meade's men: Pickett's Charge. My father didn't just take us to the top of Little Round Top. Together we walked the steps of Joshua Lawrence Chamberlain and the Twentieth Maine in the woods behind the summit. Chamberlain protected the Union flank. My dad would tear up at moments like this, particularly when recollecting some brave act by some long-dead historical figure. Such was the powerful hold history had on him. It wasn't abstract or purely intellectual: it was deeply emotional.

With my dad's coaxing, my brother Jonas and I combed the battlefields, hoping to discover actual bullets that had been fired at the bloodiest battle ever on American soil. And we did discover them. I remember being at Little Round Top, age seven or eight, where an area of grass and moss stretched down over the hill, toward Devil's Den, a collection of glacial boulders where the Confederates camped out, and my dad encouraging me and my brother to go digging around. We'd complain, "We don't see anything!" And he'd say, "Oh, keep looking—you might want to try over there."

We'd invariably find something. Only years later did I learn that my dad had bought these bullets at a local antiques store, probably for fifty cents apiece, and planted them for us to find, just as his own father had done for him. It was his way of connecting us with history in a real and tangible way.

My parents encouraged me to write letters to famous people, in hopes they'd write me back. My dad was already instructing me back then: the trick, he told me, was to say something nice, something flattering, ask something interesting, and let them know that I was a kid. So when I wrote to Richard Nixon, I asked him about opening up China. I got plenty of form letters from these people in return, but I also got real letters. Colin Powell, who would later rise to prominence as secretary of state, was then a general in the First Gulf War. He wrote me back, explaining that George C. Marshall was his greatest inspiration. He wrote of hard work, and dedication to mission.

I asked James Watson, who, along with Francis Crick, had discovered the building blocks of DNA, to draw me a double helix, which he did. I then, with my father's encouragement, sent that drawing to Francis Crick, with whom Watson had shared the Nobel Prize, and Crick also signed it. I was reading *Jurassic Park*, and Crick wrote me his opinion on the cloning of dinosaurs, something that's still a relevant topic of conversation. Matt Groening drew me a picture of the Simpsons.

For me, this was all in fun. I'd wait for the mailman with building anticipation, hoping for answers to my letters. For my dad, it was becoming a business. When he looked to sell his collection and buy better stuff, he advertised in a local publication and found active buyers. Seemingly by chance, he now had a business of sorts. He found himself spending as much time studying autographs and documents as he did working in his law practice. He set up an informal office off our kitchen, which often spilled over into the living room, and I spent many evening hours sitting in my pajamas stuffing hundreds of catalogs into the bulk mail sacks for delivery to the post office. My father's early catalogs advertised autographs for as little as $30. My mother designed the catalogs herself. It was a family operation.

When other dealer catalogs arrived, life was put on hold as my dad flipped through, page by page. Back then there were numerous dealers, and in a world where mail was delivered at varying intervals, where you might or might not have a jump start on your competitors, speed was paramount. Hesitation could be the difference between buying and losing out. The intensity and focus of those moments, as he went through the offerings, filled the room.

By the mid-1990s, my parents decided to go all in on the autograph business. They would do this full-time. The main barriers to entering the field—capital for inventory and marketing—were significant but not the barriers they are today. The initial capitalization for Steven S. Raab Autographs & Historic Memorabilia was a mere $4,500. My parents never considered the possibility of failure; they jumped in full force.

By that time, I was off to college and out of the loop, although the business continued growing, sort of the background music of my youth. One of the first autographs I remember my dad buying for his new business, when I was around twenty, was by Theodore Roosevelt, and my dad bought it from an old-school dealer, Robert Batchelder. I met him once; he had an office in Ambler, Pennsylvania, in an old bank building. He helped build many of the great twentieth-century collections. My dad had spotted in one of Batchelder's printed catalogs a letter from Roosevelt to his friend Henry Sprague, a New York assemblyman. The letter was typed on "State of New York / Executive Chambers" letterhead and dated January 26, 1900, when TR was the governor of that state. Referring to a political battle, the letter read in part:

> I have always been fond of the West African proverb: "Speak softly and carry a big stick; you will go far." If I had not carried the big stick, the organization would not have gotten behind me, and if I had yelled and blustered, as Pankhurst and the similar dishonest lunatics desired, I would not have had ten votes.

Some men and women stride across an era. Victoria gave her name to an age, Alexander and Napoléon to empires. And Roosevelt, with these words, launched a period of American leadership. He took a young country, still recovering from a devastating war that had ripped at the social and economic fabric, and through strength of will crafted an American century. No other American figure has uttered more defining words or put pen to paper in a more representative way.

The letter was priced at $4,500, fairly high for the time but not indicative of anything really special, my dad thought. But the nice turn of phrase, the reference to the "big stick," caught his attention. Was this the first use of the famous phrase, the first time TR used it? The moment of inspiration? The difference in this case between a casual reference to the "big stick" and its inauguration might be well in excess of $100,000 in what my parents could charge for it. TR might have said it more than once, but there was only one first time. My dad sensed Batchelder had not explored this angle.

Before my father had even finished going through the catalog, he called the dealer's office, found out from the assistant that the letter was still available, and placed a "hold" on it. Such a thing isn't uncommon in a trade that prides itself on its "gentlemen's agreements," where a courtesy hold allows a serious collector to consider and research an item and not lose it while doing so. Then my dad hurried out of his office in Center City, Philadelphia, to the bookstore next door. He asked for a good biography of TR and was handed Edmund Morris's *Rise of Theodore Roosevelt*. Five minutes with its index and the appropriate chapter confirmed that a letter written on January 26, 1900, was indeed the first use of that now-famous phrase. My father jumped in his car. By the time he arrived at the dealer's office, a dozen orders had come in, but his had been the first. One hour after seeing the listing, he owned the letter. This was an early coup. His excitement and collector's instinct outweighed his desire for immediate profit: He decided not to sell it immediately and put this piece in his personal collection and crowed about it.

It's hard to overstate the effect this find had on my parents. The letter would eventually sell for $200,000. My mother, who had come in full-time with my father to run the business, saw in the letter's discovery and immense value a validation of their work and knowledge. She became all the more committed to buying the best. My father's catalogs, once containing hundreds of items priced between $20 and $5,000, now began to showcase fewer pieces at much higher prices.

Joining the family business never occurred to me, not once. I lived in Rome for a while—working with the Associated Press—and returned home to become press secretary for a Connecticut congressman, which was an education in politics and the press. Next I was called on to co-manage communications for a Philadelphia mayoral candidate, Sam Katz. He lost in an election now famous for a federal wiretap of the sitting mayor's office. Fifteen years later, I'm still recovering from this riotous experience. If Katz had won, what would have happened? It's an interesting question for me because his loss represented a crossroads. What was I going to do now? I went into the public relations world full-time. But I hated it.

My dad broached the idea of my joining the business. He said it offered opportunities. And you weren't answering to anyone else. I came in part-time at first. I was noncommittal. I wasn't a collector, and the field had less of an innate pull on me than it did on my father.

He saw it as a passion; I was looking for a job.

I met with a longtime family friend, someone my father had known since he was six. I was now twenty-four. I asked the friend if becoming a lawyer was a smart move; I'd toyed with the idea for years. A prominent Philadelphia lawyer, he explained that practicing law was certainly an option, but that my father's business represented an opportunity for me. "You'll walk into any room as a peer, an equal. And rather than deal as a first-year associate at some law firm with others of equal stature, you'll meet fascinating people and command their respect." That advice stuck with me. I made the leap in 2005, committing full-time. The hunt was on.

* * *

The love of these artifacts is not idolatry. We see the best of our aspirations and motivations reflected in them. Theodore Roosevelt's "big stick" inspired my dad, but also opened the door for my father to see the business more expansively. It became the symbol of what he could build. That first true treasure he owned had showed him that the greatest of all historical documents—true instruments of history—were within his reach. A different TR letter crystallized such a moment in my own career in the business, but for different reasons.

The year was 1903, and TR was president. He embarked on a two-week retreat from politics in Yellowstone Park with a small group of companions, including famed naturalist John Burroughs. This choice of destination surprised no one. America's new president was renowned as a determined man of action, naturalist, big-game hunter, rancher, soldier, and Rough Rider. While most of his security detail and support staff in Yellowstone enjoyed the soft comforts of a nearby hotel, the president bedded down on the ground swaddled in army blankets. He sometimes tramped off for a day by himself in the wilderness, but this man who'd lost his mother and his first wife on the same day—an event that shaped his life—was never far in spirit from his home and family. He often paused during his adventures to write tender letters to his children and second wife, Edith. The letterhead he used on this trip was embossed with the words "Yellowstone Park / Wyoming."

On April 16, he wrote his youngest son, Quentin, or Quenty-Quee. Five years old, the boy was the apple of his father's eye. Many stories about this First Family included reports of Quentin's endearingly rambunctious behavior around the White House. "Dearest Quenty-Quee," his father begins. "I love you very much. Here is a picture of the mule that carries, among other things, my bag of clothes." The note breaks for the simple but effective presidential sketch of the stolid beast. "There are about twenty mules in the pack train. They all follow one another in single file up and down mountain paths and across streams." Signed, "Your loving father."

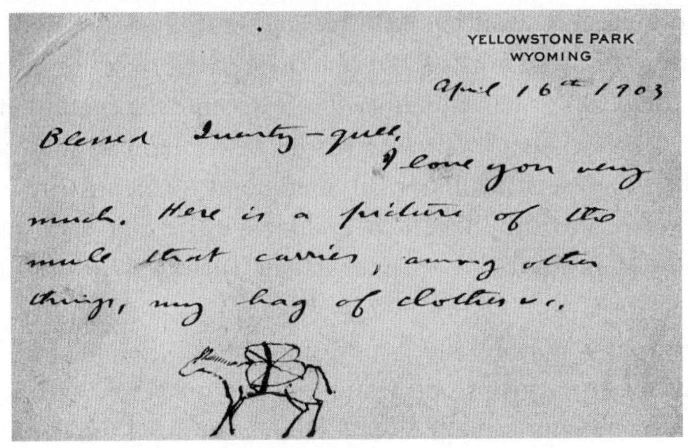

YELLOWSTONE PARK
WYOMING

April 16th 1903

Blessed Quenty-quee,
I love you very much. Here is a picture of the mule that carries, among other things, my bag of clothes &c.

The first page of Roosevelt's letter home to his son, with a drawing of a mule.

A scan of that letter appeared in my in-box one day, forwarded by its owner in the Midwest, who asked if we wanted a "little sketch signed by Theodore Roosevelt."

It seemed just a short note, and at first I made the mistake of glancing past it to the next piece we were considering. But I kept coming back to that email; there was something about TR's note that struck me. I imagined the young recipient in 1903, also living on the East Coast, staring at his father's sketch of the mule. I imagined the president of the United States, on the other side of the country, in the wilderness, indulging in such a loving embrace of his son, and I felt as if I'd caught TR in an uncensored, personal moment, as if he'd reached out from Yellowstone to me and shown me who he was. I recalled hiking with my own parents in the White Mountains of New Hampshire and Acadia National Park in Maine. (Acadia was also one of TR's favorite places.) I'd never had a similar connection to any other piece before. The poignancy of the note felt even more powerful with the knowledge that Quentin died as a twenty-year-old pilot in World War I, shot down on July 14, 1918—Bastille Day, only four months before the Armistice. The news shattered his father, who died six months later at the age of sixty.

"I want this letter," I said. "I think people will care about it." We spent around $7,000, no small sum at the time for a short Roosevelt note and far more than small notes of Roosevelt's sell for even today. Various biographies describe some of Roosevelt's letters to his kids, including some of his Yellowstone notes, but not this one. It was a new discovery.

"I love this. It really gives you a sense of Roosevelt's personality," said JoAnn Loviglio, the AP reporter who was my first call when we were ready to announce the discovery. JoAnn and I were old acquaintances from my time on the mayoral campaign. JoAnn said, "We can see a side of the man we haven't really seen before." When her story hit the wire, it went international.

So how did this piece of history go from Yellowstone to the White House to my desk? As I would learn, the path taken by historical artifacts is idiosyncratic and meandering. "Mrs. Roosevelt, after her husband died, had the unfortunate habit of giving away his letters to close friends," a Roosevelt archivist explained. This particular friend's heirs had decided to sell the gift to us.

CNN invited me on the air to discuss our find. The first call waiting for me back at the office was from the National Park Foundation, which is connected to the National Park Service. They wanted to buy the letter. When I told them that theirs was my first call but wouldn't be the last, they wired the money.

But what did I see in the piece? What is it in the nature of a person or a piece that inspires us? To each, the answer is different. But in 2007, these were questions without answers. They were questions I wasn't asking myself. Piece bought, piece sold, on to the next.

CHAPTER 2

Lessons from My Father

When I came to work for the family business, in my midtwenties, I knew nothing. Yes, I'd grown up going to baseball-card shows with my dad and accompanied him to auctions every once in a while. The business of history was always in the background. But it was just that: in the background. The phone was always ringing, and piles of catalogs and address labels were on the kitchen table, with much talk about what was selling and what wasn't. I tuned out my father's daily talk about autographs coming in and going out, mentions of this client or that, because it wasn't of great interest to me, and he didn't push it on me growing up. Plus, I was older, had my own life. At my mother's urging, my father had given up practicing law and this had become his business, not his hobby.

But now the situation had changed. This was now to be my livelihood too. I needed to learn about the business in general—who our clients were, who was our competition. I needed to learn how to authenticate pieces of history, which would take time, repetition, and attention to detail. In the beginning, I relied entirely on my dad to do this, but I paid attention. There is no school for this. One must, as the German writer Goethe wrote, "submit like a traveler who has to ascend a mountain. If the mountain was not there, the road would be both shorter and pleasanter, but there it is, and he must get over it." There is no substitute for the painstaking elements of time and repetition, no other way over the mountain.

But for the moment, with authentication being taken care of by my father, the project that gave me the most difficulty at first was to recognize value when I saw it. I understood it in a general sense: this was a book from Lincoln's library; this was a letter written by George Washington. But recognizing value and import where others have missed it, being able to sort through all those letters of General Washington's to find the best, is not as obvious as it may seem; it required a more refined eye than I had at that time.

When it came to authenticity and value, only one person could teach me: my father.

At this time, dealer and auction catalogs, physical catalogs, were the marketplace. The internet was active, but most dealers didn't list all their pieces, priced, online. Instead, when a catalog came in the mail, my father would call my attention to it. Joe Rubinfine, for example, a name well-known in our circles, is a historical-document dealer whose parents had been chicken farmers in New Jersey. Joe had caught the history bug early and had been dealing in documents since my father was a kid. Joe's catalogs were nondescript, barely illustrated, simple affairs that garnered great attention in our home. Joe had a style I liked. He didn't need to shout from the mountaintops. The quality of his material demanded respect.

My father would call me in: "Rubinfine's catalog is here." Sometimes my father would point things out to me. I remember when we bought a document signed by Walter Raleigh, he said, "These are really uncommon, Nate." Walter Raleigh, I learned, was a significant figure in Elizabethan England, a great explorer of the Americas and enemy of the Spanish, hero and then villain, prisoner in the Tower of London, and one of the most important Englishmen in history. His autographs are heavy fare, costing good money and going to sophisticated buyers. I knew none of that. Every once in a while my dad would show me something in a catalog—an autograph of Francisco Pizarro, for example, the Spanish conquistador who conquered the Incan empire—and say, "I don't think we should buy this, but you should know that you don't see these very often." Or he'd point to a letter written by Washington on the Constitution. I'd say, "Why did you circle that, it's three hundred thousand dollars—you really want to spend that much?" And he'd say, "No, obviously it's not for us, but I thought you should see it. It is a defense of the Constitution." Why should we care? Well, Washington, separate from having fought the British to win the revolution, was the chair of the 1787 Constitutional Convention, which gave us that seminal document. His copy of the Constitution would set auction records years later, selling to Mount Vernon for $10 million.

I grew up watching my father circle items of interest in dealer catalogs. He'd sit at his desk near the entry to our home, hunched over a pile of catalogs, glasses on, pen in hand, circling, crossing out, writing questions in the margins. The chair would lean back, then go forward with him as he found something of value. In the evenings, he'd spend hours searching dealer websites, looking for things he liked. He was forever on the hunt.

Now I began going through the catalogs myself. We played a game: we'd both go through a catalog circling what we thought was interesting, what was worth discussing. The catalogs were text heavy, printed in black and white, organized by last name. They looked drab, but inside there were incredibly important pieces of history for sale. It was the ultimate test—to find value. My dad's gift for doing this with catalogs and with the items offered by private sellers made him successful.

As I was learning how to authenticate objects and documents, this is how I approached the most challenging element of the business: what gives something value. It would be a decade before I mastered this skill. My father had spent decades reading, absorbing, and I was on year two. But it was a necessary step: circling items in catalogs and comparing what I circled to what my father circled. I'd trust few people to authenticate a George Washington letter. I'd trust even fewer to assign a price or historical value to the piece. Doing so requires a deeper and more profound understanding, not of the date on the page or the signature at the bottom, but of symbolism and meaning. Possessing that understanding, I'm convinced, is the difference between succeeding and failing. So I had work to do. And patience was the currency.

Usually, I'd go first, and I'd pick things that seemed obviously interesting, focusing on the headline provided by the seller. I think that in the first couple of years, I was rarely on point. The things I circled were invariably faulty in some way, because the item wasn't authentic or more likely because my dad's experience had taught him that it wouldn't easily sell, or that it was much more common than you might think.

I remember one example involving a relatively obscure historical figure: Robert Anderson, the hero of Fort Sumter.

Anderson was present at the first battle of the Civil War as commander of the Union fort, which came under assault by the Confederates. He was forced to surrender and did little else of note. His appeal lies mainly in that fateful assault on the fort in South Carolina. I didn't know his name. So I would never have circled a letter by Anderson.

"Nate, did you read it? Do you see what this is?" my dad said, repeating a phrase he would use and still uses routinely in our discussions.

It was a letter by Anderson discussing the attack on Fort Sumter. And the truth is, as I learned, nobody cares about Robert Anderson—*except* in the context of Fort Sumter. This was an important lesson for me. When it comes to assessing value, take the thing that person is associated with and from there evaluate the content. So a historically insignificant letter from Abraham Lincoln sending his autograph might have nominal value. But a letter of his mentioning slavery, the abolition of which is central to his legacy, is likely worth hundreds of thousands of dollars, if not millions. A pen used by Theodore Roosevelt certainly has value. But imagine having his hat when he was a young colonel and hero commanding the Rough Riders during the Spanish-American War. Roosevelt had left his comfortable post and volunteered to fight in battle, earning national fame and vaulting him to the vice presidency and then the presidency.

Here with Anderson, the lesson was this: the historical context matters. Anderson's only major association is Fort Sumter. He was present at the first movement of our nation's only and hopefully last civil war. And people collect that. "They're asking five hundred dollars for a letter from Robert Anderson discussing the assault on Fort Sumter," my dad said. "They obviously don't know what they have."

My father's deep knowledge of history was a backdrop to our discussions.

One of my first visits to see a collection was a drive with my father to New Jersey. We got in the car, check in hand, E-ZPass on the dashboard, and headed up the turnpike, an excruciatingly boring trip. We were going to see a man and his wife who'd inherited a private collection, including a letter from George Washington written in July 1789, a letter he signed as president. We wanted to see it in person, assess the sellers, and so off we went. The letter was short, drawing the attention of the recipient to the enclosed act of Congress, and signed, characteristically, "G:Washington." (He used a colon between the *G* and the *W*.) The collector wanted $25,000. I balked. That's excessive, I thought. Washington was sending an act of Congress as a notification to the governor of Virginia. He did this for every act, thirteen times total, counting each state. In the early days of the country, as Congress passed an act and the president signed it, the federal government had to send a copy of that act to each governor. How else would they know how to comply? Initially, for a short period, Washington did it as president. Soon, his secretary of state Thomas Jefferson took up the job. But this letter we were examining today was signed by Washington.

"Well, that's a nice letter from Washington, and we could use more Washington letters, but didn't he do that thirteen times for every act?" I asked. "And how much more than that are we going to get for it? It's not worth it."

My dad pulled me out of the couple's display room, past the entry to a small hallway. "Do you see what this is?" he said. "Did you read the date?" The letter was dated early July, my father explained, and since the first acts of the first Congress were signed in July of that year, it had to be among the first, he reasoned.

Indeed, research showed that this was one of the first two acts ever passed by Congress of any consequence, giving American customs agents the power to take in revenue from imports. This was before the income tax. The country was in debt from the Revolutionary War, customs was the only way the government made money, and it helped retire that debt and fund the country's operations. This act would prove central to the plan of the first secretary of the treasury: Alexander Hamilton. We bought the document for the $25,000 asking price.

My father had seen the true value of the piece.

I, by contrast, back home at our dining room table, had been arguing in favor of a letter I found online from former president John Quincy Adams, whose father had signed the Declaration of Independence and also served as president, priced at $2,000, in which he mentions July 4.

"I bet we can get eight thousand dollars for that," I said. "This is Adams talking about the Fourth of July."

But no: "He wrote that letter twice a day for five years," my dad said. Adams was a celebrity figure with a connection to 1776, albeit a circuitous one, and every Fourth of July, the old man was bombarded with requests from towns in Massachusetts and nationwide to speak at their Independence Day festivals. He accepted almost none. "That's worth less than they're asking—those things are a dime a dozen."

My dad had circled a letter from Lincoln pardoning a soldier, which was being sold by a fellow dealer, the now-retired and widely respected Catherine Barnes, who maintained her office doors down from my father's Rittenhouse Square law practice.

"Well, this doesn't say much," I said. "It just says, 'Pardon this soldier.'"

And my dad said, "Yes, but people care about Lincoln's clemency, and this letter represents that—and you don't see letters like this from him very often."

Lincoln's character is central to his legacy. Amid the terrors of the war, he understood that his role was to advocate for all American citizens, even those who were led by people who were claiming to be creating a new nation: the Confederacy. He also understood that these weren't ordinary times. His intercession in cases where perhaps some compassion was merited is legendary. Lincoln had a big heart, and a worn one, battered by the position in which he found himself, steward of a nation torn at the seams, husband, father who lost three of his four children during childhood. His clemency is the stuff of legend. And I missed that.

The game continued.

I circled a rather salacious letter from Benjamin Franklin, in which he was complaining about being late to a meeting because he'd had too much opium the day before. It was unusual, and amusing, and priced by the previously mentioned Joe Rubinfine at $25,000. Franklin's letters aren't common, in spite of his well-known and extensive correspondence. Even a basic letter of his will break $15,000. So I figured we had room here. My father disagreed: "You're not going to do any better than that." In retrospect, he was correct. Franklin's legacy is not centered around his love of opium; it's an anecdotal sidelight, a curiosity, albeit a fascinating one. My father's assessment of the value, the hard math, was right.

This initial lesson was to look for the things for which people are best known, admired, areas where we can learn something meaningful about the character of the person. Once we find that, we can usually make the numbers work. Follow the proverbial river to its source.

It would be years before I made the connection between my father's pursuits when I was a child and this lesson: people collect what emotionally affects them, what inspires them. At this stage, this insight came secondhand to me.

My early efforts didn't yield an entirely barren harvest. I can clearly remember the first time I persuaded my dad to buy something out of a catalog, something he'd missed.

Maggs Bros. in London is a historic firm. Back then, the company was a larger force on the autograph scene. They have historically been a vendor to royalty and the business elite. We got a catalog in the mail in Philadelphia, in which a letter from Napoléon caught my attention. Napoléon, the prophet of populist Europe, the scourge of old royalty, once said, "I have always marched with the opinion of the great masses and with events." More than a mere political or military figure, Napoléon was an idea—the embodiment of a movement.

I assumed that since we were getting the catalog now, Europeans had been picking from it for a week. This letter was written to his minister of war in 1807 and was priced at £5,000, which is quite a lot of money for a Napoléon letter. You might think the emperor's letters would be universally valuable. They're universally desired, but that isn't the same as valuable. The demand for his autograph is high, but the supply meets it head-on: Napoléon signed many, many things, sometimes as many as fifteen to twenty letters per day. He is reported to have dictated multiple letters at the same time. Not all these survive, but he must have gone through a lot of ink.

With this one, I applied some of the lessons I'd been learning: Who was the recipient, what was the date, what did it say? I was aided by my knowledge of French.

> Send a courier to General Junot in Bayonne. . . . Order him to leave, twenty-four hours after receipt of your letter, and to enter Spain with his army, and to direct himself toward the Portuguese frontier. The Spanish should have given orders for the supplying of provisions for his troops. You will inform General Junot that my ambassador has left Lisbon; and so there is not a moment to be lost, in order to stop the English.

This was a famous and widely quoted letter from Napoléon, ordering the invasion of the Iberian Peninsula. This action, along with his expedition to Russia, where he lost nearly an entire army to the Russian winter, ended up bogging him down. Turns out the

Spanish didn't appreciate his occupation. And the English would join the fight there through Portugal. The military leader of that force was the Duke of Wellington, who would later defeat Napoléon at Waterloo. So this act, the invasion of Spain, would help lead to Napoléon's downfall. I wanted it and convinced my father. The letter's price did not reflect its true value. Why? Pricing a document is an art, not a science. Maggs is experienced, but smart people make mistakes. Or maybe they just didn't think they could take a common autograph such as Napoléon's and price it higher. We sold it for $25,000.

Another early moment of success for me occurred on eBay, of all places—the first and only time I ever bought anything there. I never go on the site, but one day, sitting on my couch, during a quiet spell, I was looking to kill time. A seller had listed an autograph of William Williams of Connecticut. The seller hadn't bothered to post images of the entire piece, which was missing text in parts. Nor had he described what the letter said. And who was William Williams? I knew the answer to that question: he was a signer of the Declaration of Independence, a member of those bands of men who risked it all to defy the British monarchy.

I asked the seller for images. He refused. Weird, I thought: *I guess he's not excited to sell this.* There is something deeply unsatisfying about dealing with someone who looks on these objects as commodities or appears to take no joy in their content. It's a similar feeling to spending an hour talking to someone and then realizing they don't know your name. You get the distinct impression you're not on the same page. That was the case here.

My father and I had discussed many times our obligation to dig deeper and ask the next question. The date on this document was 1775, when the American colonists rebelled against the British. Could this letter relate to that? People collect the signers of the Declaration, and anything patriotic goes high. I read what I could of the letter and found a couple lines: "I should not fear to stake ten thousand lives if I had them, that it would end in establishing our liberties." Wow.

Again, I asked for more images. Explained that my interest was sincere. Radio silence.

I played my hunch, bid on the document, and we bought it. It turned out that Williams in March of 1775 was writing to a British loyalist—a plea for the patriotic cause. The letter was long and read in part:

> Tis beyond all possibility of doubt that a plan of despotic government has been many years preparing for America, and is now pushing into severe execution, & that nothing but the firmest union & virtuous resolution of the Colonies can prevent its accomplishment. I am sure that you have more property than you are willing to lose, & you never was very fond of being under the control of any, is it not then more than astonishing? That you should favor the principles that most certainly tend to certain destruction.

This early successful hunch of mine made us $36,000.

The early years were an apprenticeship, and experience is a demanding but effective teacher. In the beginning, my father accompanied me to see collections. But as things progressed, while we still discussed value and historical importance, my eye for authenticity developed. And I set out on the hunt alone.

Seated across from me at my dining room table were two women: a mother and daughter. They lived nearby and had come to visit me in my Main Line home. The Main Line is in suburban Philadelphia, made famous as the setting for the classic Grant/Hepburn/Stewart movie *The Philadelphia Story*. My parents were at their house in Bar Harbor, Maine; my wife, Karen, hadn't yet joined me in the business and was at her former job at Drexel, where she was a lawyer; and my daughter hadn't been born.

The women's leather briefcase was full of old papers. They laid them out on the table, and I went through the group, piece by piece, for two hours. They'd inherited a lot of things, and their ancestors had also collected documents over the years, so they had several hundred pieces. Nothing particularly earth-shattering. Early commercial documents signed by Pennsylvania notables, mostly.

There was a Benjamin Franklin letter—nice, but unremarkable at first glance:

"I send by Capt. Duncan the copies of the Accounts you wrote for, which I hope will get safe to hand. I am Sir, Your most humble Servant, B. Franklin."

Franklin was sending documents necessary for the negotiation of the Treaty of Fort Stanwix in 1768, which ceded Native American land in the West to England. Franklin was at the time agent for the colony of Pennsylvania, his adopted home, and was stationed in London. The letter was addressed to William Trent, who was representing the interests of some of the traders in claims against the other parties affected by the conflict that led up to the treaty.

When I went online, I couldn't find the letter in the known published texts attributed to Franklin. This document had been with this family and not left it for generations. No one knew it existed. I held the letter in my hand and looked at it through the light of the large window facing the street. Laid paper, nice watermark. Back then, rags were pulverized and laid wet on a rack. Once dried, the rack lines remain visible only on close inspection. The signature looked perfect, the letter entirely in Franklin's hand.

I turned the letter over to assess it for *show-through*, a word we use to describe ink penetrating the paper it's written on. A copy, a facsimile, won't have show-through. With an authentic document, the ink will often come through the verso, or the back, particularly the older ink, which was more iron gall and tends to eat through paper.

But when I turned it over, I did not see what I expected. I saw the address panel, which sent the letter to William Trent in New York. At the bottom right, another signature. But this one did not look like the other.

"B Free Franklin," it read. At the time, public officials could send mail free of charge in the pursuance of their public duties by signing their names and writing *free*. They still can, although today that signature is printed. (If you get a letter from your congressman, you'll see it.) This is called a free frank, and this was Franklin's free frank signature—allowing him to send mail without using postage.

In my effort to see the show-through, I'd found an incredible historical and autographic rarity: Franklin had put the word *free* between *B* and *Franklin* to prevent forgery. I knew these were rare and likely valuable.

I rose from the table and called my father and explained to him that I thought this material was authentic. I had texted him an image, and he agreed. I also texted him the back of the letter. "Is that a 'B Free Franklin' signature?" he asked. "Indeed," I replied. He'd never seen one in person, he said. They had become so emblematic of the US Postal Service that many stamps were created featuring this famous line. Franklin himself had served as head of the colonial post office for a time.

In many cases, the franking panel with the signature and the letter would have been separated. This Franklin letter and its free frank hadn't been. Eighteenth-century letters were not sent in envelopes. Instead, you'd use a long sheet of paper, twice the size of the piece of paper you were going to write on, and you'd fold it in half, top to bottom; write on one side of one-half; then fold the sheet of paper so the writing was on the inside; and on the outside, you'd write the address. It's the same sheet of paper. What often happens is the free frank is removed from the letter at some point over the years. Collectors have also been known to cut the sheet in half, creating two items—a letter from Franklin, and also a document signed by Franklin—the free frank—so they can have two different pieces.

I was holding in my hand an unpublished, unknown letter written by Benjamin Franklin, as agent in London, dealing with the acquisition of more land for the crown, taking it away from Native Americans, with a "B Free Franklin" signature on the back. I told the sellers what I'd found and wrote a five-figure check for the material on the spot, the first time I'd done so alone, and began my research. This was one of only a handful of such signatures to reach the market in decades, and the only one still with the letter it sent. We sold it for $50,000, and I wish I had it back.

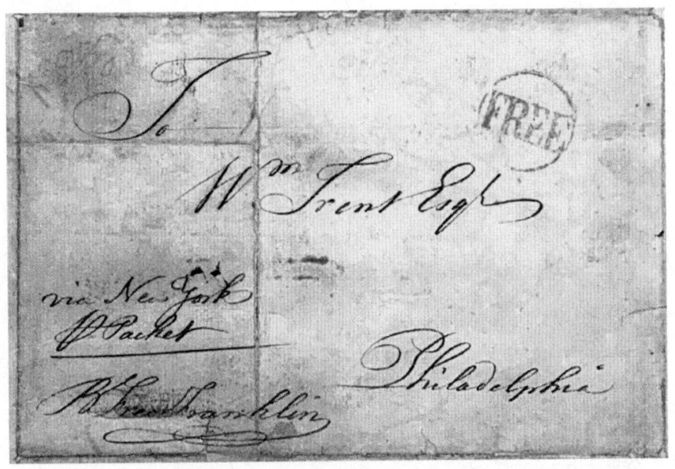

Benjamin Franklin's rare "B. Free Franklin" signature found on the back of his letter.

But my training was bearing fruit. Now I turn over everything we buy, hoping to find something interesting on the other side.

CHAPTER 3

What Is It Worth?

In 2005, within a year of my first joining the family business, Malcolm Gladwell published a book, *Blink*, which makes the point that, among other things, an expert will be able to tell the authenticity of a thing, such as art, in the blink of an eye, and that more information given over time will, in the case of that real expert, tend to confirm what that blink moment conveys.

He wrote:

> We live in a world that assumes that the quality of a decision is directly related to the time and effort that went into making it. . . . We believe that we are always better off gathering as much information as possible and spending as much time as possible in deliberation. We really only trust conscious decision making. But there are moments, particularly in times of stress, when haste does not make waste, when our snap judgments and first impressions can offer a much better means of making sense of the world. The first task of *Blink* is to convince you of a simple fact: decisions made very quickly can be every bit as good as decisions made cautiously and deliberately. . . . There can be as much value in the blink of an eye as in months of rational analysis.

Around this time, my father and I were at a rare-book fair in New York City, looking through the merchandise for sale along with many old friends, serious collectors, and a variety of dealers. If you find something interesting, chances are someone else has seen it too.

We went from booth to booth in a state of simultaneous concentration and distraction, looking, half looking, paging through documents sheathed in protective plastic, moving along to the next thing. We must have looked at fifteen hundred documents. We were shopping, but not for anything in particular, looking for we knew not what. It adds to the surprise when you don't know what you're looking for and then you find it!

Then my father said, "Take a look at this."

A letter written by Charles Darwin in 1873 to an American abolitionist named Thomas Wentworth Higginson was priced at $15,000, which was about the going rate for a Darwin letter, maybe more.

I looked briefly and said, "I don't really feel like spending fifteen thousand dollars on a Darwin letter." How much more than that could we plausibly expect to get when we sold it?

"This is different," my father said. "Read the letter."

I did:

Down House, Kent, February 27

Dear Thomas,

My wife has just finished reading aloud your "Life with a Black Regiment," and you must allow me to thank you heartily for the very great pleasure which it has in many ways given us. I always thought well of the negroes, from the little which I have seen of them; and I have been delighted to have my vague impressions confirmed, and their character and mental powers so ably discussed. When you were here I did not know of the noble position which you had filled. I had formerly read about the black regiments, but failed to connect your name with your admirable undertaking. Although we enjoyed greatly your visit to Down, my wife and myself have over and over again regretted that we did not know about the black regiment, as we should have greatly liked to have heard a little about the South from your own lips.

Your descriptions have vividly recalled walks taken forty years ago in Brazil. We have your collected Essays, which were kindly sent us by Mr. Conway, but have not yet had time to read them. I occasionally glean a little news of you in the "Index"; and within the last hour have read an interesting article of yours on the progress of Free Thought.

Believe me, my dear sir, with sincere admiration,

Yours very faithfully, Ch. Darwin.

Darwin was a monumental figure, and his legacy is still felt today. He puts truth to Emerson's observation that "genius is the naturalist or geographer . . . who draws their map; and by acquainting us with new fields of activity, cools our affection for the old." Darwin's work played out in the nineteenth century on a species-wide scale. And here, in this letter, he was talking about the American Civil War, expressing his admiration for the first regiment of freed black slaves, the First South Carolina Volunteers, which had been commanded by Higginson. When Darwin says, "I always thought well of the negroes," using an antiquated but not then derogatory term, he made a powerful positive statement on the races at a time when slavery was a recent memory. And all this he connects to his trip forty years earlier in Brazil. That would have been his famous voyage on the *Beagle*, during which he gathered samples and made the observations leading to his groundbreaking theory of evolution, described in his 1859 book, *On the Origin of Species*.

This was, it was immediately clear (at least now that I'd taken the time to read it carefully), more than a Darwin letter, it was a great letter.

In a mass of letters and books, spanning the equivalent of several city blocks, reading each as you would read the newspaper, my dad had stumbled across an evocative and powerful voice from the past, the hidden gem in the room. This was the third day of the book fair. Thousands of people had circled past this piece, which was plainly visible in a large glass case.

We checked the authenticity, though at first glance it looked right. Such a task is a requirement for every document we buy. "Start with fresh eyes," my dad would say. This meant taking the document out of the sleeve, running a hand along the letterhead, making sure that it was raised. The vast majority of old letterhead is raised, and if it's not, it can mean someone ran it through a photocopy machine. How is the flow of the pen? Do you see ink flowing on the page? Does it seem forced? Are the lines straight? One common mistake forgers make is they can't keep their lines straight. Are there crosses on the *t*? After I get to the bottom of the first page, I turn it over. Is the ink all the same strength? If there's no ink flow variation, it's possibly a copy. There should be moments when the ink gets weaker and moments when it gets stronger. Look for show-through. I check for the signature. And the signature itself: Does it look right? I see that it's signed "Ch. Darwin," which is good—you don't want to see it signed "Charles Darwin," because he didn't sign letters that way.

We ended where we began: convinced of its authenticity.

We placed the document on a hold and told the dealer we would return within thirty minutes. This was the window we gave ourselves to do research. The letter, the dealer said, was on consignment from the direct descendants of the recipient and was unpublished.

The recipient, Thomas Higginson, was an abolitionist clergyman and, in that capacity, became acquainted with Ralph Waldo Emerson, Henry Ward Beecher, and Henry David Thoreau. During the Civil War, Higginson had served as a colonel in the Union Army and commanded the first regiment of freed black slaves, which he wrote about in his book *Army Life in a Black Regiment*. He'd met Darwin in London years later, and they'd struck up a correspondence.

Darwin's views on race, as expressed in the letter, aren't surprising, given his experiences on the *Beagle*. Early on in the voyage, on February 28, 1832, the ship arrived in Bahia, Brazil, where Darwin spent a few days exploring the tropical rain forests. He was also confronted with the sight of black slaves, which offended and disgusted him. This led to a disagreement with Captain Robert FitzRoy of the *Beagle* about the ethics of treating humans as property. As Darwin later described it in his autobiography:

> Early in the voyage at Bahia in Brazil he defended and praised slavery, which I abominated, and told me that he just visited a great slave-owner, who had called up many of his slaves and asked them whether they were happy, and whether they wished to be free, and all answered "No." I then asked him, perhaps with a sneer, whether he thought that the answers of slaves in the presence of their master was worth anything. This made him excessively angry.

FitzRoy apparently banished Darwin from his dinner table, although soon apologized, and they made up. Darwin never forgot the sight of those slaves in Brazil and always opposed slavery.

The letter to Higginson is one of the few that directly illuminates Darwin's views on the question of race.

We did not need thirty minutes. People love Darwin, and here was a letter from Darwin that justified the confidence of his admirers tenfold. The value of these things is a subjective assessment, but I think the dealer misjudged the letter. We sold it almost immediately for a very healthy profit, focusing our customers' attention on the factors that made the piece uncommon, exciting, and relevant. Doing this requires a mix of historical knowledge and an understanding of the legacy of the figure in question. What is he or she known for? Why do we care about the person? An incisive and resonant description of the artifact and its historical context can increase its value significantly.

Some people have good "taste," my dad used to say. That meant they spent their money well and that their collections, as a reflection of their character, showed wisdom and a passion. To create such a collection required an ability to see a thing for what it is, beyond the paper, beyond the ink. Some don't know how. Others won't take the time. That is why any number of people can walk right by something, and another stops right in his tracks, and why something priced at $1,000 might be worth $100,000.

While the ultimate key to success in this business is the ability to determine value and recognize historical importance, the sine qua non is an ability to authenticate. Savvy collectors and other dealers can sniff out inexperience. Learning to authenticate requires a specific set of skills, honed sometimes over decades. It's a necessary first step, and my apprenticeship would require immersion in all its idiosyncrasies.

For example, some historical figures signed letters using custom-made stamps, including Albert Einstein, who would send out letters raising money for an anti-nuclear-proliferation organization with a trademark blue signature stamp. Yes, the man who helped the United States arrive at this technology recognized its danger and sought diligently to limit it. How do you recognize a stamp? "Look for bubbles in the ink, perhaps the outline of the rectangle setting of the stamp, and the lack of overlap on the crosses of a *t*, for example," explained my father. "Ink has texture, it stands up on the paper. A stamped signature appears washed-out, uniform and flat."

Some figures used machines to sign their names for them. Thomas Jefferson owned what was then called a polygraph machine, whereby he would write on a sheet of paper, and a machine tracking his every pen movement would write the same on another. This machine, invented in Europe, created exact copies of his letters, and many Jefferson letters sold today are unbeknownst to the seller actually polygraph copies. I had to learn what made them different.

The autopen, a modern version of Jefferson's signature machine, was invented in the late 1940s and first used in the White House during the Eisenhower administration. It was not all that different from Jefferson's, except that it would trace a previously created mold of a signature, reproducing it exactly. Not similar. Identical. "Try signing your name the same twice," my dad asked me. "Not close. Identical." I could not. Autopen signatures are identical. When one example precisely matches another, it's an autopen giveaway.

A machine, or autopen, signature of Reagan, with visible shakiness.

I also needed to learn how to sniff out forgeries and signatures of secretaries—what we in the trade call secretarials. "John Kennedy letters from 1958 to 1960 are almost always signed by secretaries, with a few autopens thrown in," my dad explained. I've found this to be true.

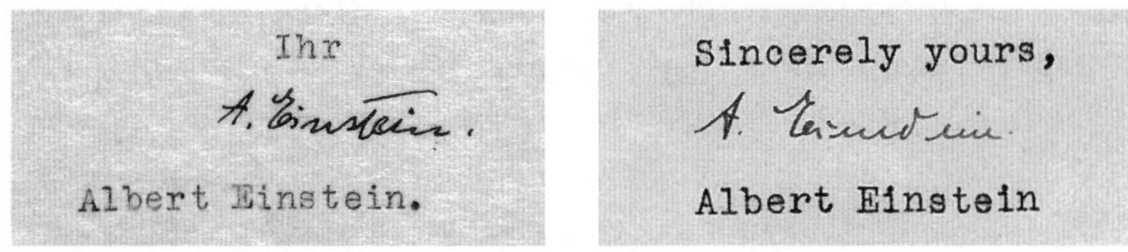

Albert Einstein's authentic signature (*left*) and one signed by his secretary (*right*).

"My client has a collection of historical documents, among the greatest in the United States," a voice on the phone told me some years ago. "You will want to buy this." If I heard this today, I'd roll my eyes; back then I assumed the collection was valuable, so my father and I went to see the client. We did our research ahead of time. This businessman had spent decades buying from one or two dealers, assembling what was purportedly a large collection. A huge collection. In particular, he had an unprecedentedly large and significant assemblage of American presidential autographs, we were told, and much more besides. He was interested in selling all of it.

When we arrived to see the collection, we found what you might expect: mahogany chairs, heavy frames on white-painted walls, a secretary behind a dark wood desk. She announced our arrival, and the agent for the collector came out to meet us, a middle-aged man dressed in a suit. The collector, we were informed, was in meetings all day and hoped we'd be able to make a strong offer for the collection.

The agent walked us down a narrow white hallway to a wooden door, which he opened slowly, carefully—almost reverentially.

The room was intended to be a museum of sorts, we soon understood: the walls were covered with hundreds of elaborately framed documents, every item identified by a small plaque. One wall was filled with a single massive frame that included the "signature" of every single president.

We looked around, and my initial reaction was "Wow, there is a *lot* of material here." The presentation was intended to overwhelm. As we admired the ornately framed displays, which must have cost $1,000 per frame on average, we were presented with an official autographed book praising and illustrating the collection. We were told we could visit the collection online. Many of the autographs, photographs, and documents were framed with large commemorative plates, each of which would have cost a great deal on its own. The enormous collection had 150 to 250 autographs, maybe more. The collector had multiple autographs from every single president.

My dad walked in and waited for the agent to leave. "This stuff is junk. There are more forgeries here than authentic signatures. And when it's not forged, it's an autopen."

Here, for example, was, if memory serves, a cocktail napkin signed by both John F. Kennedy and Marilyn Monroe. "Maybe he also has a napkin signed by Kennedy and Lee Harvey Oswald," my dad joked. We both considered it an obvious forgery. Next to it was a Lyndon Johnson autograph, which we both concluded was in fact signed by one of his aides in his stead. It was astounding, and all the more so given the lavish, deluxe presentation. We walked around the room, down the hallways where more pieces were displayed with plaques and ornate presentations. This man had spent hundreds of thousands of dollars or more on his collection, and further hundreds of thousands on its framing and presentation.

He clearly thought his collection was worth millions. But we were sure it wasn't.

Even the items that were authentic were in poor condition—or cut signatures and the like. Nothing in the group was exciting or different.

Someone had got ahold of this collector and made a small killing, selling him this stuff until he stopped buying and decided to sell.

I've spent a great deal of time considering this man's story. On the surface, the lesson to be learned is that money doesn't buy quality. This man had more money than most, but put together a collection far surpassed by people with far less money. I've helped people on fixed incomes build important collections. One of my dad's early customers was a truck driver who put aside money to buy a piece now and then and acquired some great stuff.

In this case, I'm convinced this man had been told lies—about the origin and authenticity of many of the items in his collection (that cocktail napkin!) and more broadly about the value of his purchases.

My dad and I made a small but fair offer on the few authentic things and went to have lunch at a restaurant in an adjacent mall. Three hours and a couple beers later, we called the agent. "Oh," he explained, "the owner was offended by your offer and immediately rejected it. I forgot to call you."

Months later we were on a plane to Los Angeles, or rather slightly north of Los Angeles, to visit one of my father's first-ever customers.

This man had been buying from my father since I was in middle school, from Catalog no. 1, issued in 1989. He was a lawyer turned businessman, perhaps not wealthy but certainly comfortable, and had set about collecting his primary interests, which were in the field of American history.

"He's a very deliberate buyer," my father explained. "Some people call and buy things having read the first line of the description and the price. This guy will take a week or two before pulling the trigger, regardless of the price. He has great taste. Money doesn't buy taste or a discerning palate."

Now he had decided to sell much of what he'd collected.

We rented a car at LAX before heading to a late lunch and glass of red wine in Santa Monica, at a small Spanish tapas place just a block from the beach. It was a warm day. A small street fair was taking place up the street, and after lunch my dad found a place that sold "the best pistachios in the world." Years later he's still ordering them online in bulk. We talked about this man, our client. "You're going to be impressed by what he has."

We walked into his home the next morning; his circular driveway led up to a modest house, close to the highway. It was dark inside, with dark wood floors and furniture to match. The man had a small table set up in the entryway. No agent, no middleman, just him. His wife was off to pick up the kids.

He and my dad riffed for a little about things I knew nothing about, the old days. Then the man disappeared and returned with a large folder, made of thick card stock, housing documents in plastic. He pulled them out to show us one by one:

- An important letter written by General George Washington at the Winter Encampment of Valley Forge, the moment of greatest peril for the Continental Army in their fight against the British.
- The call from the Secession Convention floor in South Carolina urging all the other Southern states to secede and a form a confederacy.

- A missive of the Marquis de Lafayette praising the heroics of his "father" George Washington, and longing to return from his injury during the Revolutionary War to fight alongside his American brothers.
- A letter from Winston Churchill during World War II calling for "the defeat of Hitler and all he stands for."
- A letter from Charles Sumner on his sickbed discussing how he had been attacked on the Senate floor by the pro-slavery South Carolina representative Preston Brooks in the lead-up to the war. Sumner is a relatively marginal figure in the grand scheme of history, but his brutal caning on the floor of the Senate came to symbolize the hostility between North and South. And remember, when it comes to documents and artifacts, connecting the historical figure to their greatest achievements or strongest legacy always adds significant value. It meant this Sumner letter was worth not $1,000 but $8,000.

You get the picture. It was historical gem after historical gem. All authentic, each acquired with the deliberation of a collector fascinated by and knowledgeable about the subject.

He had no elaborately framed documents in his office, no intermediary dealing on his behalf. Watching my dad and him discuss and negotiate was like watching two old friends and collectors talk about the respective historical merits of each document. "You don't see many winter letters from Valley Forge of Washington anymore, let alone one with this urgency," my dad noted.

There were a few things the collector didn't want to sell. He had a letter from Thomas Jefferson inviting over a Muslim friend on Ramadan. And some other pieces from the nineteenth century, the period that most interested him.

But he wanted, as I recall, around $120,000 for the above pieces and a few others, and we agreed. He'd probably made some profit over the years, collecting these things; and we'd sell them again, and so would we.

* * *

These three interactions, coming in such proximity, one in New York, another in the DC suburbs, and yet another in Los Angeles, were educational for me. They spoke to me of the ability to assess historical importance, to understand the true meaning of these pieces. The LA buyer was steeped in the history, knew his stuff better than I did, bought from reputable dealers, was deliberate and thoughtful in his purchases, not overly impulsive, and a fine person to deal with. His hunt was in the pursuit of history, proximity to these great figures and events that interested him. His pieces weren't elaborately displayed. They were housed in a folder that he could bring out, hold, enjoy, for himself and his close friends.

The DC buyer's primary reason for collecting was for show and ego. He didn't seem to care about the authenticity of the material, and he saw nothing in these objects beyond the shine of the frame. Nothing was particularly important. The value had never been higher than on the day he bought them. To quote Goethe again: "What gleams like tinsel is but for a moment. What's true remains intact." And the man seemed like a jerk.

Early on in my career, I saw the value of quick and accurate judgment, experienced Malcolm Gladwell's blink, and had met the polar opposites of our potential customers. I knew which I preferred. And I learned another lesson: with the more discerning customers, the chances that the material they've acquired is authentic are much, much higher. Money doesn't buy taste, but with taste comes authenticity.

CHAPTER 4

The Gold Medal, the Top Hat, and the Martini Shaker

"Friends, I shall ask you to be as quiet as possible," said Theodore Roosevelt. "I don't know whether you fully understand that I have just been shot."

In 1912, while running unsuccessfully for a third term as president, Roosevelt had been the victim of an assassination attempt, shot just before he was to give a campaign speech. At the time, before FDR served four terms, there was no term limit on the presidency.

"It takes more than that to kill a bull moose," he continued, referring to his hunting days in Canada. "Fortunately I had my manuscript, so you see I was going to make a long speech, and there is a bullet—there is where the bullet went through—and it probably saved me from it going into my heart. The bullet is in me now, so that I cannot make a very long speech, but I will try my best."

Those fifty sheets of paper saved his life. Nearly a hundred years later, I was looking around in an antiques shop belonging to a man who sold curios and other objects, coins, flags, trinkets, and some pieces of paper. A dark, musty room, quiet and a bit dingy. We were in suburban New York, viewing an unrelated collection of documents, and wandered into this shop along the street near our hotel. We'd heard the name of the dealer before but had never bought from him. His shop had pictures of him with his pets throughout—a comical ambience, mixed with perhaps some mold.

"It's just a piece of paper with a hole in," I said.

"Look on the back," my father said.

I turned it over, and on the verso was an inscription from Roosevelt's wife, supporting him at his bedside as he healed, gifting it to a friend. The bullet hole was visible as a tear.

The dealer was asking $5,000 for it. The page wasn't signed by anyone famous, but the context and provenance together gave voice to its authenticity, and we bought it on the spot. And sold it one week later for $40,000.

Objects and artifacts, as opposed to autographs or documents, hold a unique fascination for people: Ernest Hemingway's typewriter, Abraham Lincoln's stovepipe hat, Franklin Roosevelt's hankies (he used to send them to children named after him), books from a prominent figure's library. You can imagine the historical figure owning the object, holding it in his or her hands; an intimacy and closeness attaches itself to these things. They are relics, full of emotion and significance.

The challenge with objects is to make sure they're real. As with the Roosevelt speech, which is more an artifact than an autograph, context is everything.

If I gave you a fountain pen and told you it had belonged to Theodore Roosevelt, how would you know that? What if I showed you a picture of Theodore Roosevelt writing with the pen? You would still be confronted by the same problem: How do you know that the pen isn't simply a replica of the original or another one made at the time by the same manufacturer? Establishing the provenance of an object can be very, very difficult.

How would you keep track of the provenance of a fountain pen? Think about how many hands something like that would pass through. One possible scenario would be if you had a letter from the owner of the pen sending it to someone else and describing the pen in detail.

We all want to believe. We want to believe the pen is the real thing. This vein runs through our hunt for history. We've all treasured objects that our parents or grandparents gave to us—these intimate objects have deep meaning. And so it only makes sense that we look beyond family to history. There is something innocent and almost childlike in our desire to suspend critical judgment and accept what is before us.

But in my experience, the more glamorous the story, the less likely it is to be true. A relative of mine, for example, told me he had a signed photograph that Frank Sinatra had given to him because he helped launch Sinatra's career in New Jersey. The story is obviously self-aggrandizing, it puts my relative close to a major figure, and it isn't true. Frank Sinatra's studio sent him the photo, and it was signed by a secretary. As things get passed down from one generation to the next, the story is likely to grow, not shrink.

A collector approached us not long ago with a collection of military correspondence and the writing desk of Winfield Scott. In the nineteenth century, military men had boxes that opened to expose pens, ink, and paper and folded out to provide a platform for writing letters in the field. Winfield Scott was the great general of the Mexican-American War, which expanded the nation and made the military career of future Confederate general Robert E. Lee. Scott's career spanned an era. He commanded troops in the War of 1812 and the Black Hawk War, as well as the Mexican-American War, and was the most senior army officer at the start of the Civil War. Remarkable. We wanted the letters and so acquired the whole collection, along with what *might* be Scott's writing desk.

But when we got it, we posed a series of questions to ourselves.

"Well, it's clearly from the era, and it says Winfield Scott on it," my dad noted. The name Winfield Scott was inscribed on a silver plaque at the top of the box, where you'd expect it. "But could it have belonged to a different man, also named Winfield Scott?"

How would we ever know?

We decided to keep the collection for the letters and we still have the box. It's likely the real thing, but that element of doubt has set us back on the research trail, and for now, it's simply a beautiful object sitting in our office, not for sale.

Scott's writing box illustrates the conundrum posed by such objects: you have to rule out other possibilities. And you have to know what questions to ask.

With the Roosevelt speech fragment and the Scott desk, I was learning about the complexities of authenticating such objects, but I also learned that while caution is necessary, it often pays off.

In 1818, on the floor of the House of Representatives, with the War of 1812 three years past, Congressman and eventual four-time presidential candidate Henry Clay listened to a speech from former general, now congressman, William Henry Harrison, who rose from his seat to accept a solemn honor, given to him just days earlier. He wanted, as it was published in April of that year, to "bear testimony to the gallant services of the gentlemen of the Northwestern army, and took the opportunity of expressing briefly his sense of the distinguished honor to which he had recently himself received at the hands of Congress—a reward more dear to him than any other that could be conferred on him, but which he must look on as due to the gallant army which he had the honor to command rather than to his merits."

General Harrison had defeated the Indians in the 1811 Battle of Tippecanoe and was appointed commander of the Army of the Northwest in September of 1812, a pivotal moment in what came to be known as the War of 1812 against Great Britain and its allies, including numerous Indian tribes. The following year, 1813, Harrison led his men in the Battle of the Thames, in Ontario, winning a stunning victory, one that claimed the life of the Shawnee Indian chief Tecumseh and held the old Northwest for the United States.

Harrison, with the help of lobbying from Clay, had received the Congressional Gold Medal for these acts. In a ceremony at the White House, presided over by President James Monroe, the medal was bestowed on Harrison.

Almost two hundred years later and some sixteen hundred miles away, I picked up a small box. The box felt heavy in my hands, much heavier than I expected. It measured four inches by four inches and weighed almost a pound. The exterior was made of a board of some kind. I opened it slowly, with bated breath. The contents had been the reason for our hurried visit to Colorado. Inside, a maroon cloth setting, both on the bottom and the top of the box, housed a gold coin, larger than two and a half inches in diameter. The medal pictured a bust of General William Henry Harrison, facing right, in uniform. The reverse showed America personified by a maiden wearing a tunic, with her right hand resting on the US shield inscribed FORT MEIGS and BATTLE OF THE THAMES, major battles for which Harrison was being honored. Above was the inscription RESOLUTION OF CONGRESS, APRIL 4, 1818, and below, BATTLE OF THE THAMES. The man who'd faced down foes, British and Native American, and who'd distinguished himself on the battlefield, also held the distinction of serving the shortest term in office as president—thirty-one days—dying of pneumonia contracted a few weeks after his inauguration. This was in theory the very gold medal awarded to him for his military exploits. This would be no minor discovery: it would be the unearthing of an American treasure, a find that no one was looking for.

My father and I had flown out to see a large collection belonging to a direct descendant of William Henry Harrison and also of Benjamin Harrison, our twenty-third president (from 1889 to 1893). This family had been involved in politics and military service since before the Constitution was signed and could claim to be one of the great political dynastic families in America, even though relatively unknown now.

The first Benjamin Harrison had arrived in America around 1630, when the colonies as they were then known were nothing more than vast forests and Natives. He built Berkeley Plantation in Virginia. The fifth Benjamin Harrison signed the Declaration of Independence and was governor of Virginia. His son, William Henry, moved to

Indiana Territory and served as its governor before his military heroics and brief presidency. His grandson became the first grandson of a president to assume that office, following in the familial footsteps of John and John Quincy Adams. The next such dynasty would be Franklin and Theodore Roosevelt, who were cousins, and the Bushes, who were father and son.

The man had told us that he had the Congressional Gold Medal given to William Henry Harrison in 1818, among many other items and documents. We knew that only a handful of such early medals survived. Nowadays, Congressional Medals of Honor are given out more freely. But those early medals are buried treasure, an actual hidden golden medallion. No one knew where the Harrison medal was. A small handful of others, including Andrew Jackson's medal, had surfaced over the past century and were quickly acquired by one institution or another. Could this be the real Harrison medal?

We were now looking at it in what was an unremarkable suburban split-level house. Nothing of historical note was hanging on the walls, with no other sign that this was the home of a descendant of the Harrisons'. This man was rather stern-faced. Straightforward, not unfriendly but not friendly either.

He hadn't brought out his material all at once, but rather in waves. Folders, framed documents, all from the basement. The first piece was an old book that had belonged to William Henry Harrison and later to President Benjamin Harrison. It bore the signature of the former and an inscription from the religious leader who eulogized him. A book from the libraries of two presidents, it was titled *Fletcher's Works, Volume 1*, a religious text. Fletcher was a contemporary of John Wesley's (Wesley founded Methodism), a key interpreter of Wesleyan theology in the eighteenth century, and one of Methodism's first great theologians.

The man brought in a rather large framed document signed by Abraham Lincoln, appointing his ancestor governor of Nebraska Territory. There was President Benjamin Harrison's inaugural address, which was bound into a book and signed at the end, not a copy he'd signed later but the one he delivered—the very document he held as he gave it. Objects in the collection included a walking stick that belonged to Benjamin Harrison, another book from the library of the signer of the Declaration of Independence, also Benjamin Harrison. A set of dinner plates had apparently—according to family lore—come from Abraham Lincoln's White House. These, we decided, after looking at the manufacturer's name on the back of the plate, were reproductions. This well-known set was done later, around the time of President Benjamin Harrison, to commemorate the assassinated president. Not an uncommon occurrence at all: the family lore was wishful thinking. Here were files of the ongoing correspondence of the Harrisons with William Howard Taft and Theodore Roosevelt.

Finally, there was the gold medal, in its maroon cloth setting. It gleamed, and its weight spoke to its import, at least I hoped. This beautiful and mysterious object on the surface matched the known description of the lost gem.

The medal presented us with a dilemma. A coin dealer is focused on the physical properties of a piece—is it in mint condition? Coin dealers care about a number of technical aspects that don't apply to us in the same way. They examine small imperfections. The closer the coin is to how it first appeared, the better. Even a scratch the size of a needle point can be frowned upon. To me, the medal was in beautiful condition. But we cared first and foremost whether it belonged to William Henry Harrison. What is the historical importance of the piece? Only two other such medals had ever been awarded to future presidents in that early-American period—Andrew Jackson and Zachary Taylor. And here we were, looking at what we hoped was the very thing. But, as the dinner plates reminded us, and as Ronald Reagan so memorably put it, trust but verify.

We matched the size on the spot and concluded that the known size of the original medal and the dimensions of this were identical. All the markings were right, the engraver's signature where it ought to be, and the right person. It was still with the heirs. All good signs.

We had to think through all the scenarios: Maybe it was a reproduction, a souvenir copy, perhaps with every member of the family getting one at the award ceremony. If so, it wouldn't be gold. Or perhaps it was made as a commemorative coin years later. This wouldn't explain the size, which usually changes with reproductions, but we couldn't authenticate the medal on the spot. We needed to know its metal composition, compare it against more contemporary descriptions of the medal, and consult colleagues, whose experience with coins would be worth tapping into.

The man wanted many tens of thousands of dollars for the medal alone. That seemed expensive to us but not totally unreasonable. We had little precedent to go on, with the medal being as rare as it was. We told the family that assuming we could authenticate it, we would buy it at their price. That meant we'd end up paying well more than $150,000 for the entire collection of historical documents and objects.

"I need to think about it," the man said stiffly. He looked away. It wasn't clear to us that he wanted to sell the medal, let alone permit us to authenticate it. And so we left with nothing.

To look discovery in the face and be forced to turn away is the ultimate frustration. We offer our advice, spend our valuable time, and also get our hopes up. An acquisition is often accompanied by excitement—we have found and bought something cool. But the man had no obligation to sell anything to us, and we were polite on our exit. When we left, he had the same stern expression on his face with which we'd found him. His wife was the opposite, smiling, offering us food for the road. An odd situation overall, and we went home and tried to put the collection behind us, the medal disappearing into the same cellar from which it came.

The undeniable nature of true historical treasures is that once you've seen them, you can't forget them. Or, as Thoreau famously wrote in *Walden*, "You seek it like a dream, and as soon as you find it you become its prey."

Fortunately, less than a week later, the Harrison heir unexpectedly wrote to us: we had a deal, but with one caveat. He understood we had work to do before wiring him the money, but we had one week to do it. I was in Washington, DC, at the National Portrait Gallery with Karen when I got word of his acceptance and the timeline. We were in town for other business and enjoying the museum between meetings. We set up shop in the spectacular inner courtyard by the café—usually a tranquil space where we enjoy a bite to eat and a glass of wine—but we were now frantically booking Amtrak seats back to Philadelphia and a last-minute flight to Colorado. We rushed home, and less than three hours later I was in a cab to the Philadelphia airport.

I went through the same routine, renting a car, driving to the same hotel. When I arrived at the Harrison descendant's house, he was again as blankly reticent as he'd been the week before. Not a reaction to me, I thought at the time, but an essential character trait. Not hostile exactly, but not warm. He led the way silently into his living room.

Since then, I've thought about his attitude regarding the whole transaction. I wonder in retrospect whether he'd been wistful about his decision to sell his family documents. Generations had passed these down and down and down again, and it had come to him and he'd made the call to sell, with no one in the next generation to care for them. Maybe he was just sad to see the material go and, though recognizing the propriety of his decision, still found his emotions mixed with bitterness.

Collectors have a hard time selling their pieces. That is in part because they've invested emotional energy in buying them, living with them, drawing inspiration from their presence. But imagine if that inspiration is also familial—rather than merely seeing the reflection of greatness in the object, to know that your blood is derived from it. I'm sympathetic when the hard decision to sell has been made.

I inventoried the documents, took the medal, the books, and other objects, including President Benjamin Harrison's pen, and put them in my bag.

The understanding was that I would now take the medal to be authenticated, within his time frame, and would pay him if it was. If not, I'd bring the medal back. "One week," he said. He wanted the money or the medal. It wasn't clear to me if that meant everything, all the documents, books, and other artifacts, or just the medal. I decided to toss pessimism to the wind and hope for the best.

I agreed, telling him that I planned to take the medal to the Smithsonian.

As I went through security at the airport with the objects in my bag, I carried the presidential cane and used it, tapping the floor as I walked. It was a lighthearted end to step one of the saga.

Karen and I met David Miller at the Smithsonian National Museum of American History. A congenial fellow, he was the museum's weapons expert and curator. He bore a striking resemblance to the actor Jeff Bridges.

Miller led us into the vast backstage research and storage areas of the museum. A long hallway reminiscent of a high school. People with badges filing past their offices, doing the work reflected in the exhibit spaces out front. We made a left through one doorway and walked past several thousand swords, knives and axes, antique rifles, muskets, and pistols, and various other relics from the annals of battle and warfare. The room was the size of a small soccer field—it reminded me of the government warehouse where the army secreted the Ark of the Covenant in the final scene of *Raiders of the Lost Ark*.

I had the medal carefully wrapped in my briefcase. We expected the Smithsonian to be particularly helpful in authenticating the Harrison medal because they had, as part of their collection, a gold medal from the same era. Called the Truxtun medal, it was awarded in 1800 to the naval hero Thomas Truxtun, one of the first commanders appointed to the new US Navy by President George Washington. The idea was to compare the two medals, and specifically, the *metal* in the two medals.

We rounded a corner of the room, behind a stack of antique knives, to find a woman in her thirties standing over a machine that looked as if it were a distant cousin of a photocopier. The woman, Dawn Wallace, was an "objects conservator" at the museum, and she explained that this machine was an X-ray fluorescence spectrometer (XRF), and that we'd be able to compare the precise metallic compositions of the exteriors of the two medals. The spectrometer displaces electrons from their orbital positions in a fashion specific to an element—a safe and noninvasive method of analysis.

Here is what we knew at that point:

1. The medal was the precise size of the original. Copies made from an original are often different sizes and have other markings that would give them away.
2. Copies of this medal had been made but were not of the same metal. They were bronze. I seem to remember a couple were made of silver. But gold back then was rarer than today and more expensive. Copies were not generally made in gold. Experts in the field confirmed all this: a gold medal of the right size would be authentic. Or, as Miller jokingly put it, "Congress is cheap, but not when they're stamping their name on something."
3. There was a record of the awarding of this medal to Harrison, and this medal had two holes showing it had been worn, hung from a long-lost string or necklace.
4. No other contemporary copy of this medal had ever surfaced.

One other fact worth mentioning: In researching this medal, I found an obscure publication in the library at the University of Pennsylvania—one that had been issued by the Daughters of the American Revolution. Caroline Harrison, the wife of President Benjamin Harrison, was a member. The booklet showed this very medal, down to every facet, and an article thanked Caroline for allowing it to be on display at some exhibit the organization had organized. The seller of the medal today was the heir of Caroline Harrison.

This was a compelling and nearly definitive set of facts. But it all required the *metal* being the right composition for a medal created in the first twenty years of the 1800s.

Wallace put on latex lab gloves and placed the Truxtun medal on the machine's sample platform so as to assure that the scanning beam would strike the flattest portion of the engraved surface, yielding the most accurate analysis. The results appeared on the computer screen in only a few seconds. The Truxtun medal was mostly gold, but not 100 percent; imperfections in the blending of metals were characteristic of coins fabricated at that time. A graph recorded those imperfections. Gold from this period is not as pure as gold today, Wallace explained. That's what the spectrometer numbers represented.

Now she placed the Harrison medal on the machine and I held my breath. We all did. The anticipation that comes in such moments measures in direct proportion to the potential of the find. And there was plenty of anticipation. Even the curators, who had no stake in the authenticity of the medal and were simply providing research help, felt the anticipation. We were reconstructing a story generations after the fact. If the medal was authentic, it ought to produce a similar series of numbers to the Truxtun's, having been made less than twenty years later. A much-later copy would have a different chemical composition. Wallace hit the switch and the machine spit out another series of numbers on her computer screen. She was seated, and we were behind her. Only she could read the results. She turned her rolling chair around and faced us: "It matches." She smiled. The two medals were effectively identical: their compositions matched. The gold in the two medals had been made with the same early nineteenth-century process. When Wallace overlaid the two graphs, it was difficult to even tell there were two samples. Our medal was authentic.

A month later, I was on national television unveiling it.

And I still have that spectrometer report.

* * *

Aside from the science, the Harrison medal had excellent provenance going for it, which is especially important for the authentication of *objects*, as opposed to documents. We buy documents all the time with incomplete provenance. This is the norm. Not bad provenance, where we have reason to believe the item is either not good or improperly on the market. But incomplete, as in, all you know is that your great-grandfather bought an autograph from noted nineteenth-century dealer Walter Benjamin in New York City. How would you know where Walter Benjamin got it from? It's uncommon to be able to track a document from the moment it was signed to its arrival in your hands, every step of the way. But ironclad provenance isn't necessary for authentication of documents, which can prove themselves. In the lingo, they self-authenticate (or fail to) thanks to all the technical factors such as signature, paper, folds in the paper, ink, historical content, other known examples for matching, and more. Provenance is a good second opinion supporting the authenticity of documents and can shed light on the document's story, the journey of the piece of paper or animal skin, but it is not mandatory.

With objects, provenance is, in most cases, mandatory. Consider Nicolas Cage's sleuthing in the movie *National Treasure*. He finds what he says are Benjamin Franklin's glasses. How does he know? We want to believe, an "expert" tells us it is so, and onward we go. In this case, the provenance of the Harrison medal was what enticed us to take a closer look. If a John Doe had brought it in, stating that the medal had somehow resided with the Doe family for generations, we would have approached it much more carefully. The direct Harrison connection is what caused us to take it seriously. We examined its authenticity through that lens. Even the idea of a copy, that the family had multiples, was something we examined and had to definitively dismiss.

The absence of solid provenance, my dad explained to me once, undermines the numerous claims regarding caps allegedly worn by General U. S. Grant, or the claims (there have been at least three) that *this* pen, not the others, is the one Abraham Lincoln used to sign the Emancipation Proclamation. No less than three bloodstained suits have been presented as the one worn by Lincoln on the night of his assassination, but how can we know which of these, if any, is the one? Often impossible. So paper documents and their signatures have an advantage: they can be forged, yes, but technical factors and connoisseurship can establish authenticity. Often, no equivalent factors can provide the same assurance with the general's cap, the fountain pen, or the bloodstained suit. They require solid provenance. William Henry Harrison's Gold Medal had everything: science, research, plus provenance.

Take the case of Lincoln's stovepipe hat, recently the subject of much controversy. The hat resides at the Abraham Lincoln Presidential Library and Museum in Springfield, Illinois, and is a centerpiece of their marketing, fund-raising, and exhibition efforts. In 2018, a report surfaced that this hat, which the museum had acquired from Louise Taper, a well-known collector of Lincoln autographs and artifacts, might not be real. It had cost the museum a whopping $6 million. Lincoln had allegedly given the hat to an early supporter, a farmer named William Waller, in 1858—two years before Lincoln was elected president. Waller had passed it down to his children, and for a few generations the hat remained in the family, and the story was passed down as well. By the time it was sold and Taper had evidently acquired the hat, the story had evolved, and the hat had supposedly been given to Waller a few years later, during the Civil War. The extraordinary step of testing for DNA was undertaken by the FBI. The result: inconclusive. DNA is almost never used to prove such things. That it had become an issue here was not good news. The hat had the right production city, Springfield, Illinois, and was reportedly the proper sit to fit on Lincoln's head, but lacked any verifiable provenance.

So ask yourself, Was this Lincoln's hat? Here is my perhaps unsatisfying opinion: maybe. Right style, right manufacturer, stories stretching back generations. But with those shifting stories of its origins, could it also have been one of many other hats this hatmaker made in Springfield matching what was not a unique style?

What is certain is that the emotional energy in creating such stories and believing them is significant, and the gravitational pull of the desire to believe can be difficult to escape. But if you're interested and have an extra $6 million, I hear the hat might be coming up for sale.

When I was living in Rome, years ago, I stayed in a charming neighborhood across the Tiber, not far from the Pantheon. The central piazza was Piazza di Santa Maria in Trastevere. I worked hard to learn Italian and effectively succeeded, but a small slice of home was the movie theater around the corner from the piazza, which screened English-language movies. I would pass by on my way into the city center, looking at the posters showing the most recent movie to make its way to Italy, usually six or eight months after it had debuted in New York. The only movie I saw there was *Thirteen Days*, a drama starring Kevin Costner as President John F. Kennedy's assistant Kenny O'Donnell. O'Donnell was a good ol' boy, a friend from home whom the Kennedys brought along to the White House. He was a trusted political consultant and close friend to both John and Robert Kennedy—a member of the inner circle that was sometimes dubbed the Irish Mafia.

Around fifteen years after I saw the Costner movie, O'Donnell's family called my office and wanted to meet. The elder O'Donnell had died rather young.

O'Donnell's daughter-in-law drove to our office in Pennsylvania from upstate New York in an old blue minivan. She'd called to tell us she was coming, noting that she had a document appointing Kenny O'Donnell as special assistant to the president, which was signed the day Kennedy walked into the White House on January 20, 1961. It's likely the first document that Kennedy signed as president, and that's why we were interested. It symbolized the dawn of a new era, a hopeful era. She had other things too, she said.

She was warm and jovial. We looked at the documents she'd brought, spread out on a table in my office. The first thing I wanted to see was the 1961 document, to make sure it was authentic. It was beautiful—set in a battered frame, the glass a little dirty, but the document was clearly genuine. The signature was good: it clearly wasn't secretarial and matched no autopen pattern. It had been in the same frame all this time. No one had cleaned the glass or polished the frame in the last fifty years. I suspected it was just as it was when O'Donnell received it from the president.

We turned to another document she had, a memo from O'Donnell to JFK that had also been signed by RFK, which had to do with race relations in the 1960s. This document was also signed by J. Edgar Hoover and had landed on Attorney General Robert Kennedy's desk. He then sent it to the president. So this document had been touched by Hoover, RFK, and then JFK. Remarkable.

Sadly, one of the items was a reproduction: an act of Congress signed by Lyndon Johnson, framed with the pen he'd used to sign it. It was a photocopy of the original act, which was in the National Archives, although the pen was authentic. Johnson created these and gave them to supporters who'd played some role in the passing of the act. The frame was original and matched others I'd seen.

Then she said, "There are a few things in my car you might want to look at."

We walked out to her car, which was in chaotic disarray. She asked me if we bought things other than documents. "Yes, we do—anything of historical significance," I replied.

She opened the hatch of her car and removed four large paintings, each wrapped in a household blanket. These artworks had hung in the White House during the Kennedy administration, she explained, and I said, sure, I'll make you an offer on those.

Then she unwrapped a silver martini shaker. "Do you want this too?" she asked rather skeptically. Turns out the martini shaker was the vehicle through which I would better understand O'Donnell. Back in the office, we laughed together as she remembered the 1960s and the good times they used to have: Vice President Lyndon Johnson relieving himself on someone's lawn during a raucous party, everyone stumbling out of the party past him. *Mad Men*–era Washington. The joy, fun, and innocence before the Kennedy assassinations.

O'Donnell had the unique distinction of being the only person present for the assassination of both JFK and RFK. He watched both of his friends die. He slipped into drinking and died years later as a result.

But we didn't focus on the negative, we focused on the good memories. The good work they'd done. She explained that the martini shaker was a gift Bobby gave to each of his groomsmen at his wedding to Ethel Skakel in 1950. It was inscribed RFK TO PKO'D with the date June 17, 1950, etched into the silver on the next line—a unique artifact connecting Kenny to the golden era of the Kennedy family.

I keep this object in my office to this day, a reminder of the romantic age of American politics, the glamour and subsequent tragedy of our political royalty, the way the past can haunt the present.

CHAPTER 5

The Auction Game

"Imagine you are in an auction room and watch a George Washington letter sell for one hundred thousand dollars," my father said to me. "Do you think that if we waited one month, it would sell for that exact same sum at the same auction?" The question was rhetorical. It likely wouldn't.

I'd seen an Abraham Lincoln letter for sale, written during the campaign of 1860. The estimate was $15,000–$20,000, a reasonable price for a good Lincoln letter. It "passed," meaning that it failed to meet the reserve set by the seller, the number below which he or she would not sell it. Six months later, the document reappeared at the same auction priced at $10,000–$15,000. This time it sold for $35,000.

An auction sales result is nothing more than that. It is the amount of money one person is willing to pay for one object on that day in that room. That is a function of the marketing of the piece and, sometimes, buyers' schedules and moods, the economy, and perhaps what sold yesterday at a different auction.

"Just because a document sells high," my dad noted early on, "doesn't mean it's worth that. And if it sells low, it might be worth much more. Don't assume. Examine with fresh eyes."

The example he had used was a 1996 auction featuring the estate of Jacqueline Kennedy. As the *Los Angeles Times* reported, "The auction fever of the Jacqueline Kennedy Onassis estate sale ended Friday with frenzied Camelot souvenir hunters ringing up $34,457,470 during four days on Sotheby's cash registers, over seven times the original estimate of $4.6 million. . . . Sotheby's savvy marketing, which tapped into a rich vein of nostalgia, yielded big profits for John F. Kennedy Jr. and Caroline Kennedy Schlossberg."

Arnold Schwarzenegger paid $772,500 for a set of the late president's golf clubs, which was 858 times more than Sotheby's estimate.

For years after the sale, we would be offered materials from that auction at prices reflecting what the buyer paid, and not anywhere near where we thought we could price them.

"So what is that stuff worth?" my dad asked. "Is it worth the estimate that the auction gave it? Or what the person paid? Or the lesser sum we'd pay? Or what that person will eventually get?"

I saw all of these dynamics in play at my first New York auction, just a year or so after I joined the business.

Malcolm Forbes was the publisher of *Forbes* magazine; he'd spent a lifetime fashioning himself as the very embodiment of fantastic, eccentric, extravagant wealth. He named his private jet the *Capitalist Tool* and his yacht the *Highlander*. He owned a half dozen residences and hosted elaborate, multimillion-dollar birthday parties. He was also a voracious collector—of art and antiques, Fabergé eggs, motorcycles and hot-air balloons, toys and toy soldiers, and rare books, autographs, and documents.

Forbes had put together one of the finest collections of historical documents in the twentieth century. He simply bought the best material, some of it from us. He combined seemingly unlimited financial resources with a keen eye, a formidable arsenal. And after he died in 1990, as often happens, his heirs decided to sell the collections. Numerous auctions of his prized possessions took place over many years. Christie's got the coveted auction of the autographs and historical documents, with so much material they divided the collection into a series of six auctions, which were held between 2002 and 2007. The stuff was incredible. Everybody wanted a piece of this collection. The hype was just one notch down from that of the Jackie Kennedy auction. The first sale alone brought in nearly

$20 million. The manuscript of Abraham Lincoln's last address as president brought in $3 million; a letter from Einstein to President Franklin Roosevelt warning of the devastatingly powerful potential of nuclear weapons netted approximately $1 million. Christie's sold a cut Button Gwinnett signature for nearly $300,000. Who is Button Gwinnett? He signed the Declaration of Independence and was then promptly killed in a duel, so if you are collecting the autographs of the signers of the Declaration, you need him, and his handwriting is rare.

I went through the large catalog with my father, circling the things I liked, and waited for him to do the same. I'd circled a lot of pieces with high estimates, big names, and big headlines. But my father had found something that puzzled me. "Why do you like this?" I pointed to a document signed by President William McKinley in 1898. He'd not only circled it, but placed a star next to its listing.

"That might be the most important document in the catalog," he said. "Do you see what it is? It's a sleeper. Remember the *Maine*?"

He was referring to the explosion and sinking of the USS *Maine* in the Havana harbor in 1898. This incident is the origin of the phrase "Remember the Maine," the rallying cry for people agitating for war against the Spanish, which maintained a colonial hold on Cuba. Thus began the Spanish-American War, which reduced Spanish influence—and expanded American influence—greatly. The war launched the career of Theodore Roosevelt, who commanded his Rough Riders to legendary fame. And it joined a list—a small one—of official declared wars. Congress voted to declare war against Britain in the War of 1812, Mexico in the Mexican-American War in the 1840s, Spain in the Spanish-American War in 1898, Germany in both world wars, Austria-Hungary in World War I, and Japan, Bulgaria, Romania, and Italy in World War II. (In the case of World War II, it was Japan that spurred the vote to declare war against the Axis Powers.) That's it. The rest of the wars were undeclared.

The document that had caught my father's attention ended the third of these: it was McKinley's order to certify the peace treaty ending the Spanish-American War. In many ways, this war launched America onto the international scene and began a period of increasingly bold activity, symbolized by Theodore Roosevelt.

"There has been a lot of publicity around these auctions, and I expect everything will sell at substantially higher prices than they would any other time because of the excitement," my father said. "But I want that piece."

Christie's is in Rockefeller Center in midtown Manhattan, an iconic address. It is designed to feel museum-like. Galleries display art and other items for sale or from upcoming auctions. At the end of a long hallway are a pair of staircases leading to a mezzanine. This is where the auction takes place. The large room has an elevated platform at the front, and a large screen off to the side showing the current bid in multiple currencies. That's not all that relevant in the book and manuscript world, which tends to be American and English, but the art world is international. Another screen displays a photograph and lot number for whatever is being sold. At an art auction, the artwork itself is sometimes displayed, though not always; at a document and manuscript auction that's rare.

The auctioneers at Christie's are suave Englishmen in bespoke suits. Or at least, that's the general sensibility, regardless of gender or nationality. They are understated, and wry. They specialize, so you recognize them from auction to auction. They speak clearly, slowly, and conversationally.

I stood in that room and watched letters go for ten times what we'd budgeted to pay: Washington letters went well into the six-figure range, and Lincoln documents ten times the estimate, then the McKinley document came up.

We bid $4,000, then $6,000. Someone else bid $7,000. We bid $8,000, someone else bid $9,000, and then it was silent. We bid $10,000. Then it was silent again. We waited. Fifteen, twenty, thirty seconds can pass. As the seconds tick by, your heart beats a little bit more quickly. You think you're going to get it. Then someone else steps in: $11,000. There's a psychological element to this. People who step in having bided their time may be playing a game. The game is: because they're just stepping in at this level, they want you to think they're willing to go a lot higher. The goal is to get you to bow out. But that may not work. In this case we were back in at $12,000, and they bid $13,000, and the bidding continued up.

You can bid a lot more than you want to, or ought to, because you're in the thick of it. You're bidding incrementally, and it's a game, it's a gamble. It's not as if somebody comes to you and offers you a document for a certain price, and you can make the decision separate from the action. It's like the story of the frog thrown into cold water, not realizing it's getting warmer and warmer and then it's too late: the auction is over and the collector can be left thinking, *Did I overpay for this piece?*

Some pieces we're willing to pay anything to get. Well, not literally *anything*, but we're willing to substantially exceed what we think anyone else will pay because we see something in the piece, or we think it's incredible and we want to have it.

In all cases, knowledge is key. Auctions are not perfect markets, and it's very much a "buyer beware" environment. These events are not for the uninformed.

When the final hammer came down, we'd won it; we paid $20,000, far less than we would have had it come to us privately, and far less than we felt it was worth. We eventually sold it for $60,000.

This is the process by which my dad had built his business in the early years: he'd looked at page after page and found something hidden in plain sight.

The hardest part of my apprenticeship wasn't learning how to authenticate documents and artifacts. That can be done in a few years. It was learning how to assess value, learning to spot the gems in a sea of mediocrity, taking that "blink" moment and translating it into action, and putting money on the line as a result. That takes a long time, a decade or so.

What we did with the Forbes catalog became a regular challenge: If I was given ten documents and told to pick the best one, could I do it? My father and I were looking for things to buy, but it was also an intellectual game we played—a formative part of my learning the rare-document trade.

The stamp, book, and autograph fields are intertwined. After all, letters that were sent had their own stamps. One day, we were looking at a catalog from a New York City stamp auction, which included many letters, including from Benjamin Franklin and Sir Walter Raleigh. The glossy, perfect-bound, illustrated catalog was fifty pages long, with around two hundred lots, many highlighted with larger descriptions, images, and bolder headlines.

My dad handed me the catalog and challenged me: "Can you find the best piece in the catalog?"

I looked through, page by page, and I said, "The Walter Raleigh document?"

"No. Walter Raleigh documents are uncommon and this is a nice one, but no. The piece that you're looking for is treated as minor in the catalog, takes up two or three inches there, and it's incredibly important."

Now I was frustrated. The significant documents were showcased with photographs, while the lesser items simply quoted the letters and details in small print. I looked through the catalog again. What was he talking about? I couldn't figure it out. Then my father pulled out a pen and turned the pages of the catalog and circled the description of a letter. As he'd said, the listing was small, unremarkable.

I read it and remained dumbfounded.

"What is this, Dad?" The letter was signed by someone named Hutchinson. Who the hell was that? My father said only, "Read the letter."

Dated September 13, 1801, it was written from "Headquarters" in Egypt.

> I shall be very much obliged to you to copy the inscription from the Stone. I send you the former copy which you say is inaccurate. Tell Colonel Turner that not only the Stone but every thing which we get from the French should be deposited in some place of security. I do not regard much the threats of the French savants. It is better however not to trust them. Have you heard of any more Coptic or Arabic manuscripts?

The letter was written to Edward Clarke and signed by John Hely-Hutchinson. None of the names meant anything to me—or apparently, to the organizers of the auction, who'd consigned it to a tiny spot in the catalog.

"I guarantee you that if I look up the dates for this—September 1801, in Egypt—they're referring to the Rosetta Stone, and if so, I bet this is the order to seize the Rosetta Stone," my dad said. And he was right.

Napoléon had conquered Egypt in 1798, and the following year a French army engineer had discovered a large stone on which the same text had been inscribed in three scripts: hieratic, Greek, and Egyptian hieroglyphics. Since people could still read ancient Greek, that meant there was a hope—which proved well-founded—that by comparing the texts hieroglyphics could at last be translated. This translation feat made available to us much of the wisdom and experience of the Egyptian civilization. The army engineer's find was named the Rosetta Stone and was hidden away in Alexandria a few years later when the British arrived to take Egypt from the French. General Hutchinson took Cairo and dispatched a civilian scholar, Clarke, to take possession of the Egyptian artifacts Napoléon had collected.

Clarke had found the stone and reported as much to Hutchinson, who, in this letter, ordered him to seize the artifact from the French. It was soon transported to the British Museum, where it remains, one of that institution's most prized possessions.

The letter was sitting in plain sight. That same day we paid \$25,000 for a letter sent by Benjamin Franklin from Paris while he was there negotiating funding for the American Revolution, and we also bought the Walter Raleigh. But we only paid a few hundred dollars for the Rosetta Stone piece. I can't remember what the Franklin letter said, but I think about the Rosetta letter all the time.

This phenomenon of serendipity is important to note. The line that separates what gets lost to history and what gets found is thin. It can be as thin as an intuition that a document is something special, or a family member recognizing that an inherited treasure is, in fact, a treasure. In this case, if my dad hadn't seen it, the Rosetta Stone letter may not have sold at auction at all and been returned to an estate and possibly thrown away. Instead, now it's in the British Library, which bought it from us. The line between those two events was our raising our hand, bidding on the piece. There were no other bidders.

My father knew the history, he saw the writer was in Africa, he recognized the reference to the "Stone." (He'd always been fascinated by the Rosetta Stone; years earlier he'd made a point of taking our family to see it when we visited London.) I think the bigger picture is, he had an intuition and bothered to read the letter. He didn't look at the name Hutchinson and say, "Never heard of him, I don't want that." No—he took the time to actually read the piece. He took nothing for granted. He didn't assume that because the auction company hadn't given it any attention, it wasn't important.

We search the world for these artifacts, these documents, but if we can't recognize them when we see them, what good is the hunt?

A classics professor at Bryn Mawr College was retiring some years ago. She'd inherited a collection of material from her father and grandfather—letters and documents from the Duke of Wellington, Ernest Hemingway, Rube Goldberg, cartoonist Reamer Keller, Presidents Andrew Jackson and James Madison, Henry Clay, Orville Wright, the painters Maxfield Parrish and Norman Rockwell, and many others.

The woman had sent us a long list with a brief description of each document. My dad took one look and said, "Most of this we don't really need, except for the Orville Wright letter, and the Ernest Hemingway letter." Of the hundreds of pieces we were looking at, those two stood out above all the rest.

How had he honed in on the Wright and Hemingway letters so quickly? It was because the content of the letters connected to the historical significance of their authors. The letter from Orville Wright described him and his brother as they "intently watched birds fly, in a hope of learning something from them. I cannot think of anything that was first learned in that way," he wrote.

> Learning the secret of flight from a bird was a good deal like learning the secret of magic from a magician. After you once know the trick and know what to look for, you see things that you did not notice.

This spectacular letter puts us inside the inventive mind of Wright. You can almost see the two young brothers staring at the sky, watching the birds above their Indiana home.

The Hemingway letter was about fishing. "We always gaff a marlin in the head no matter where he is hooked," he wrote, laying out detailed instructions and opinions about landing these enormous fish.

> When you get the head up by the boat the tail may be fourteen feet away if the fish would be big enough. How are you to lead their tail toward you when the hook is in the fishes mouth? Also the gaff holds best in the fishes head and you can then grab the bill and hang on while you club him across the top of the head between the eyes. A gaff in the head kills the fish too and does not spoil the meat. . . . Everyone in Cuba where I learned to fish for marlin gaffs them in the head and out of about a hundred and twenty that I have caught would say that all but four or five have been gaffed in the head and those were gaffed elsewhere by slips or by accident.

Hemingway was a man of action, forging his high-literary tough-guy style by writing about bullfighting and war. He took up marlin fishing in the 1930s in Key West, Florida, and in Cuba, where he described first learning the sport in this 1935 letter. He would return to the subject in *The Old Man and the Sea*, published in 1952 and written in Cuba—the story of an old fisherman, Santiago, battling to capture an eighteen-foot marlin. (The struggle does not turn out well.) This was the book that won Hemingway the Pulitzer Prize. So fishing was a key part of his legacy.

One year later: The drive into rural Maryland wound past redbrick barns, cornfields, soy fields, and along dusty dirt roads, ditches on each side. Such was my entrée into the auction world as a solo bidder. My father was in Maine for the summer, and the task fell to me. My destination was a converted farmhouse and barn that had become the seat of an obscure auction house, or at least obscure in our world. Inside was mayhem, with well over a hundred sweltering bidders watching the action. This was Crocker Farm, and you could hear the raucous bidding and auction hammer pounding from outside the old barn. At the front of the room was a small dais, where a man stood talking a mile a minute in the chanting drone common to livestock auctioneers.

The item up for sale was a quilt.

I couldn't understand a word he was saying. This was very, very different from the Forbes sale at Christie's.

I looked around in awe. In the back were the auction "offices"—a couple of small rooms and some folding tables and chairs. In the loft above, where I guess the hay bales had been stored, were more folding tables covered with refreshments: small cubes of cheese, crackers, wine, and Bud Light. Many were drinking. A handful of people were visibly intoxicated.

I was in search of one of the first Thanksgiving proclamations—in fact, the first issued by a man with the official title "president of the United States." The auction company described the piece as an "extremely Important John Hanson Thanksgiving Proclamation, March 19, 1782, signed 'John Hanson,' President of The United States in Congress Assembled, and 'Chas Thomson,' Secretary of Congress, two pages, folio, each 12 1/2" x 8". Ink of document remains dark and bold, including that found on Hanson's signature. Extremely rare, signed document, *the first Thanksgiving Proclamation issued in the United States under the Articles of Confederation*" (my emphasis).

John Hanson was never President of the United States, you might say. Well, you would be wrong. In March 1781, the country's first constitution was passed, the Articles of Confederation, designed to bridge the English colonial government and the permanent constitutional government that lay ahead. In November 1781, Congress elected the first leader under those articles—Hanson. So in November, when Hanson took his seat, he was technically the first "President of The United States in Congress Assembled," and forever after the answer to a common trivia question.

Hanson's calling for Thanksgiving might also seem odd to our ears. No talk of turkey, no discussion of family getting together around the dinner table, no Lions or Cowboys game. The overall tone of the proclamation is not exactly joyous, referring to Great Britain's "lust of Dominion" and "lawless ambition" causing "all the horrors and calamities of a bloody and vindictive war" and "the cries of the distressed." Today we know that by March of 1782 the Americans had effectively won the war for independence, but back then, at that moment, the Americans could not have been *certain* that the British wouldn't return to the field after the surrender at Yorktown. This was where Lord Cornwallis surrendered to General George Washington after a great siege that featured heroics by one of Washington's battlefield aides, Alexander Hamilton. But tens of thousands of British troops were still stationed in New York City—which had been the hotbed of loyalism—and elsewhere; the pitiful state of American finances left the soldiers unpaid and debts to European lenders mounting; and the Treaty of Paris that would end this war wouldn't be written for six months, or signed for another eighteen months.

At this moment, Hanson declared a day of thanksgiving for the American people, and that's what I was looking for at the end of that dirt road that day.

Hanson's proclamation, though early in 1782, wasn't the first. A form of Thanksgiving had been declared by the Continental Congress, with Samuel Huntington and John Hancock as president, starting in 1777. But these men didn't have that now-coveted title president of the United States, and this one was early, predating the formal end of the war and the forming of our government.

The Hanson family had kept this piece for centuries; the current generation had decided to sell it, along with an old bottle of Hanson's port "approximately ⅔ full," and an early Revolutionary War diary. And they'd consigned the items to what I imagine was their community auction house, as often happens.

My job was to examine the piece in person before bidding, then to bid high enough to get it. My dad had sent me an email that was in effect a small history lesson, laying out the importance of the proclamation.

I made my way to the back of the room to register and to study the document. The room was crowded and loud. I continued listening to the auctioneer, struggling to understand him. My fear was that I'd somehow miss my lot altogether since he was going so fast.

The man who showed me the piece was my age, in his late twenties, the son of the owner of the company. The hustle and bustle of the auction crowd faded as I looked at the proclamation. The auction house had sent me a photograph, but seeing it in person was a prerequisite to bidding. You often can't tell a copy from an original in a photograph, which removes the features that you can see viewing an object in person and makes the whole image flat. You can't hold a photograph up to the light to see the watermark, check the back for show-through of iron gall ink. When the original document is there in front of you, you can run your hand along the paper to judge its consistency. So that's what I did, without my father's guiding eye, like the inaugural sailing of a vessel pushed out from dry dock. I felt a little wobbly, I suppose, but I was sure: the document was authentic.

I waited for lot 279, watching the surreal scene. The bidding was frantic and exuberant, and the items were more quilts and other household items—carpets, ceramics, silverware, and so on. It seemed to be an estate sale, and the auctioneer was racing through more than fifteen hundred lots. The prices were modest, in the hundreds of dollars, far less than the thousands I was prepared to spend.

The auctioneer's voice ebbed and flowed, his thick mustache and large, wide body moving as his two hands pointed left, right, up front, and at the back of the room.

I figured I'd bid on the Revolutionary War diary, which came up before the Thanksgiving proclamation, just to see how it went. And immediately I realized that my impression of the auction as an unsophisticated country affair wasn't 100 percent accurate. The bidding on the journal climbed fast, past $20,000, and I dropped out quickly. Revolutionary War diaries are uncommon, and those that contain detailed descriptions of people or battles sell well. They're primary resources for our study of the revolution. This is how we know what happened on what date and where. But what I wanted was the Thanksgiving proclamation.

The winner of the diary wasn't in the room—he or she was on the phone. And now I noticed a folding picnic table where the telephone bids were being processed. I realized I wasn't alone in this.

I was standing near the back of the room. The bidding started at $4,000, and I raised my bidding "paddle." Most people envision a paddle with a number on it, and those do exist. But generally bidders are just raising their hands, only showing their paddle and number at the end. Nowadays when I go to an auction, I have a more seasoned approach, tending to wait until the end before jumping in and then bidding more strategically. But this was my first solo auction, and I was still worried that I wouldn't be able to understand the auctioneer's high-speed, unconventional style, and I didn't want to inadvertently miss the hammer altogether. I put my hand up early to alert the auctioneer that I was in this game. I wanted him to know that he needed to come back to me.

In the barn, only a couple of other bidders took part. Most of the competition came from an unknown number of bidders on the phones.

The bids were going up, and as they did, my heart began beating faster, the building of a heat that drives bidding exuberance. I could barely understand the guy. I just listened to the numbers. All the babble in between I just filtered out.

Soon enough, most of the other bidders dropped out, and it was just me and someone on the phone. I bid $14,000 and waited for the hammer.

Back and forth we went. The pauses between bids had gotten longer.

Then suddenly *Bang!* the gavel struck, and it was all over, including the shouting. It was mine.

I'd won the Thanksgiving proclamation for $18,000 plus the 15 percent buyer's premium, for a total of $20,700. (The auction house takes this commission on the "hammer price" from the buyer and the larger 20–25 percent commission from the seller.)

I also bought the bottle of port for a little over $1,500. A visibly drunk man stumbled over to offer his congratulations. I still have that bottle and it sits on my mantel.

CHAPTER 6

The Art of the Fake

The signature looked pretty good I thought. It read "A. Lincoln," as Lincoln's letters always did. If you see a letter—not a formal document—signed Abraham or Abe, run in the other direction. The *Lincoln* ended with a two-tiered signature, with the final two letters set on a slightly higher plane. Indeed, Lincoln's autograph typically takes three distinct steps upward, and a flat signature is suspicious. This had those steps. Yet I had a feeling in the pit of my stomach. The writing had a labored look to it throughout the letter. A few letters looked deliberate, even traced, and the dateline was scrunched. The lines weren't straight—they bobbed and weaved up and down. Something was wrong. Yet this was a famous letter, widely published, being sold by a reputable dealer, referenced in one of the biographer and scholar Carl Sandburg's great works and illustrated there. My father had suggested, before seeing the scan, that we buy it. This important letter was about Lincoln's pardoning a soldier to be executed during the Civil War, an act for which the president would earn a reputation for fairness and clemency. Yet it wasn't passing the blink test.

On my first day on the job, my dad had walked over to his bookshelf of reference works, many now rare and out of print, and picked one out.

"Read this," he said.

Many years earlier, when I was about eight years old, my father began putting together what would become a large reference library, with books about authenticity, great auction catalogs of past years, biographies of famous people, and illustrations of authentic autographs, against which he compared the autographs he would collect. By the time I joined the business, his walls were covered with books.

He reveled in discussing the history of the field. "Aristotle collected manuscripts and maps; so did the ancient Romans," he said. "The elder Pliny wasn't merely a collector of autographs, but made the earliest known comments on their rarity, remarking that in ancient Rome, in their bookshops, the letters of Cicero, Virgil, and Augustus Caesar weren't uncommon, but that those of Julius Caesar were very rare."

As Mt. Vesuvius erupted, and Pompeii was being buried, Pliny the Elder was across the bay with his book and document collection. His nephew Pliny the Younger wrote:

> On 24 August, in the early afternoon, my mother drew his [my uncle's] attention to a cloud of unusual size and appearance. He had been out in the sun, had taken a cold bath, and lunched while lying down, and was then looking at his books. . . . My uncle's scholarly acumen saw at once that it was important enough for a closer inspection, and he ordered a boat to be made ready. . . . He hurried to the place which everyone else was hastily leaving, steering his course straight for the danger zone. He was entirely fearless. . . . Ashes were already falling, hotter and thicker as the ships drew near, followed by bits of pumice and blackened stones, charred and cracked by the flames: then suddenly they were in shallow water, and the shore was blocked by the debris from the mountain.

My father's interest in the history of the sellers of history has made him something of an expert on the subject. While Europeans began opening historical shops in the early mid-nineteenth century, the historical professional trade in the United States was decidedly newer. The early collectors, motivated by a growing realization of the importance of the American story and the collecting spirit of the Victorian era, put together collections that would today be nearly impossible to find. The material cost little, $5 or less for a letter by George Washington, for example. The Victorians notoriously clipped signatures off documents. William Sprague, America's first renowned collector, wrote to George Washington's biographer Jared Sparks asking for a sample of Washington's handwriting for his growing collection. Sparks obliged by taking a scalpel to Washington's inaugural speech, slicing it into collecting pieces, an unfortunate symbol of the era. All this my father told me the first week on the job, perhaps even the first day.

The first book my father pulled off his shelf for me was a battered copy of a memoir by early collector Adrian Joline, *Rambles in Autograph Land*. Joline had been alive during the lifetime of Darwin and a bit after. If he wanted a letter from Theodore Roosevelt, Joline had no need to buy one—he'd write the White House himself. His was a noble passion, an educated pursuit. Joline decries the Victorian collecting mentality and writes of the difference between collecting for the sake of collecting and the true hunt—the search for the history and its meaning.

But the book I liked the most was called *Great Forgers and Famous Fakes*, written by twentieth-century dealer Charles Hamilton, who died during my lifetime and whom my father knew. Hamilton gives detailed accounts of some of the scoundrels of the age, men adept at handwriting and forging, the equivalent of an actor doing a great impression, but with a more sinister intent and legal implications. Hamilton writes about men content to steal and misrepresent.

From him I first learned of Joseph Cosey. Cosey was the greatest forger of his generation, Hamilton felt. Cosey's works appeared (and still appear) in major auctions and continue to dot the landscape. Many libraries have his forgeries without knowing it.

And if you wanted one in the early twentieth century, you needed only to pull up a stool at the bar, where Cosey could often be found, and buy the man a drink. It could plausibly be said that Abraham Lincoln posthumously fueled Cosey's alcohol problem.

"Practically everybody has been stung by Cosey," Mary A. Benjamin told Hamilton. She was heir to the Walter Benjamin firm, the first major dealer in the United States. Cosey loved Lincoln, but he also forged the letters of George Washington, John Adams, Alexander Hamilton, Benjamin Franklin, and many more. He had access to period paper, period ink, and he'd practiced so extensively that he could write full letters fluidly. Cosey wasn't his real name. It was Martin Coneely.

And yet, in spite of his obvious talents, Hamilton wrote, Cosey had an Achilles' heel when it came to Lincoln. He never got the signature just right—that three-stepped shape. It goes up almost uniformly. Lincoln would write the tent of the *A*, place a dot or two after the letter, then cross it with a counterclockwise loop. From there, without picking up the pen, he'd start the *L* of *Lincoln* and keep it on a platform raised above the *A*, before proceeding through the *o*, from which he'd step up again for the *ln*. Cosey wrote the entire name on a horizontal line.

Even Cosey wasn't perfect. Everyone has an Achilles' heel.

Eight years later, I was staring at that Lincoln letter.

"Dad, I don't know why yet, but there's something wrong with this letter," I said. "We shouldn't buy it."

It was no small thing to evaluate the holdings of a seasoned dealer, a generation older than me, and pronounce his material fake. I've done that since, but I'd never done it before. I had to be sure. Moreover, this was not an unknown letter. It had come from the collection of the revered Oliver Barrett. Barrett put together the most significant collection of Lincoln documents ever, then or since, a collection he sold for many millions. He was friends with Carl Sandburg, and Sandburg had reproduced this very letter in his book *Abraham Lincoln: The War Years*. The Papers of Abraham Lincoln noted the existence of this letter and cited the Barrett collection as its source.

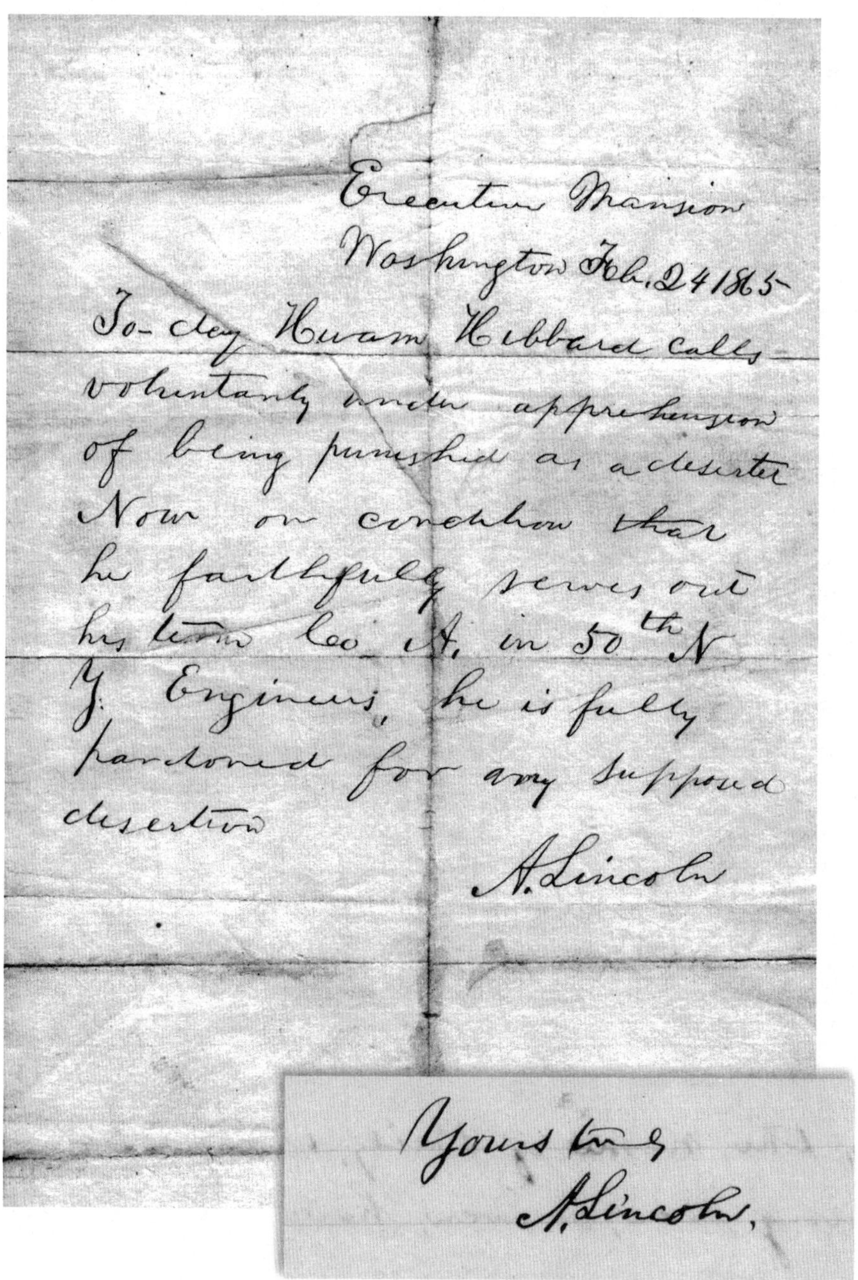

Executive Mansion
Washington Feb. 24 1865

To-day Hiram Hibbard calls voluntarily under apprehension of being punished as a deserter Now on condition that he faithfully serves out his term Co. A. in 50th N. Y. Engineers, he is fully pardoned for any supposed desertion

A. Lincoln

Yours truly
A. Lincoln.

The forged letter from Abraham Lincoln (*top*) and his authentic signature (*inset*).

I looked at the handwriting. Many of the letters superficially looked right. This wasn't traced. Care had been taken to re-create a few of Lincoln's more idiosyncratic letters, such as the distinct capital *F*. The paper had been folded properly to mimic a piece that had gone through the mail. But from there the similarities to an actual Lincoln letter were few.

The entire letter sloped down, left to right, as if the writer had lost interest at the end of each line. Some of the letters were just wrong if you looked at them individually. The dateline was smooshed together, as if the writer had run out of space. A couple of the letters were shaky, and the entire letter was uneven. In Lincoln's time, people studied handwriting, and the lines of a letter were straight, not uneven. This was the first time I had this instinct, this gut feel.

It took about an hour of active discussion with my father for me to become fully confident in my assessment. "Do you think it's Cosey?" my father asked.

I looked at the signature. This forger knew what Cosey never got: Lincoln's signature was three stepped. Yet Cosey's letters were far more convincing taken overall. Cosey's forgeries fail on one elemental level, the autograph, but generally succeed in the overall texture of the handwriting. This sloppy attempt was both corrective of Cosey's work and not worthy of it.

We didn't buy the letter, and the dealer who'd listed it for sale agreed with my assessment after I explained my thinking. But more than that, the forgery matched none of the known examples published in my father's extensive library. We'd found a new forger, an unknown counterfeiter. The dealer pulled it from his inventory, acknowledged his mistake, and the episode ended.

All this I began to learn on my very first day at the office, thanks to my father's bookshelf.

My dad had another book by Charles Hamilton, *Scribblers and Scoundrels*, which recounted more stories of the infamous men and women who preyed on gullible and not-so-gullible buyers. They were both forgers and thieves.

Hamilton himself was taken in by one such Bonnie and Clyde team, a husband and wife who stole historical documents from the National Archives and then sold them. Hamilton was incensed and helped the FBI track down Sam and Elizabeth Matz. "How the Matzes had managed to elude arrest is difficult to understand," he writes. They traveled with five children, one of whom was an infant. Wanted posters everywhere read, "Sam . . . dresses well, talks big, and smokes cigars." Hamilton reports that Elizabeth was "very messy looking and seemed rather beaten and pathetic." Yet they were adept at disguising themselves. "Sam had grown a shaggy moustache; and Liz's warts had almost disappeared." Hamilton engaged in a sting to take them down. I loved the Men in Black, "Just the facts, ma'am," 1950s-style descriptions. But his tales of the industry during his time gave me an important insight: some people are willing to bend or break the rules to profit from history.

"I recognize these things, but I can't quite place them."

Karen and I were walking down the temporarily carpeted aisles of the New York Antiquarian Book Fair at the Park Avenue Armory, where it has been held for as long as I've been doing this. Inside one of the booths was an array of letters, mostly by American presidents, and I knew I'd seen them before. I remembered one piece clearly: a letter by then general Zachary Taylor, writing from a battlefield of the Mexican-American War in the 1840s. Taylor's fame in that war led him to the presidency. There were also letters by Washington, Adams, Jefferson, Lincoln—valuable material.

Then it came to me—I remembered where I'd seen these documents. It had been a few months earlier.

My father and I had driven to a one-story house in New Jersey to look at a collection, checkbook in hand. The documents were owned by two men—old friends—who'd bought the collection together.

They were in their early forties, had no experience in the field, and seemed honest and well meaning. We spent three painstaking hours analyzing the documents, looking at them one by one and figuring out what we'd offer. We wanted the whole collection or nothing, and it made little sense and might encumber the negotiation to itemize the offer piece by piece. Every once in a while, as we calculated, my father and I would step into the small garden behind the house and discuss valuation. We finally agreed to pay our hosts around $80,000, as I recall, a fair number and one that would guarantee us (and them) a sizable profit. But when it came to the question of provenance, as it always does (or ought to), we ran into trouble.

The men had purchased the collection from a Haitian woman who'd taken care of an elderly man who'd died. It was the man's collection, and she had told them that he'd given it to her as a gift. She was a professional live-in health-care aide. I couldn't help but think of this old man, anonymous to us, who'd spent a lifetime collecting these beautiful documents. I tried to imagine the scenario in which he'd give his entire collection, something worth a great deal of money, to someone he knew only in the final year or so of his life. How would we untangle this?

I had an idea: I asked the men to call the former caretaker to see if she'd sign and notarize a letter declaring that she'd been given the documents as a gift, so we'd have proof of legal ownership, and her identity would be known to us. But the two men explained that, no, she wouldn't. She wanted the gift to be kept quiet and she would remain anonymous.

We didn't know who the original owner of the collection was. And the woman who'd supposedly been given the documents refused to attach her name to the transaction. To us, and I think to any reasonable person, it was pretty clear what had happened. We told the two men that we couldn't in good conscience sell our customers material that we suspected might not be legitimately on the market. The health-care aide's story seemed implausible to us, and her refusal to sign a letter was flat-out incriminating.

We walked away. Day wasted. But all the wiser.

Now, months later, I was looking at the same collection. The very collection of historical documents we had *not* purchased was on display in this man's booth.

He came up to me, bragging, as he always does, this time about purchasing such a stellar collection. I looked him in the eye and asked, "Was it two men from New Jersey?"

"Yes, it was."

"I recognize this material." I said that we'd been offered that collection too, but we'd been concerned about the provenance. He smiled innocently, told me the two men had mentioned we'd passed and why, and did not remove the material from his booth. I noticed later that he didn't advertise any of these documents on his website. I imagine he sold most in direct pitches to his customers at discount prices to move them along. I remember thinking to myself, *That's a polluted stream*—a metaphor we come back to all the time. "If you fish in polluted streams," I say now, "you're going to get sick."

And Hamilton's message, one I absorbed at the beginning of my career in history, came right back to me: some people are willing to put aside their morality for money.

CHAPTER 7

The Real Ronald Reagan

A collector and longtime friend rang up my father on the phone: "I have this amazing collection of Reagan letters. Are you interested?"

The collector had purchased the letters from an agent of the stepdaughter of Senator George Murphy, who'd married her mother years after his first wife died; Murphy himself had died in 1992, and she'd waited until Reagan's death to sell the documents. The collector chose us because, back before I joined the business, my dad had handled the enormous collection of Reagan letters to his pen pal, written over half a century. That collection, still the largest of Reagan we—or perhaps anyone—had ever seen, ended up at the Reagan Ranch.

Part of the hunt is a network of hunters. This collector and friend of my father's had found these new Reagan letters at a jewelry consignment shop near Chicago where he lives. He wanted our opinion on their value, and perhaps to have us as a partner in their ultimate sale.

Looking through the letters, I saw an opportunity. I wanted a chance to test a theory: people care about these figures, and we could reach potential clients effectively with an experienced public relations operation. People are interested in Reagan; and this stuff was spicy. I'd give it a run. I'd been a press secretary to a member of Congress and to a Philadelphia mayoral candidate, then had gone into PR consulting in the private sector. Why not apply my experience to my new business?

George Murphy paved the way for Reagan's ascent in many ways—he'd been a Hollywood star before becoming a US senator. They were old friends, and the correspondence spanned Reagan's eight years in the White House. The forty-one letters covered everything from his opinions about political rivals and world leaders to his takes on political scandals and thoughts on media bias. They painted a picture of Reagan as leader of the free world, powerful and connected, conversing frankly with an old friend. Nothing like it had ever been on the market.

Reagan's first impression of Gorbachev, in 1985: "It would be foolish to believe the leopard will change its spots," he wrote. "He is a firm believer in their system, and he believes the propaganda they peddle about us. At the same time, he is practical and knows his economy is a basket case." In 1988, Reagan visited the Soviet Union, the first visit by an American president in fourteen years. "For the first time, I believe there could perhaps one day be a stirring of the people that would make the bureaucrats pay attention." He was right: the Berlin Wall came down a year later; and the Soviet Union dissolved two years after that.

In terms of domestic politics, the letters contained his assessment that he'd been successfully maligned when it came to taxes: "There is no question but that we're vulnerable on that one," he wrote to Murphy in 1983. "They've done quite a job on me as 'favoring the rich' in our tax policies." He described former vice president Walter Mondale as "lying through his teeth" about Reagan's plans to cut Social Security and referred to Senator Ted Kennedy dismissively as the "playboy from Massachusetts." Reagan defended himself as entirely innocent in the Iran-Contra affair and complained bitterly about the "daily poison of the *New York Times* and *Washington Post*."

I looked back at old political press releases I'd written, adopted a template for our firm, wrote up a press release, and contacted a reporter I knew at the Associated Press in Philadelphia. I had an interesting story: an intimate and revealing collection of letters by Ronald Reagan. Was this something she might want to write about?

She wrote a small item about the letters and put it out on the wire.

What happened next was like being unexpectedly caught in a windstorm. A light breeze hits, you balance and relish the fresh air, then another, much stronger breeze comes in and nearly knocks you off your feet. I was sitting with my parents on their patio, drinking a glass of wine. I was tracking the story on the internet and watched as that small item went from the Pennsylvania papers to the New York papers to California papers and then overnight to the international wire. The next day we were bombarded with phone calls. I did numerous interviews, and television wanted the story. I went on CNN and Fox News, saying we estimated the collection was worth $225,000. The collection sold immediately. We got a call from an old friend who worked at Maggs in London, Hinda Rose—since deceased. She was representing an Israeli businessman who'd seen the news in Israel and wanted to buy the letters. This was the first sale I'd orchestrated, in my midtwenties, from start to finish. It had taken a single day, and we'd sold something for a quarter million dollars to a man whose agent was in England and who lived in Israel. I discerned in all this a powerful message: that public relations in this business works. A current of historical interest was out there. With both the buyer and the general public, we'd reached people we never would have otherwise.

But I didn't have time to explore this thought any further.

The telephone rang again. A man identified himself as the son of George Murphy, the recipient of the letters. He said, "You have a problem. Those letters belong to me." His stepmother had wrongfully taken them, at least in his view.

We calmly explained what had happened. We were good-faith purchasers and had no way of knowing about any internal family disputes about ownership. This sort of thing can happen when a family has two sets of children. But the son had his father's entire archive, the chair he sat on in the Senate, movie posters from his years in Hollywood, and boxes of other stuff.

His story was believable, so we offered him a deal: we'd make him a financial partner in the transaction. He accepted, the collection sold, he made his money, and indeed he asked us to sell the rest of his father's things. We became friends and stayed in touch for years before he passed away. He'd met Reagan many times, hosted him and been to the ranch; he knew all the bigwigs in California during those years and regaled us with stories of having Walt Disney visit his house. His father had been a Republican when California was Republican.

More than that, conversation with him gave the letters context and texture, like having them annotated. He took those letters and amplified them, giving us a deeper perspective on Reagan.

Although I never met Reagan, I feel I know him pretty well. The letters we've carried, and we've carried many, are warm. I suppose I'm not alone. Reagan is a widely beloved figure, though many people see him through a partisan lens. But Reagan was a leader, and a mass of men and women see in him their dreams and aspirations, and they long to live in his world. Rather than jump into the partisan fray, ask yourself, Why? What does this tell us?

But regardless of what I thought I knew, I was unprepared for the deeply personal nature of the letters that would next reach my doorstep.

I answered the phone one morning and the voice said, "Hi. This is Patti Davis. I have some letters my dad sent me. Who can I talk to about selling them?"

She could talk to me—and did—but first, who was Patti Davis? I scrambled to google the question, and a minute later I was wondering whether this was *really* the former president's daughter. Whoever was on the other end was certainly friendly and disarmingly honest about a *Playboy* spread (news to me; though I googled that too) and about her relationship with her parents. We talked for forty-five minutes—a long time. I asked her to forward a scan of one letter. She did so immediately, and it floored me. The letter was written in 1990, two years after her father had retired to the ranch in California. Even during Reagan's presidency, it was widely known that he and Nancy had a complicated and contentious relationship with their daughter, who would confirm this in the memoir she published in 1992. Reagan had learned about the planned memoir and wrote:

> Patti, you are hurting us—your parents—but you are hurting yourself even more. We were not a dysfunctional family. . . . I have memories of a little girl cuddled in the chair with me asking me to marry her. Across the room, her mother signaled me to say yes. . . . We have many happy memories of her childhood. We have no thought or desire of interfering with her life, but now and then we'd like to see her and know how she's getting along. After all, it's sunset time for us.

The letter's wistful closing spoke volumes: "Please Patti don't take away our memories of a daughter we truly love and who we miss. With Love, Dad."

Reagan was pleading with his daughter for a reconciliation. It nearly brought me to tears. And there was more. There were two copies of the letter: he'd sent one to Patti. And he'd kept a copy in his desk at the ranch, Patti explained, where it had been found after his death. We bought and sold both versions, but it was the letter that Reagan retained that touched me—the *idea* of that letter, its evocation of loss and the regrets about what might have been, and most of all, that he kept it always within reach. A deeply humanizing moment from a president, the kind of glimpse one rarely gets of any person, let alone such a public one.

Selling your family's heirlooms can be difficult; so much emotion is attached to them. Some people have a sense that any individual or family that decides to sell a valuable document is guilty of the worst crassness. This isn't fair. In most cases, the motivations are logical, rational, and reasonable. It is common for the steward of a family's treasures to find that no one else in the family is interested in caring for the pieces, so with a sense of stewardship in mind, the person wants us to find appropriate homes for the material. It is the *rule*, not the exception, that eventually one heir, or a committed group of them, or the stewards of an estate, will decide to sell or donate their documents. Even George Washington's heirs sold his papers to the Library of Congress. Then, at public sale, they parted with the suit he wore to his inauguration, and thousands of additional documents. Indeed, we've carried items that were part of this original sale. Einstein's descendants sold his correspondence. First Lady Edith Roosevelt gifted many of her husband Theodore's letters, and some of these recipients or their descendants sold them. We've carried some of those letters as well.

When Reagan's letters to Murphy had been brought to my attention, I'd considered them scandalous and eye-catching, objects to be bought and sold. (For outsiders peering through the glass at correspondence intended as an exchange between two people, there's always an element of voyeurism.) But these letters that Patti Davis had engendered entirely different feelings. I got drawn into the family saga, and the personalities jumped off the pages. They touched me, offered an intensely personal perspective on a very public person. In a subtle way, the experience also changed the way I saw our business.

These letters have a universality, a sense that you can look past the author and the recipient and feel the emotions. Look beyond Reagan's stationery and see his pain. Look beyond Patti's decisions and see her struggle. See in yourself the president's love or sense in yourself the daughter's defiance and independence. This was the moment, I think, that I transformed from being primarily a salesman to a passionate advocate for the importance of history.

For me, the Patti Davis letters drove home a point my father had implicitly been teaching me for years: We're not selling investments or objects or mere souvenirs. We're selling a meaningful, powerful, and often emotional connection to the past.

PART II

THE HUNT

CHAPTER 8

The Mystery of the Washington Survey

In 1771, George Washington was thirty-nine years old and working on a survey of his plantation in Mount Vernon, Virginia. In the previous two years, he'd purchased large parcels of land, expanding his property by hundreds of acres. He'd discovered what he believed was an unused, triangular slice of land—situated conveniently near his other holdings—that he wanted to acquire. This survey would measure its size and location and would be submitted to Lord Fairfax, the English proprietor of the Virginia land grant, who owned and therefore could grant Washington the rights to the land.

Washington was a war hero, having led hundreds of men in the French and Indian War in the 1750s, and was a member of the Virginia legislature in the 1760s. He'd been married for ten years, helping to raise his wife Martha's two young children from her first marriage, to Daniel Parke Custis. Custis had died in 1757, leaving Martha and the children a vast inheritance, including an eighteen-thousand-acre estate and eighty-four slaves. Washington was born to a prosperous family, but his marriage had made him truly wealthy.

The Mount Vernon plantation had grown tobacco, mostly, until a weak market for the stuff in the mid-1760s convinced Washington to grow wheat. He built a large flour mill and operated multiple farms on the property—including the River Farm, the Muddy Hole Farm, the Dogue Run Farm, and the Union Farm. Washington added land to his holdings with some regularity, acquiring neighboring farms.

What we think of as Mount Vernon today, when we go on our school trips, is the homestead and surrounding property of what was once a sprawling collection of tracts that Washington accumulated over a generation.

It was when buying seventy-five acres next to Dogue Run the previous year that he'd stumbled on this 20.5-acre plot. Lord Fairfax had become friendly with Washington, and Washington longed for Fairfax's status: socially prominent, well-connected, landed. Some of this Washington would achieve, some not, but perhaps one of the great mistakes made by the British crown was not granting Washington a British royal officer's commission. This might have kept him from becoming a patriot and taking the position he held in the revolution. Now Washington was on Fairfax's land, surveying a portion, not in use, bound on the south by a small river, Dogue Run, and the west by the Piney Branch, a small tributary that entered heading southwest.

The American taming of the frontier landscape and our relentless push westward is tied to the profession of surveying. Something about this passion for land and the growth of our nation is uniquely American. More than a century before Frederick Jackson Turner wrote in his essay "The Significance of the Frontier in American History" that our democracy was shaped by our westward frontier expansion, men such as George Washington were putting land on the map, so to speak.

Turner wrote, "Thus the advance of the frontier has meant a steady movement away from the influence of Europe, a steady growth of independence on American lines." More famously, Turner summed up his frontier thesis thusly: "The existence of an area of free land, its continuous recession, and the advance of American settlement westward explain American development."

Some of the land Washington surveyed was closer to his home and some was farther west. He wasn't alone among our presidents in his passion for mapping the land. Abraham Lincoln, born on the frontier, was a surveyor before he became an attorney. His handwritten surveys rarely reach the market, but we have had one. When they do show up, they go high. In the American story, one need only look at Mount Rushmore to understand the tie between the western land and our nation. Every single president there has his own tie to it and to our expansion. Washington and Lincoln were surveyors. Roosevelt was a renowned explorer of the American West and national-park trailblazer. His ranching days in the Dakotas and tour of Yellowstone are legendary. And Jefferson, himself a prodigious landowner and farmer, was the visionary who—against strong opposition—concluded the Louisiana Purchase, nearly doubling the size of our country. He then sent Meriwether Lewis and William Clark to explore it.

Washington came to surveying young. He'd inherited his father's surveying equipment; at the age of sixteen, he'd been invited by George William Fairfax, a cousin of Lord Fairfax's and whose Belvoir estate was close to Mount Vernon—he was a neighbor—to join a month-long survey party on the western edge of Virginia. This led to a commission from the College of William & Mary to survey the newly formed Culpeper County the following year, when he was seventeen. The tools of the trade were a compass called a circumferentor, which had perpendicular sights and was mounted on a tripod, and long metal survey chains. He produced some two hundred maps over the years.

Washington was, in effect, a surveyor for the king—a dutiful servant of the king of England—creating maps for the king's representative in the colonies. This career ended when he joined the British military to fight the French, but he never gave up his devotion to the craft and the land. And as Mount Vernon grew, he recorded its dimensions. He'd surveyed this land numerous times over the years, marking off his new land acquisitions, his various farms and lots. And now he was making another.

Along with his equipment, he took pen and paper out into the field. The laid paper he wrote on, made from rags, as was the custom, was around eight by thirteen inches. In surveying the plot he sought to acquire from Fairfax, he drew a map on the top of the page with all the key locations and features marked and numbered. Below he drafted a description of the property and its precise parameters:

> The above is a Plat of the waste & ungranted Land entered by George Washington in the Proprietors Office in the year and found to contain by actual survey Twenty and a half Acres and bounded as followeth, viz: Beginning at a large Hickory standing about 4 poles [also known as rods, or 16.5 feet] from Dogues Run [a creek running north-south] Corner to a Tract of Land which the said Washington bought of George Ashford [in 1762] and extending with a line thereof (corrected) No. 86 W till it intersects a South thirty five degrees East Course of Harrison's Patent.

There were many mentions of different trees—Spanish oak and water oak and sweet gum—and the various farms that had been incorporated into Washington's property, and his neighbor's property lines and how they all intersected, resulting in "20 ½ Acres as above & all the waste & ungranted Land that is or may be lying between the Lines of the Land now held by the Subscriber."

In other words, these twenty and a half acres would be granted from Fairfax to Washington.

The use of natural boundary markings, such as trees or streams or rocks, was the standard system back then, adapted from the English method. Before the time of GPS and more precise methods of calculation, this was the best they could do. What happens when a tree falls or a farmer reroutes his stream? This would eventually lead to the Public Land Survey System, which used grids of precise measurements in miles, but leading up to this time, dating back to the land grants written under the authority of Governor William Penn in the seventeenth century in Pennsylvania, such natural boundary markers were a reality.

Surveying was rugged, invigorating work. It was also careful, meticulous work. Washington took detailed measurements and wrote precise descriptions of the features of the land.

When he'd completed this draft survey—a project that took days—he began again, preparing what would be the final version of the survey. The draft was marked up with corrections and cross-outs; the final product would be pristine. He kept the draft and sent off the final version for approval by Lord Fairfax, who granted Washington ownership of the 20.5 acres. But that was only the beginning of the story of this survey.

More than 240 years later, I received an email from a dealer who told me he'd acquired a handwritten George Washington survey, or rather a fragment of it: "It is believed to be the only Mount Vernon survey handwritten by Washington in private hands and is accompanied with a certificate of authenticity signed by Charles Hamilton."

I recognized that name from Hamilton's books about the autograph trade, where I'd first seen the handiwork of Cosey and many of the other forgers and had read about some of the more unsavory characters one sometimes finds in this profession.

The dealer sent along the certificate of authenticity—the COA. A stamp of approval from someone who theoretically ought to know. The dealer was wrong that this is the only such survey in private hands. There are others. But still, it was interesting.

He offered to sell it to me for $35,000.

Now, this was a strong but not altogether unreasonable number: George Washington surveys are highly desirable. Not many are on the market. Sometimes they're signed, sometimes not. In this case, it was from 1771, and the signed portion had evidently been cut off. Gone was the schematic, the map that would once have been present, but still surviving was a portion of the multisentence description of the property.

This thrilling find, a rare Washington survey of his own property, Mount Vernon, was of real historical value. I did a quick search of public records: it had come up for sale recently at a major public auction, which had touted the COA.

So it had gone through this major auction company and carried with it a certificate attesting to its authenticity from a respected man in this field. But something about it seemed off to me. The paper was right in texture, wrong in size, and the handwriting was off, in a familiar way. It was a little too bubbly at the edges of the letters. A little too weirdly cramped. The letters seemed forced, uneven. And the lines weren't straight. In the eighteenth century people were trained to write in straight lines, even when no lines were on the paper. But these lines weren't straight. And come to think of it, why was the ink bleeding on the paper? I took another look. Sometimes that first initial reaction, like having a bad taste in your mouth, causes you to stop and think and look further. What was it I just ate?

You run your eye across the page, looking for inconsistencies between what you would expect and what you are looking at. Is the spacing off, the handwriting unfamiliar, the lettering cramped, the signature unconventional, the ink bleeding, the paper the right size? You get a deep-down gut feeling that something is off, and that is sufficient to take out a proverbial magnifying glass and look in the dark corners.

My suspicion started me on a journey to find out what this thing was. I immediately contacted a colleague of mine, Michele Lee Silverman, who now works at the Folger Shakespeare Library. She was for many years a curator at Mount Vernon and is interested in Washington forgeries. She and I go back and forth all the time about documents we come across. She loves the stuff.

I sent her the photograph of the 1771 Washington survey and asked her what she thought. "This one does seem to have some inconsistencies and like you, I'm not convinced it's GW," she wrote. So we began digging. If it was indeed a forgery, it wasn't dreadful. Someone had taken time making it—this wasn't a casual affair. And it was clearly not a contemporary forgery: it was old.

The first thing we uncovered in our search was that another version of the same 1771 Washington survey had sold at Christie's, at public auction, in 1994, and then again in 2004, fetching just over $130,000. The "Christie's version" had the very same cross-outs and corrections as the fragment offered to me, which I suspected of being a forgery. The Christie's version had the schematic plot of land diagram still there and was signed. On the one I'd been quoted, the "slice" was apparently taken from the middle. Suspicious.

Of course, Washington might have prepared more than one draft as he was surveying his property in 1771. Perhaps he'd written a draft, made corrections, and copied a new version on a new piece of paper, then made a second series of corrections and another final draft. Setting aside that I'd never seen such an example on the market, in what world would two drafts have *identical* corrections? Sometimes authenticating a document is logic as well as experience. Would you create a rough draft of a document, then reproduce that rough draft with the same cross-outs in precisely the same locations? No. You'd incorporate your edits into a final version.

Something else: The handwriting on the Christie's version was notably different—not uneven, not cramped. The lines were ruler straight. It looked right.

My next discovery: Sotheby's had carried what appeared to be yet another version of the 1771 Washington survey of Mount Vernon. The "Sotheby's version" was a beautiful piece, with no cross-outs, as you would expect from someone producing his or her work in final form. It sold again publicly in 2007. (Collectors frequently buy and sell as their collections evolve; both the Christie's draft and the Sotheby's final had appeared to change hands multiple times; both of those documents remain in private hands, as far as I can tell.)

Right around the same time, I got a call from Michele, who was then working at the Society of the Cincinnati. She'd found yet another version of the survey, this one at Colonial Williamsburg, which also has a significant collection of revolutionary era and pre-revolution documents and artifacts.

A fourth copy of the same Washington survey? This was getting stranger and stranger. Michele sent me a link to a blog item on the

Colonial Williamsburg website that included a photograph of the fourth version. It was another draft—and it had, once again, nearly identical cross-outs and corrections to the "slice" and the "Christie's version." So, we now have three of the same draft document, the above two and the Williamsburg copy (plus the final copy sold at Sotheby's).

The handwriting on the Williamsburg copy matched the handwriting on the one sent to me via email—the same loops, the cramped style, the uneven lines. In both cases, the ink was bleeding slightly, which is a sign of a potential forgery—when new ink is applied to old paper (plenty of it is around for forgers to find), it can bleed a little bit.

I said to Michele, "I think Colonial Williamsburg has a forgery. Whoever did the forgery I am looking at I think also did the one at Williamsburg. It's written in the same hand."

We were now presented with a rather unusual and incriminating set of facts. It seemed to us that the forger had somehow gained access to the original draft, the one that sold at Christie's, or had seen the image that appeared in an auction catalog and created at least two forged versions. I contacted Mount Vernon, which sent me an image of the survey as it was displayed in the auction catalog of a company called Parke-Bernet Galleries (now part of Sotheby's) in 1946. The catalog referenced the first sale of the draft, in 1931, by American Art Association/Anderson Galleries, which may also have published the draft survey in their catalog. The forger may simply have received one of these catalogs, had on hand a piece of laid paper, and done it by sight. The forged versions weren't traced, they were done freehand. We know this because the lines aren't even, the spacing is wrong, pieces are missing, and the pagination is different.

Where the slice and the Williamsburg versions had the same author, so did the Christie's and Sotheby's versions. The latter are authentic and have the warmth and strength of Washington's script. The other two fill me with a sense of deception.

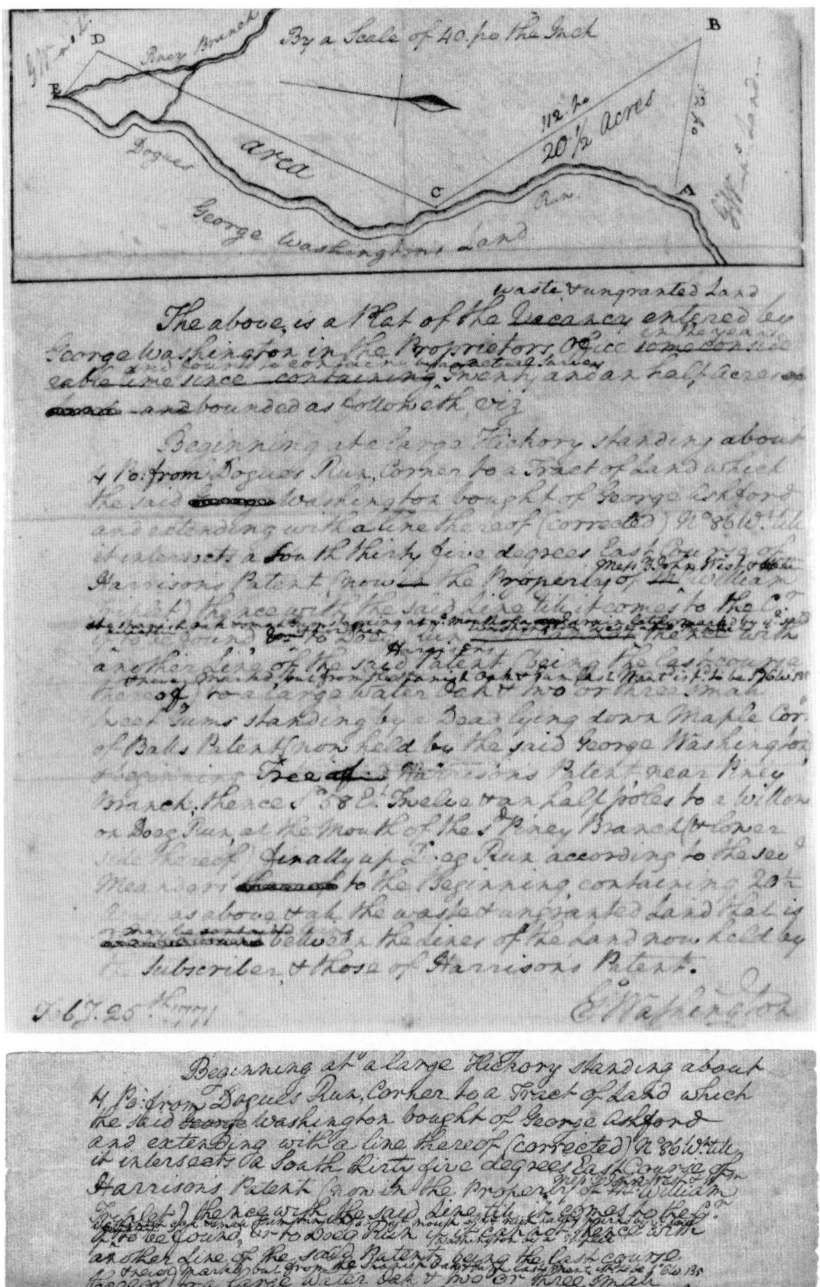

The above, is a Plat of the Vacancy entered by George Washington in the Proprietors Office some considerable time since containing Twenty and an half Acres and bounded as followeth, viz

Beginning at a large Hickory standing about 4 Po: from Dogues Run, Corner to a Tract of Land which the said Washington bought of George Ashford and extending with a line thereof (corrected) N° 86 W. till it intersects a South thirty five degrees East Course of Harrisons Patent (now the Property of Mess. John West & William Triplet) thence with the said Line till it comes to the Cor. if to be found, or to Dogue Run; thence with another Line of the said Patent being the last course thereof to a large Water Oak & two or three small Red Gums standing by a Dead lying down Maple Cor. of Balls Patent (now held by the said George Washington) Beginning Tree of Harrisons Patent near Piney Branch, thence S° 38 E. twelve & an half poles to a Willow on Dog Run, at the Mouth of the sd Piney Branch & lower side thereof, finally up Dog Run according to the sev. Meanders to the Beginning, containing 20 1/2 Acres as above & all the waste & ungranted Land that is between the Lines of the Land now held by the Subscriber, & those of Harrison's Patent.

Feb. 25th 1771 G° Washington

Beginning at a large Hickory standing about 4 Po: from Dogues Run, Corner to a Tract of Land which the said Washington bought of George Ashford and extending with a line thereof (corrected) N° 86 W. till it intersects a South thirty five degrees East Course of Harrisons Patent (now the Property of Mess. John West & William Triplet) thence with the said Line till it comes to the Cor. if to be found, or to Dogg Run; thence with another Line of the said Patent being the last course thereof to a large Water Oak & two or three small

The George Washington survey, authentic (*top*) and forged (*bottom*).

So now to identify the culprit. At first I focused on Robert Spring.

Robert Spring was an Englishman who emigrated to the United States and opened a small bookshop in Philadelphia in the late 1850s. He sold authentic pieces, but "supplemented" them with forgeries.

And it turned out he was pretty good at it—good enough that you still see the forgeries around today, much like those of his successor Joseph Cosey. People think they have originals when they're actually "Springs." He was the first great American forger of autographs, the first to realize he could profit from tapping into the passion we feel for proximity to the great men and women of our past. Most often, he'd get access to a real document and make copies to be sold. He'd cut blank pages out of old books and portions of letters that were unused, matching the paper to the era, all so the paper would feel right. He used ink that sat right on the paper and could fool people.

Though he forged autographs of many people, he was a production shop of Washington forgeries, which typically took one of two forms. He'd either write a check drawn by Washington on the Office of Discount and Deposit in Baltimore or a pass through American lines during the American Revolution. Spring's genius was to approach local Philadelphians and present them with a pass bearing the same name as an ancestor. What a fortuitous find, the buyer might say, unknowingly buying a document written the night before. Charles Hamilton himself quipped that if all the passes had been authentic, having Ramapo as their destination, it would have created the first traffic jam in American history.

As the Victorian era progressed, interest in collecting only increased. With interest in Shakespeare spiking and odd theories about him proliferating, the Victorians had an idea. They'd ransack old churches, local archives, and the like, looking for his autograph. They were hunting for treasures left behind by Shakespeare, and to dispel theories that he was a composite of many people or no one at all. To admit that would rob the English language of its heroic bard, a painful rewriting of the historical record. This hunt, which was ultimately unsuccessful, is emblematic of the era's growing interest in the accumulation of things, whether scientific specimens or autographs.

Spring saw this, and his illicit business took off, at least for a while, right alongside the legitimate autograph business. The first serious American autograph dealer was Walter R. Benjamin, whose father was the writer Park Benjamin. Walter grew up in a literary milieu—one might find Henry Wadsworth Longfellow sitting in his living room—or Ulysses S. Grant. Walter had the excitement of seeing all these great figures, and that was the inspiration for his business, launched in the 1880s. He figured out that autographs weren't just something that might pop up at a book auction every once in a while, but that a market for them existed.

Spring's operating procedures were outlined at his trial for forgery in Philadelphia in 1869: "He would obtain, by some means, a genuine letter and then trace it on a sheet of paper, which he stained with coffee grounds to give it the appearance of age. The bogus letter would be inclosed in a note and addressed to some gentleman who had a fine private library. The note stated that the writer was in want of money, and if the recipient desired the autograph letter he could send money to a certain address. He received a number of replies containing remittances varying from $10 to $15, the letters being addressed to several post offices within a few miles of this city."

Spring fled to Canada, then returned to Baltimore, where he conducted business, posing in letters to collectors as the daughter of Thomas "Stonewall" Jackson, who was forced to sell her family letters because she needed money. The cover was plausible enough for Spring, who churned out hundreds of forgeries. He was finally found guilty at trial and sent to prison.

So had Spring made copies of the 1771 Washington survey?

I revisited my initial perceptions and what seemed to be the facts.

Did I believe I was correct that this was a forgery? Yes, clearly.

Was this the work of Spring? Forgeries as a rule lack consistency in that they are the product of someone mimicking someone else and not that person's actual handwriting. It's not always obvious who the forger was. But each forger does have his own style, with some consistency within that.

So we pulled at the threads. The roundness of the handwriting had some similarities. But the dissimilarities irked me.

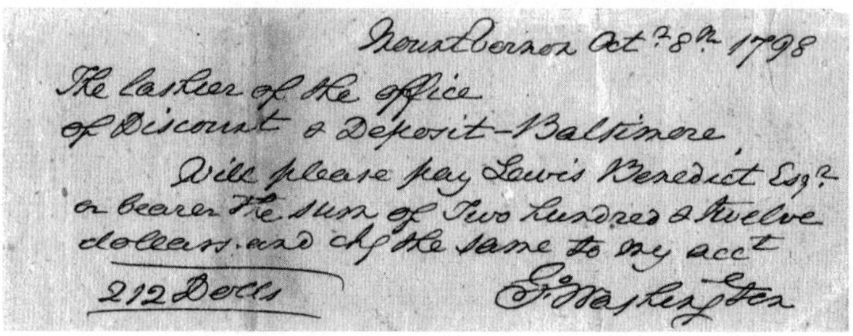

Mount Vernon Oct. 8th 1798
The Cashier of the office
of Discount & Deposit—Baltimore
Will please pay Lewis Benedict Esqr
or bearer the sum of Two hundred & twelve
dollars and chg the same to my acct
212 Dolls
G. Washington

Robert Spring's forgery of a George Washington document.

I made an appointment with a special collections librarian at Colonial Williamsburg. I remembered going there as a child with my parents and welcomed an excuse to return as an adult.

Karen and I were met by Doug Mayo, one of the research librarians—a reserved but friendly man in a blazer and khaki pants. He took us into the back, where we sat at a long table, and he brought out a folder. This was the library's 1771 Washington survey.

As we all looked at the surveys, the Williamsburg version presented a number of red flags. The ink was bleeding, indicating the wrong-era ink on the previous-era paper. The size of the document (7¾ x 10) was more like a regular sheet of paper, not the larger size of the real documents from that time (8 x 13). Where one looked long, the other looked closer to a square. There were sloppy mistakes: Karen turned to me and pointed out that on the versions we thought were authentic, you can see Washington has marked points A, B,

C, and D on the map. But the Williamsburg document is missing point A. This is not a mistake a seasoned surveyor would make.

The handwriting on the Williamsburg survey sloped up and down; a tributary of one of the rivers on the survey was completely missing; there was no watermark, which would give you a better idea when the paper was made or where it was from, although it was rag paper.

I'd walked in thinking that the Williamsburg document was *almost certainly* a forgery, and I left thinking that it was *most definitely* a forgery. The dealer who'd offered me the survey to begin with ended up donating it to the collection at Mount Vernon—which accepted it as a forgery. I took that as vindication enough.

So who was the culprit? Spring?

Probably not Spring, I finally concluded. It was, as with the Lincoln I'd uncovered years earlier (and initially thought was Cosey), a newly discovered forger. No previous survey forged by Spring had ever surfaced. Spring's forgeries were better than this, not as much sloping and slanting, cramping and missing elements. The signature was all wrong for Spring's handiwork. And it was not a pass, a check, or a tracing. The handwriting was similar but not identical. And the bleeding of the document felt amateurish for Spring.

I considered the implications of this discovery, which went beyond this one document. It was for me a mark of my own progress: years after I could barely read a Washington letter without help, I was now sniffing out forgeries at first glance that had fooled generations. Where years earlier I might have taken out a magnifying glass, turned the piece over, compared one letter to another, now that first gut feeling had been its own form of authentication. The months of additional research only confirmed what I "felt" that first moment.

So was the forger an artist, for clearly a good forger has a skill; or merely a cheat; or both? I decided the forger has a skill but is a thief. Why? He has taken nothing that does not belong to him. He has sold something and gotten money in return. Yes, but he has stolen. He has stolen our affection for the great figure and attached it to a fake.

The experience marked a nice bookend, from my first days in the business reading Hamilton's books to challenging one of his certificates of authenticity. The auction company that had offered the piece for sale and illustrated it in their catalog had relied on that COA, not their own research. That buyer would have received a COA, where the buyer of the Christie's or Sotheby's would have received nothing of the kind, but left with the real deal.

Months later I went to see the movie *Can You Ever Forgive Me?* with Melissa McCarthy. It's based on a true story: McCarthy plays Lee Israel, who learned to forge literary letters and autographs and duped many seasoned book dealers into buying them. This was the 1990s. At the end of the movie, she is in a rare-book shop looking at an autograph that she herself had forged, and the dealer comforts her by saying, "It comes with a certificate of authenticity." Without missing a beat, she turns to the store owner and says, "Does that certificate of authenticity come with a certificate of authenticity?"

CHAPTER 9

Taking the Reins

When Lord Nelson took a command position in the British Royal Navy, he paid homage to his late uncle, his mentor, by acknowledging the passing of the torch: "Trust I will continue as long so as I shall prove myself, by my actions, worthy of supplying that place in the service of my country, which my dear uncle left for me."

I had no such grand moment when I realized my apprenticeship had ended, that I was now a full partner with my father and mother. It happened slowly. My parents spent more time at their summer house in Maine, leaving me to run the show. As I've described, I had pushed to rename the company and relaunch our website. The Raab Collection was a luxury business, and now it was branded that way. I'd been inspired by the example of the Phillips Collection, in Washington, DC—a small modern art museum. It's a jewel of a collection, well curated, and it's beautiful. It's most definitely not the Smithsonian, but it doesn't need to be. This would be our model at that stage: a curated, boutique-style business. I did not want to run a mom-and-pop business, so I changed it. We would be more like an art gallery or small museum than a catalog business. As we were enhancing our internet presence, I also made a point of getting our name out in the news.

A lot of family businesses flounder because of power issues between the two generations. But my parents readily accepted me as an equal. They had confidence that I wouldn't sink the thing! This is how we run the business now: Karen and I oversee day-to-day operations, and my parents are still very much involved. We make the big decisions as a committee of four.

But the real shift for me wasn't anything as mundane or practical as running the finances of our business, or figuring out a brand strategy, or even the long learning curve of document authentication. It was something more elusive: I had found my way to the emotional yet intangible heart of this trade in history. I came to understand what binds people to the physical traces of our history and its great men and women, why these artifacts and pieces of paper have such power. This isn't an easy lesson, and no one can teach it to you. You have to learn it yourself.

This is a story I think about frequently—a formative experience. I was contacted by a man in his mideighties who wanted to sell his collection of historical documents. This pretty large collection, maybe thirty pieces, appeared to contain, from his description, some interesting things. He had a nice Eleanor Roosevelt letter, and he had letters from impressionist painters including Renoir and Monet. The collection, in retrospect, wasn't that memorable. A rather formulaic collection of interesting but not important documents, the kinds of things we acquire without great planning or excitement.

I drove to his home in suburban New Jersey. The comfortable split-level house had 1970s-style wall-to-wall carpeting, rather thick, giving away that the house had been designed with some care but perhaps thirty years prior. Strikingly, the owner had his entire collection on display, framed and hung on the walls. As you entered his house, a Franklin Roosevelt letter greeted you on your right, the stairs leading up past George Washington and George Bernard Shaw, reaching at the top steps Claude Monet, before pivoting to a wall where Renoir hung alongside Eleanor Roosevelt and James Madison.

This collection was clearly important to him. The documents looked as if they'd been hanging on these walls for decades, carefully arranged with the help of his wife.

While she served me cookies, I went through the collection piece by piece. I was authenticating and buying a large collection on my own for one of the first times. I was comfortable doing it, but cautious. These are expensive mistakes if you make one. I spent a lot of time with the material. Many of the pieces were nice—I'd never bought a Monet or Renoir before, for example—but I could read the French script and nothing was particularly spectacular. Nevertheless, I liked the collection, felt we could make money, and I wanted to buy it.

Once I'd gone through everything, I stepped outside to call my father, and we went over how much we thought we should pay. Twenty-five thousand dollars, we concluded, was the right price.

I went back into the house and told the man what I thought the collection was worth, the price I was willing to pay, and anticipated perhaps a little negotiation and an easy transaction. But I've never forgotten his reaction.

He sat down, totally silent. Visibly shaken. Devastated. He nearly collapsed into a small wooden chair set at the bottom of the steps, under a minor document signed by Thomas Jefferson. He sighed, looked blankly ahead, and deflated into the chair.

I realized what only experience could teach, what I could only learn by experiencing that moment emotionally with that man: I had put a price on something he loved, and it would never be high enough.

My offer was perfectly fair and reasonable. I don't think the disconnect was caused because he'd spent a fortune building his collection, but rather because he'd spent a lifetime doing it. This is an important distinction.

We agreed on a price, and he said not another word. He wasn't angry at me, he was just deflated. He was heartbroken. His wife pulled me aside and said, "Don't worry about his reaction. He just loves these things."

I took each piece off his wall and packed them into my car. As I left, I turned back, looked at those empty walls, with small dust windows where the pieces once sat, and below them sat that man in his chair, with no documents behind him, still staring ahead.

I think about that old man all the time, and I almost wish I hadn't bought his collection. He was so upset. It was such a hard thing to witness. *Experience* is a better word. His emotions activated my own. We went through it together. This man reflecting back on his lifelong pursuit, all while I was looking through the same lens.

Understanding this strong emotional pull is a lesson that seeps into you, without any action required, any book to read. It's a strong, sometimes painful, sometimes joyous lesson. There is no school you can go to for this, no master teacher. It's the creation of your own link to the history forged through experience.

One day, rather early in my career, a woman called our office. She was retired and her grandson was going to college. She explained that the family didn't have a lot of money, but she'd inherited from her parents a letter written by George Washington, and the time had come to sell it so she could honor her promise to send her grandson to college. Her husband had passed away. She could make this contribution to her family and was prepared to part with the letter.

She wanted to come visit us, a six-hour drive from her home in northern Connecticut. I imagined this wasn't a trip she'd normally undertake, and the duration of the trip was commensurate with the importance of the sale to her.

I said, "You can certainly come down if you want, but I encourage you to send me an image before. If it's not for us, I would hate to have you make the long trip for nothing."

She insisted, "My parents told me it's authentic. I'll come down."

Again I protested, but she was adamant.

I think you can see where this is going. She drove down and entered our office full of energy and optimism. She was a youthful gray. She sat down on our couch and pulled the letter out of a paper grocery bag she'd carried it in. I took one look at the piece and knew. This was a rather primitive forgery. I looked up at her expectant face. This was not going to go as she hoped. Rather than negotiate a price, I had to break the bad news to her. This was just what I'd feared.

I decided subtlety here was not a benefit. I looked her in the eyes and said, "I'm sorry to say I think this is a forgery."

I'll never forget what she said back to me: "That's not good."

She took it better than I did, I think. It crushed me to know the story of her family and deliver the bad news, as if I were a member of that family and experiencing the crushing blow. I felt as if I were keeping that grandson from going to college. I like to think that they figured out a way or that perhaps she was exaggerating.

She left that room and faced the long drive back. I wished she'd sent an email.

Shortly thereafter, I received a call from a farmer from New Hampshire whose ancestors had been prominent religious figures. He was a descendant of the first Episcopal bishop of New Hampshire, Carlton Chase. Chase wrote President Lincoln on May 22, 1862:

> I cannot longer restrain the expressions of my grateful emotions as I contemplate the manner in which you, under the divine providence, are shaping the destinies of this afflicted country. God be praised, that such a man lives for us, and that to our chief leader in this momentous crisis is given such wisdom, and such moral and intellectual powers, to inspire us with confidence and hope. Of all men here, with sincerely are exception in any rank of life, you have now the perfect confidence. Thanksgiving for the good you are doing, and prayers for your health and safety into all the devotions of Christian people.

One hundred and fifty years later, I was on the phone with Chase's great-great-grandson. He had some papers.

"I don't know if they're worth anything," he told me. Such a statement is often used as a cover by people selling forgeries, but when it comes from a place of modesty and not presumption, as I thought was the case here, it often portends a great historical find. When he sent me images, I wasn't disappointed.

This man had two letters by Abraham Lincoln, written during the Civil War, to Carlton Chase. I had never seen such letters before and haven't since. They referenced God in support of the Union, an incredible rarity: "It is most encouraging to feel that in the midst of the labors and perplexities of war and policy, we are supported by the confidence and sustained by the prayers of good people. It is only less than the approval of God upon our endeavors. . . . A. Lincoln."

He and I spoke again on the phone.

"I figured they're not worth much, but it can't hurt to ask, right?"

"This is what you have," I responded matter-of-factly, and I offered him tens of thousands of dollars for them, as I recall. I figured we could net around $80,000, and we offered him just over half.

Silence. More silence.

"Hello?"

I was met with yet more silence. Had he dropped the phone? Had a heart attack? What had I done?

In these cases, we often get a counteroffer, then meet in the middle. Making an offer can be the start of a negotiation, assuming we're in the ballpark. The seller will occasionally tell us about some estimate he has received from Christie's or another auction company. Rarely does it involve another dealer. Our entire inventory is stocked with material that we have bought ourselves, paying cash up front, on the assumption that we will eventually sell it at a profit. I'm not aware of any competitive autograph dealer operating like this anymore. So our primary competition is an auction estimate. But in this case, no counter, no reaction at all.

Turns out he was speechless. It's difficult to explain how you can hear excitement in silence, but I did that day. His silence was interrupted by his acceptance of our offer, in a near-giddy voice. He'd never seen that much money in his life at one time and had thought he never would.

But the final story I'll tell shows yet another reaction.

I got a call from a prominent Hungarian-born historian who had for years been a professor at Chestnut Hill College, serving as a visiting scholar at a great number of other places. He'd long been retired.

His life was fascinating. A Jew, he'd survived World War II but barely. He was part of a Hungarian labor battalion with other Jews, and during the German occupation had survived the siege of Budapest. From this experience, and after years of further education, he crafted a view of the world forged by the atrocities of Hitler and Mussolini. He raged against populism and those who appeal to mass culture as a base for power and wrote more than fifty books, many with this theme. His work was both historical and scientific, drawing broader moral conclusions from his experiences. For decades, he explained, he'd corresponded with the actress Sarah Churchill, Winston Churchill's daughter. They were friends. But he'd also corresponded with a number of notable scientists, including Werner Heisenberg, who'd come up with one of the most important scientific principles of the twentieth century. Shortly after Einstein's statement of his two great theories of relativity, Heisenberg stated in his uncertainty principle that you cannot know with mathematical certainty the exact location and velocity of any particle at the same time. This professor claimed to have two Heisenberg letters on this principle, relating it to relativity, so I went to visit him.

This collection was unusual because the owner had been the correspondent. He wasn't selling a collection of other people's material—he'd received these letters himself, in many cases as a much younger man. He had a personal connection to the writers of these letters.

He lived not far from me, maybe twenty minutes, a rare coincidence in a field where we buy from all over the world. He lived on one of the Main Line's great old estates, separated from the road by a long, private driveway, which emptied into a circular drive that wound past a guesthouse and left me parking in front of the entryway. The old building was beautiful, although fallen into some disrepair, as many of these Main Line estates have. The man greeted me at the door and we walked into his home, which was cluttered. Ahead of me, I saw walls filled with old maps and prints, large living rooms, and a beautiful dining room. The small kitchen might have felt cramped were it not for the view it offered overlooking a pond. We sat at the kitchen table. My host was jovial and began telling me about his life while showing me his letters. His friendship with Churchill; his letters back and forth with various theoretical physicists. This was more than a transaction, it was a conversation. He asked me about my family—where were we from? He'd seen the name Raab on a map of Austria. He offered to give me the map. I declined.

We talked for some time, but then I cut to the chase: "I'm afraid I really don't want most of this material, as interesting as it is—there's just no market for it. But I will certainly buy the Heisenberg letters."

They were as advertised. And better. They spoke to the great scientific debates of the era. Einstein was working on a unified field theory, his final work, which would meld various scientific theories, a view of the nature of reality that he could not then prove but that scientists now think quite likely. Here, in 1963, Heisenberg noted that Einstein's work would eventually take primacy, extolling Einstein, now deceased, and writing that their theories weren't in conflict: "I do not see how a conflict could arise between the uncertainty principle and such a mathematical formulation. . . . The uncertainty principle is always a part of such mathematical formulations."

I offered him $3,500, and he countered with $500 more, and we met in the middle and shook hands.

As I got up to go, he said, "Oh, no, you're not leaving yet! Have you ever tried apple brandy?"

I laughed and agreed to try his apple brandy. It was 10:30 a.m., but no matter. He wheeled out a small bar cart and poured two apple brandies, and we raised our glasses.

"I've never sold anything like this," he said, "and I think it deserves a proper toast."

We were sealing the deal.

In the grand scheme of things, that day in the Main Line was a minor transaction, but it stretched over two hours of conversation and connection. My host spoke of his deceased wife, his son who lived with him, and his work and friends, spanning his time in war-torn Europe, and our exchange was wonderful, greased by our morning drink. I've never forgotten it, or the apple brandy.

Unlike the man in New Jersey, this man I'd come to visit wasn't sad about parting with these remnants of his life. But he did recognize their power all the same. These letters Heisenberg had written to him were part of his personal story, and now they'd been passed on. That's what we were toasting: history, changing hands.

CHAPTER 10

The Report of the Death of Napoléon

Each day, we're contacted by at least twenty people looking to sell us their historical treasures. Distinguishing the forged from the authentic, the important from the mundane—that is a great deal of what we do. Learning to spot the diamond in the rough is a skill learned over decades and put to the test each day in a multitude of ways. I came to this skill last, and it still tests me. The key lesson from my father was to always pay attention, examine everything. Take nothing for granted. The greatest gem can be buried under a mountain of rock; and likewise, many are taken in by fool's gold. It shines like the real thing but it's not.

To put it another way, could you recognize a gem if it was sitting in front of you? These things don't come to us with a sign around them that reads THIS IS IMPORTANT. We have to hunt, then find, and lastly understand and recognize. With five or even two things in front of you, could you pick the more valuable? True finds are often in plain sight but unlabeled and raw.

In a large auction with many lots, some of which have many items, don't assume that the auction house has necessarily highlighted the most important items in its catalog. Don't assume the descriptions of each of the lots is complete and accurate. Perhaps you see something in a piece the auction house doesn't. Hidden gems may well be found.

A few years ago, Christie's was selling the estate of a major collector who'd recently died. To judge by the catalog, he'd primarily been a collector of American documents. Half of the few hundred lots were rare books. There were some beautiful pieces—a great Washington address to Congress; another document was signed by Henry VIII, a rare and interesting piece. Some relatively minor items were also being sold in individual lots: I recall a land grant filed by Thomas Jefferson, for example. These land grants, while having some value, were signed by the thousands, offering land to Americans seeking to conquer the frontier and build their homes in the American West. Many of the recipients were veterans of the revolution, and they received their land for free. These grants are not unique. They're a more affordable way to own Jefferson's signature.

Christie's divided the material into two auctions because of the sheer quantity, and at the first auction we bought a few items, among them the Washington address, but this first auction turned out to be the appetizer. The second would offer the main course. Among the individual offerings, grouped into single lots, were "group lots," where the auction house has decided that the individual pieces aren't sufficiently important to stand on their own and are, therefore, grouped together in one large lot. These latter were sorted geographically—European-related material, American-related material. They read in the catalog as afterthoughts in the mind of the salesman, like the baby's breath in a bouquet of five dozen roses. But they can be much more.

After looking through the auction catalog, I contacted the specialist at Christie's and asked about these group lots. What was in them? Did he have any more information about them? So much miscellany was in these lots, he explained, he couldn't possibly describe it all in any detail. If I was interested, I should come to New York and look for myself. (Generally speaking, the auction companies make all the lots available for viewing before the auction takes place.)

And so that's what we did.

Karen, my father, and I went to New York, to Christie's familiar midtown offices.

It was the day before the auction (the second and final auction of this large collection), and the viewing room was crowded. Long glass cases sat alongside wooden tables, the former containing the more valuable pieces and the latter housing the larger lots. The high-profile lots were getting the most attention: this was a bidder's opportunity to take a close look at that Washington or Jefferson document. Dozens of boxes contained the group lots that we wanted to look at. So sitting next to the document signed by Henry VIII, offered as a single lot and gathering much attention, were these lots with minimal descriptions. The individual lots were hung dramatically on the wall, well lit, with that light shining on the gilded frames that had been put together decades before. Those documents penned by Washington, Jefferson, King Henry, and others were displayed, but the large group lots sat in nondescript blue archival boxes stored in glass cases. One you could easily see and the other required a special request.

We decided to divide and conquer. My dad and Karen would focus on the English-language material; I'd take on the European material. I'd studied abroad in France, taught myself Spanish and Italian, and spent a year after college working for the AP wire service in Rome, so I speak and read all three languages. This would turn out to be a crucial advantage. Moreover, I had studied paleography, the study of writing, for a few months in Rome, so I was comfortable reading the script from different eras, as the style of forming letters and words evolved over time.

I saw immediately that the catalog description had left many things out. It listed just nine or so pieces. Among them was an uncommon early document from the wicked King George III appointing his royal representative to a prominent position in colonial New York City. This was before American independence, when the king could still stock American commercial committees with his own men. Valuable, sure, but nothing groundbreaking. At nine pieces, I expected a manila file folder, something small enough to sort through in minutes. I would then move on to help my dad and Karen with the American lots, where we thought the real meat and potatoes were. But here I was confronted with three large boxes containing dozens and dozens of documents. I looked closer at the description. It did note that there were forty-eight pieces, I saw. This was not just one file folder. It was several, jammed into a box that could barely contain the history. The documents were literally overflowing the boxes, way too large to fit into the allotted space. Presumably, they listed the more important pieces.

The first piece I pulled out blew my mind. The letter was written by King Louis XVI of France, in April of 1792, addressed to the king of England. I recognized the paper and the script and the signature was distinct. This was entirely in Louis's hand. "I thank you that at a time when certain Powers have come together against France, you have not allied yourself with them. . . . Together we must bring peace to Europe."

As the noose (I suppose guillotine is more historically accurate) was closing in around him, Louis had sent this letter to be hand-delivered to George III via a secret mission, with a simple proposition: our two countries, long enemies, should now become allies. His hope with this was to draw the English into the action, assuming that if they were involved as allies, they would protect him. Nothing came of this clever statecraft; Louis XVI was guillotined the next year, in 1793.

This powerful letter, written entirely in French, at a turning point in history, from the king of France to the king of England, as the revolution raged all around Louis, was sitting loose at the bottom of a box with no identifying notes or catalog entries, untranslated, a document of incredible importance for Western Europe.

My God, what else is in this box?

As I looked further, I found one royal treasure after the next. Here was an ornate manuscript signed by Louis XVI and his wife, Marie Antoinette—together. The two great doomed monarchs on one sheet. The catalog had described one document from George III relating to New York City. But I found another more important item: an invitation to his coronation in 1761 from King George III to a prominent supporter. This was the last coronation of a king to preside as monarch over America. There was also a letter from George VI to the Archbishop of Canterbury, announcing the engagement of his daughter, the current queen, Elizabeth, in 1947. George wrote, "My father set before us and my family a high standard of duty. I am sure that our daughter will always keep King George's lofty ideals before her and endeavor to follow his example." She reigns still. The finds continued. Here was a document signed by Catherine the Great of Russia, which I couldn't read (I don't know Russian), but I could see who'd signed it.

Here was a certificate for a young couple's marriage, signed by Napoléon and his wife, Joséphine, in their official capacity as emperor and empress of France. During the era of Louis XIV and his successors, the monarchs would sign the marriage contracts of important and well-connected people. Napoléon, who styled himself as a supermonarch, continued this practice, and if you were one of his officers—as this man was—Napoléon and his wife would sign your wedding documents as witnesses.

But most striking, with the possible exception of the letter sent by King Louis of France to King George of England, were the documents from the end of Napoléon's life: a group of letters from the man watching over Napoléon in his exile on the island of St. Helena, announcing his illness and death and describing it in great detail.

More than any other man of the nineteenth century, Napoléon captured the world's attention. Some Americans excoriated him, others idolized him. Continental Europe, while the English for a time looked on, waged violent war against him. Napoléon was the people's emperor, an original populist, a man born nowhere near Paris with an imperfect grasp of the French language.

His men fought for him, died for him. He called out to them, "Death is nothing, but to live defeated and inglorious is to die daily."

Napoléon had a keen sense of history and his place in it. In Egypt, at the feet of the monuments, he said to his troops, "From the tops of those pyramids, forty centuries look down on you." He knew the power of his appeal, his legacy. "A great reputation is a great noise:

the more there is made, the farther off it is heard. Laws, institutions, monuments, nations, all fall; but the noise continues and resounds in after ages."

In his great opus, *Representative Men*, Emerson described Napoléon this way: "Every one of the million readers of anecdotes or memoirs or lives of Napoléon delights in the page, because he studies in it his own history."

By 1814, Napoléon had been exiled to Elba, then escaped to regain power. But he'd famously lost at the Battle of Waterloo to the allied forces led by the Duke of Wellington. This was the last of the so-called Napoleonic Wars. Napoléon was banished to St. Helena, more than a thousand miles off the coast of western Africa.

Even in defeat, he claimed the mantle of victory: "They charge me with the commission of great crimes: men of my stamp do not commit crimes. Nothing has been more simple than my elevation; 'tis vain to ascribe it to intrigue or crime. . . . I have always marched with the opinion of the masses and with events."

His death in 1821 shook the world as much as his life.

The first letter in the group was from a British admiral stationed on the island, Robert Lambert, who first reported that Napoléon was ill, in a communication to his superior:

> Be pleased to inform Their Lordships that General Buonaparte has been attacked with a dangerous illness which is expected by the medical attendants to prove fatal. In the event of his demise I shall immediately dispatch a vessel to England with the intelligence.

This was followed, five days later, by the announcement of his death:

> Sir, I have to acquaint you for their Lordships' information that General Buonaparte departed this life at a little before six P.M. on Saturday the 5th Instant. My letter No. 9 of the 2nd Inst, by the Bristol Merchant Ship will have apprized you of his dangerous illness. On that day a consultation was held, in which, by the

> Governor's desire Dr. Mitchell, Surgeon of the Vigo, joined. He continued in attendance until the demise, and afterwards assisted at the opening of the body, the report of which, signed by all the medical attendants, I enclose. From the importance of this event I have judged it proper to confide my dispatches to Captain Henry, the Senior Commander on the Station, who has visited the body with me, and can give their Lordships any further details required. I have sent him in the Heron, that vessel being the fastest Sailer, and the next for relief; and I trust these measures will have their Lordships' approbation.

The autopsy report, entitled "Report of Appearances on Dissection of the Body of Napoleon Bonaparte," was also part of this group of documents. This detailed, even gruesome account of Napoléon's organs and viscera was written on May 6, 1821:

> On a superficial view the body appeared very fat which state was confirmed by the first incision down its centre where the fat was upwards of one inch and a half over the abdomen. On cutting through the cartilages of the ribs and exposing the cavity of the throat a trifling adhesion of the left pleura was found to the pleura costalis. About three ounces of reddish fluid were contained in the left cavity and nearly eight ounces in the right. The lungs were quite sound. The pericardium was natural and contained about an ounce of fluid. The heart was of the natural size but thickly covered with fat. . . .

The former despot was pronounced dead, stricken, the doctor said, by cancer of the stomach. Napoléon's death has fascinated historians ever since. High levels of arsenic in hair samples taken during his life fueled speculation that he was poisoned—speculation that continues to this day.

I like to think of the path these documents take in their own lives, their own existences as pieces of history. So let's look at these

Napoléon documents relating to his death. He died on St. Helena, an isolated island sitting off the coast of Africa, far from most points of civilization. From there, the documents journeyed thousands of miles to London, where they informed the Western world of the death of Bonaparte. From there, they traveled thousands of miles more to the room in which I was sitting, unearthed at the bottom of a pile of papers.

None of these documents was in the printed description of this lot. It simply offered to provide a list to those who wanted more information. I hoped that no one else would notice what I'd found.

I called my dad over and said, "This is the lot. I don't know what you're looking at, but this is the lot. We need to get this."

In cases such as these we must play our cards close to our chest. We went home and had a long conversation about what I'd seen and what it was worth. We expected (and feared) the lot would go much higher than the auction estimate.

We were right. I was not the only one who saw something in that lot. The next day Karen and I walked through the same doors and down the same hallway and sat in the middle of the auction room, watching the auctioneer on his platform, the large screen above depicting the lots and their prices as they came up for bidding.

Christie's had estimated our lot at a ridiculously low sum of $6,000–$8,000. To get this lot for that price would be too good to be true. In the room were several dozen serious collectors, agents, and a few dealers with modest practices—the usual suspects, most of whom I knew. The bidding on the European lot started low and stayed there initially. Only two or three of us in the room were interested, with one other bidder on the telephone.

It seemed as if the bidding were going to go to about $14,000, which would have been absolutely incredible, but then it went higher. And higher. My heartbeat quickened in a mixture of excitement and irritation as I focused on the one other person still bidding, who was on the phone. The auction had become a duel between the phone bidder and me.

Once we got past $30,000, then $40,000, people began looking around, saying, "What did we miss in this lot? Why are these two people bidding it up so high?" They'd read the description and took it as complete, more or less.

Karen began nudging me—when was I going to stop? When we crossed $50,000, Karen said, "You really need to stop." And I thought, *I really think this lot is worth it. We will make money from this lot.*

The person on the phone *also* understood the value of these documents. The drumbeat of the auctioneer quickened as the price rose higher and higher. We settled into a back-and-forth as each bid was mirrored by a bid $2,500 higher, then $5,000 higher as the price went up. The auctioneer appeared equally confused as neither of the bidders showed any sign of slowing. I looked ahead, raised my hand intently. I believed in this group, had read the lots in their original languages, and wanted it. The room got warmer, then hot. I finally got the documents for $68,750, the most expensive lot sold at the Christie's auction that day.

I remember taking Amtrak home that evening, carrying the documents in a heavy box. It was a huge lot, a massive group. The experience drove home to me that people miss things. Certainly, speaking a few European languages helped me spot the value of these documents. But more than that was the willingness to be diligent, patient, and focused—the cultivation of those qualities reaps the greatest rewards. Think of the Benjamin Franklin letter I'd seen earlier in my career: sometimes coming away with a great prize is as simple as turning a thing over to see what's on the other side.

In this case, I was able to bring *my* knowledge to bear. I'm not sure my father or Karen would have seen what I saw in that lot. But they backed me 100 percent in my decision to go for it, and it paid off. We more than made our money back selling the documents we bought that day—the announcement of Napoléon's death alone brought in close to what I paid for the entire box and more than that Henry VIII document that had sparked so much interest in the sale originally.

CHAPTER 11

Provenance, or Where's This Stuff Been Hiding?

Historical documents often don't survive. Countless have been thrown away, tossed in the fire, ripped up, buried, thrown overboard, and otherwise just lost to time. That some survive is a credit to the people who've shepherded them, the people who've carried them from one place to another. Learning the historical importance of a document is clearly an element of what we do. But understanding how a piece of papyrus, parchment, or vellum got from a noted person to our hands can be just as interesting. Knowing that Abraham Lincoln issued in his own hand a protective order allowing a Southern family to return to their plantation during the Civil War, and that while doing so he mentioned the conflict—that is intriguing. But understanding that he issued the order to a family member, and that family passed it down through consecutive generations, carrying it from Washington to Arkansas to California to Connecticut and then to us—that awareness of the document's journey as an artifact produces a different type of satisfaction.

This journey can take many forms. Understanding this journey can shed light on who owns historical items and what that ownership means.

The heirs to a huge collection of letters sent by Abraham Lincoln to his secretary of the treasury Salmon Chase had abandoned the family home, with the entire archive inside. This was a half century or so ago. When some local kids later stumbled across the letters in the empty house, they recognized their good luck and walked door-to-door like they were selling candy—except here they were asking a few dollars for a letter by Abraham Lincoln, a bargain even at that time. The house was abandoned, they figured, so "finders keepers." When a local historian discovered what had happened, he phoned a community attorney, who took up the case pro bono, involving the police and scaring the pants off the kids. The original family who'd abandoned the home returned to claim their prize. The attorney convinced the kids they were not in legal jeopardy if they simply returned the historical documents, which they did. The family then sold the letters to Brown University, where they remain. But the attorney who helped reclaim the family treasures, and who had requested no money for his work, did ask for two letters of Lincoln of his choosing to give to his daughter, who had an interest in the sixteenth president. This meandering journey ended when that young girl's son sold them to us. From president to secretary of the treasury in the heat of the Civil War, to family heirloom, to an abandoned home, to the hands of the neighborhood kids, to a young girl, to her son, to me.

Another, more powerful example: Consider the Confederate general Evander Law, who saved hundreds of historical documents with other Confederate papers as William T. Sherman's army approached. No one knew exactly how these had been saved, only that they'd been among the official South Carolina papers removed from the state capital and set to be burned. The documents formed the backbone of the historical record of the secession period in that crucial Southern firebrand state. Among them was the official call from the floor of the South Carolina secession convention in December 1860 inviting other Southern states to secede. Law saved reams of historical records, salvaged pieces of the American legacy from the trash bin, and this service was repaid with legal action against his family. His descendants attempted to sell the documents to libraries and other research institutions, but failed. They sold a few privately, including that secession-convention call from 1860, which we bought at a small bookshop. The rest the family sent to an auction company, and South Carolina moved to block the sale. State authorities took the position that the Law family didn't own these pieces and had merely been caretakers. The case went to the district court, which concluded that the Law family had saved these pieces from the trash, and that the documents had been abandoned; the US Supreme Court refused to hear an appeal of the case. So the family got to keep the pieces and sent their entire archive to auction, where it sold for $330,000. Our document, meanwhile, which had cost us $60,000, was now legitimately ours; we sold it to a real estate developer in California for more than $100,000.

Another episode from early in my career relates directly to this question of provenance. Imagine my surprise when we received an anonymous email one day in 2006 from a man saying he had some of Saddam Hussein's personal items, taken from one of his palaces in Tikrit, Iraq. The man had Saddam's military uniform, with his rank on the lapel. He had some nice family portraits.

He'd also come across an archive of sorts, with filing cabinets and numerous papers. Here he was in the middle of the desert, and he'd stumbled on a trove of historical documents. They included the official diplomatic appointments of the ambassadors to Iraq by Presidents Harry Truman and Dwight Eisenhower, when the country was ruled by King Faisal II, before he was overthrown in 1958. This soldier had taken a folder filled with these documents and now wanted to sell them.

On the surface, the story fascinated me. What the man must have seen: the lavish beauty of the palace, the white marble and sandstone, the many gilded rooms, all abandoned.

Deciding if an artifact or document is real, and what it's worth, starts with a close examination of the item, but quickly turns to an examination of provenance.

As we always do, we asked follow-up questions to better understand the journey of these documents. Was the man who contacted me civilian or military? Were the items he had gifted or taken? His answers: military and taken, or, rather, "rescued."

So let's follow the journey of these documents: signed by an American president, carried by a diplomat overseas during times of peace, handed to the ruler, who then placed them in the nation's archives, where they remained during revolt and a change to autocracy, only to survive yet another revolt and an American-led invasion, when they were found by this soldier.

The soldier told us exactly where he got them. He didn't include his real name and used an email address that was clearly chosen at random for this communication.

We talked internally about what to do and decided that with such uncertain provenance, and the man's right to ownership so unclear, it was best to pass. We could not buy them or sell them.

I later learned that this was a widespread problem during the Iraq War: theft from the country's museums and archives, of art and artifacts, which were evidently being smuggled out of the country amid the fog and confusion of war, mostly by Iraqi citizens.

But our credo with these things is to be overly cautious and, when in doubt, walk away.

I told the soldier we weren't interested. I see Saddam Hussein letters on the market from time to time, and I wonder about them. I certainly couldn't authenticate a Saddam Hussein letter; and where are they coming from?

Ascertaining the provenance of historical documents and artifacts starts with knowing whom to trust. In the case of Barry Landau, my instincts for spotting someone who is *not* whom he represents himself to be served me well. Some people wear their honesty, or lack thereof, on their sleeves. Or, as Winston Churchill brilliantly quipped, "Men occasionally stumble over the truth, but most of them pick themselves up and hurry off as if nothing ever happened." This man looked as if it had never crossed his path.

We met at a rare-book fair in New York City. He shook my hand enthusiastically. "Barry Landau," he said, handing me his business card. It identified him as "America's Presidential Historian," though I'd never heard his name before. No one else around me had. He was in his sixties and spoke self-importantly about his encounters with Presidents Ford and Nixon; about how he had a great collection of historical documents.

As he talked to me, his bragging put me off, and I attempted to escape the conversation. I noticed he was accompanied by a young associate who was studying the items for sale at our booth and writing down all the prices. Our pieces were locked in a case so he was looking at them through the glass. They were an odd couple: the young man prim and buttoned up, hair slicked back, pen in hand. He looked like a Broadway version of a sailor in white uniform. And the older man posturing, a bit disheveled. Their behavior and demeanor seemed odd, and it wasn't just me. Midconversation with Landau, Karen stepped away and positioned herself, arms crossed, so that she could keep an eye on both men, acting as a guard. Since she stands just over five feet tall, it's unclear what she had in mind, but something was just not right and we both felt it instinctively. Landau asked me for my business card, and I explained that I didn't have one with me and that I never carry them. He chastised me, "What are you doing in this business without a business card?"

I couldn't get out of that conversation fast enough. He asked for my contact information later and I wouldn't give it to him.

Fast-forward about a year later: I read that a man had been arrested for stealing documents at the Maryland Historical Society in Baltimore. I looked at the picture and it was the same guy—I recognized the man!

The *Wall Street Journal* reported:

> Mr. Landau and an associate, Jason Savedoff, are awaiting federal trial in Baltimore, accused of conspiring to steal irreplaceable historic documents and sell them for profit. Paul Brachfeld, inspector

> general of the National Archives and Records Administration, says that of the 10,000 pieces removed from Mr. Landau's New York home, at least 2,500 of them—potentially worth millions of dollars—were stolen from historical societies, university libraries and other institutions along the East Coast.
>
> Prosecutors said in court that they found in Mr. Landau's apartment jackets with extra-deep pockets specifically tailored for stashing documents.
>
> Lee Arnold, senior director of the library and collections at the Historical Society of Pennsylvania, recalls a duo with a voracious appetite for documents. He says the pair handled hundreds of boxes of items, visiting 21 times between December and May, and gave out Pepperidge Farm cookies to staff. At the Maryland Historical Society, where the indictment alleges the pair stole roughly 60 documents, a staffer says they tried to charm employees with cupcakes.

I called Karen to my computer and asked if she remembered him too. She did and had the same recollection: he was creepy. Our caution and instincts were well rewarded. Others in the business he'd met that day had received calls from him offering documents for sale and had in many cases bought them. They were all stolen: an 1861 document signed by Lincoln from the Maryland Historical Society; a 1780 Benjamin Franklin letter from the New-York Historical Society; seven "reading copies" of speeches with the president's notes on them from the Franklin D. Roosevelt Presidential Library and Museum.

The pair were prosecuted in federal court in Baltimore by US Attorney Rod Rosenstein, and Landau was sentenced to seven years in prison. The younger man got a lesser sentence.

They'd removed the documents, then done the due diligence of also removing the card catalog entry associated with each one, covering their tracks. So the seizure by the Feds yielded not only the original documents but also card catalog entries typewritten decades ago.

The documents, collected by some of our nation's premier historical organizations and representing centuries' worth of archiving, had been carried out, en masse, in pockets built into the jackets of these two thieves, then packed into Landau's New York apartment. Amazingly, the documents, we were told, all made it back where they belonged.

Landau is different from Cosey or Spring. His motivations appear altogether unrelated. His modus operandi was not to trick collectors but rather to sell to dealers, mainly book dealers—people who would recognize forgeries but might not investigate provenance.

In his narrative poem *Metamorphoses*, Roman poet Ovid tells the story of Narcissus, the young man who, having deceived his townsmen and then the nymph Echo, is cursed by the goddess Nemesis. He stops in the woods for a drink and spots his reflection in a pool, falling in love with his own image and wasting away, never able to escape it. As Ovid writes, "While he is drinking, being attracted with the reflection of his own form, seen in the water, he falls in love with a thing that has no substance; and he thinks that to be a body, which is but a shadow. . . . While he pursues, he is pursued, and at the same moment he inflames and burns."

Landau was cut from the same cloth. The praise he received as a historian, a friend to presidents, given awards and generally feted, was perhaps not enough. He surrounded himself with the trappings of history, and the more he had, the more it bolstered his self-image. The edifice he'd built, shaky as it was, was reinforced with letters written by Jefferson, Washington, and Roosevelt. Landau had fallen in love not with his own image, but with the historical characters whose letters he treasured, and the prestige they conferred upon him. His was a doomed venture because—like that of Narcissus—it came from vanity.

The old historical societies have magnificent halls for research, decorated with centuries-old works of art. Some of these halls are two stories high, filled with long wooden desks adorned with reading lights, and given an air of grandeur by the dark wood paneling and the near silence. The only sound is the footsteps of archivists carrying original historical treasures to the researchers.

As the archivist of the Historical Society of Pennsylvania approached me, she held out a small manila folder, which contained a letter written by Benjamin Franklin. She smiled and walked away. I opened that envelope only to find a photocopy, a reproduction of the letter copied from the original. This was one of the more worrisome moments I've ever had concerning provenance.

My problem was that, in my bag, to my left, I had this very letter, the original. I was considering acquiring it for $25,000. As part of my research prepurchase, I dropped by the Historical Society, which has an extensive collection of Franklin material. In the folder was a copy of the letter I had, which would in itself be unremarkable. But the copy was complete with the same folding creases and the same small smudge in the center-right portion of the letter as the one I was carrying. And now the worrisome part: the clear implication was that the society owned the original, which would be unfortunate for me.

I gulped, concerned about the situation I found myself in. I was on the board of directors of this organization, which made it all the more potentially embarrassing. How could they have a copy of this letter and I have the original? There was no record of any sale. For forty-five minutes I sat there wrapping my head around the possibility that the original may have been *stolen* from this folder, and there I was holding it.

My anxiety turned to curiosity when I finally noticed, behind the copy, a *very* small note that made oblique reference to the minutes of the society.

I requested the minutes from that date from the same archivist, without referring to why or to my latest discovery. Half an hour later, those same footsteps echoed through the hall and brought me my salvation. The minutes indicated that though they weren't setting precedent, the board had agreed to give, in the 1970s, the original of this letter to a longtime supporter, who sold it to another collector,

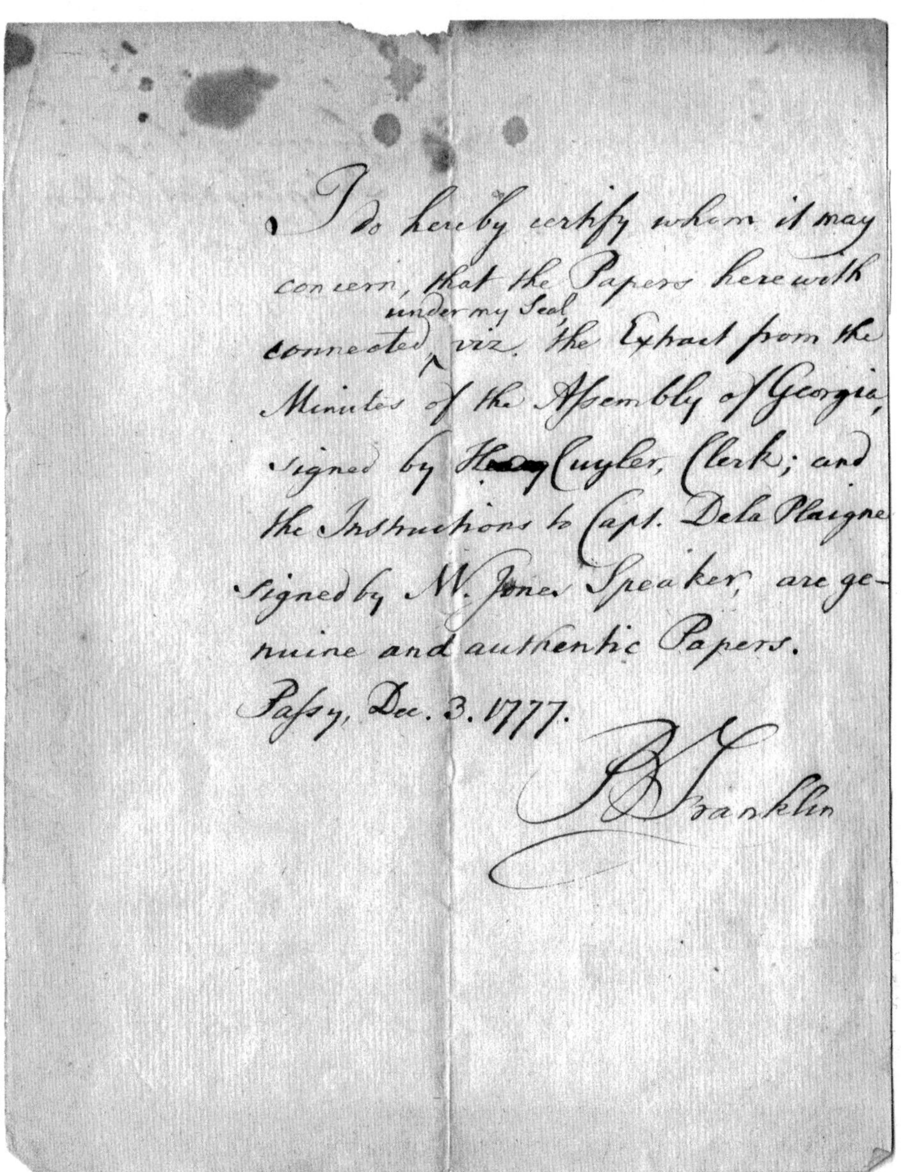

I do hereby certify whom it may
concern, that the Papers herewith
connected, under my Seal, viz. the Extract from the
Minutes of the Assembly of Georgia,
signed by ~~Henry~~ Cuyler, Clerk; and
the Instructions to Capt. De la Plaigne
signed by N. W. Jones Speaker, are genuine and authentic Papers.
Passy, Dec. 3. 1777.

B. Franklin

The Benjamin Franklin letter I feared had been stolen.

who then sold it to us. We in turn sold it to a telecom executive in North Carolina for around $40,000.

My favorite illustration of the power of the "journey" of a document, or its provenance, is Winston Churchill's famous POW letter to his captor in South Africa more than a century ago. The year was 1899. The ambitious twenty-four-year-old future prime minister was a correspondent for London's *Morning Post* when war broke out between England and the descendants of the original Dutch immigrants in that distant land—the Boers. He immediately embarked for South Africa. In-country, the only way he could reach the front was by boarding the armored train sent out for reconnaissance every day, and he did so on the morning of November 15, 1899. The Boers set a trap for the English train, which crashed. Churchill had no weapon, and the train's armor did no good, so he surrendered, along with everyone else on board. His captors realized this confident young man came from an esteemed family back home and was therefore a valuable bargaining chip; as such, Churchill was treated as an officer POW. One Hendrik Spaarwater was ordered to escort the prisoners and hand them over to the local police, who would then escort them to the POW camp in Pretoria. Spaarwater showed real consideration for his prisoners, and as he handed over Churchill to the police, Churchill took from his pocket a small pad of paper and scribbled a note dated November 17, 1899: "The bearer, Mr HG Spaarwater, has been very kind to me and the British officers captured in the Escort armoured train. I shall be personally grateful to anyone who may be able to do him any service should he himself be taken prisoner. Winston S Churchill." Churchill would cite this letter in his book *London to Ladysmith via Pretoria*.

This small pencil note in hand, Spaarwater headed back to the front lines, but he was never captured and had no need for it. Yet he kept it. A year later, he was killed in a friendly fire incident. His belongings, including the note, were returned with his body to the small, isolated rural town where he'd lived. The note now had new ownership: his wife, and then his children, who appreciated its power. After the family had held the letter safely for a couple of generations, Spaarwater's great-granddaughter loaned it to a small village museum, where it was displayed along with other artifacts from the Boer War for the occasional visitor who happened by. Keep in mind, this museum is in the heart of old Dutch Boer country, far from any major city, so essentially the note remained where it had been signed.

In 2016, we received an email from the owner of that museum. "We met a great granddaughter of Hendrik Spaarwater during this time. She was in possession of the letter. She donated it to our museum after visiting us, because according to her, her sons were not interested. After two years of a display in our museum she made contact and wanted the letter back. My husband offered to purchase the letter and she sold it to us. My husband passed away in 2015 and my children and I are continuing with the museum."

They weren't yet interested in selling the letter, but we learned more about it and marveled that it had survived all this time. Then they recontacted us, wanting to sell it. Were we interested? Museums and other institutions divest themselves of material all the time, for all kinds of reasons, but private museums such as this, which work more like family operations, do so somewhat more informally. I immediately responded to this inquiry and almost just as immediately agreed to buy the letter, with the usual "after inspection" stipulation.

Something about this piece was special, as if I'd cheated the order of history and had caught Churchill far away from home, long before he was famous, just a young man claiming his place in life.

But now a quandary lay ahead of us: How to get the letter from a ranching district at the bottom of Africa to the Main Line of Philadelphia? The only solution was a six-hundred-mile round-trip journey to the nearest FedEx office—in Johannesburg—by the museum owner.

From Churchill's pen to HG Spaarwater's pocket, then to his children's and great-granddaughter's safekeeping, then to the village museum, then to FedEx, then to me, eight thousand miles away.

Finally, the letter found a new home with a collector in the American South—the owner of a military-contracting business (also a veteran whose son is serving in the military abroad) who has taken up the task of preserving this piece of history. Though the writing of the letter predates Churchill's time as prime minister, the story of the document is so central to his life and so evocative of his character that we had many orders for this piece at $36,000. I love to unearth and then contemplate such a chain of ownership. No, it wasn't necessary to further establish authenticity in this case.

But it is a reminder that each document survives for a reason, because of a series of steps that several people have taken, people who'll never meet one another, often separated by thousands of miles. How much history has been lost because of just one break in this chain, one careless person, or one person who simply didn't understand what he or she had? Books could be written, history changed, if we had what has now been lost.

CHAPTER 12

Thomas Edison and Albert Einstein

Rarely do we enter a room without instinctively reaching for the light switch. Most of us turn on the lights in our homes without thinking twice. But life wasn't always this way. Although we understand the invention of the light bulb and its commercialization as a major advancement, few of us give it the credit it merits as a revolution.

Imagine a world before the light bulb: Once the sun went down, most serious work ended, save what could be accomplished by fire and gaslight. Candles were expensive and out of the reach of most, and both they and gas were serious fire hazards. Life essentially ground to a halt with the setting of the sun. Thomas Edison lit the world, and he did so by changing that dynamic entirely. He wasn't the only one working on the idea of artificial light, but he invented the light bulb, figured out how to wire homes with electricity, then sold it to the world, converting nighttime into modified day.

While the invention of the light bulb took place in 1879, perhaps the greatest demonstration of its power to change the world came a year later, at a now little-remembered event. Edison would prove to humanity that the light bulb could provide light not just under lab conditions, but everywhere. He would bring his invention into everyone's home.

But it wasn't easy. Think about it: You can't just take a wire, stick it underground, and expect it to last uninsulated from weather, movement of earth, and decay. You have to insulate it and make sure the current travels.

W. S. Andrews, one of Edison's first employees, described the system they created: "In 1880, Mr. Edison laid out a system of underground distribution from his laboratory in Menlo Park, to supply 1000 lamps, placed on wooden lamp-posts along the streets and roads of the village of Menlo Park and also in the dwellings. As no electric circuits had ever before been placed underground, there was absolutely no experience to guide in the proper laying and insulation of the conductors."

All this work was being done at Edison's laboratory in Menlo Park, New Jersey, the first such research-and-development operation in the world. There the great inventor employed a large staff, including his head engineer, John Kruesi, a Swiss man who'd trained as a locksmith but whose real talent was making Edison's inventions come to life. Together, they worked on a system for getting electricity into people's homes.

This was crucial: What was the good of an electric light if you had no electricity? So Edison's team set to work figuring out how to lay electric wires underground, and they used their own neighborhood as a test case. Both Edison and many of his staff lived close to the laboratories.

They experimented with different insulation materials, ultimately arriving at a mixture of Trinidad asphalt mixed with oxidized linseed oil and a little paraffin and beeswax. Then the wires, buried underground, were run into the buildings.

On Election Day 1880, the electric line along Christie Street in Menlo Park was completed, streetlamps were in place, and Edison's home, as well as Kruesi's, across the street, were connected to power. When Edison was told all was ready, he said, "If Garfield is elected, light up that circuit. If not, do not light it." Garfield was the Republican candidate, favored in most northern states, and he won. That night, Christie Street in Menlo Park lit up, and everyone cheered.

It's hard to overstate just how momentous an achievement this was. This was only the beginning: electric power soon lit up entire cities all across the world.

* * *

One hundred forty years after this test, we received a portentous email:

> I am the family historian and grandson of Paul J. Kruesi, whose father, John Kruesi, was one of Edison's principal associates, the foreman of his lab, the one who built the first phonograph, the one who moved Edison's electric works from New York to Schenectady. I have about a dozen signed letters from Edison to Kruesi and also a piece of a cable in Menlo Park.

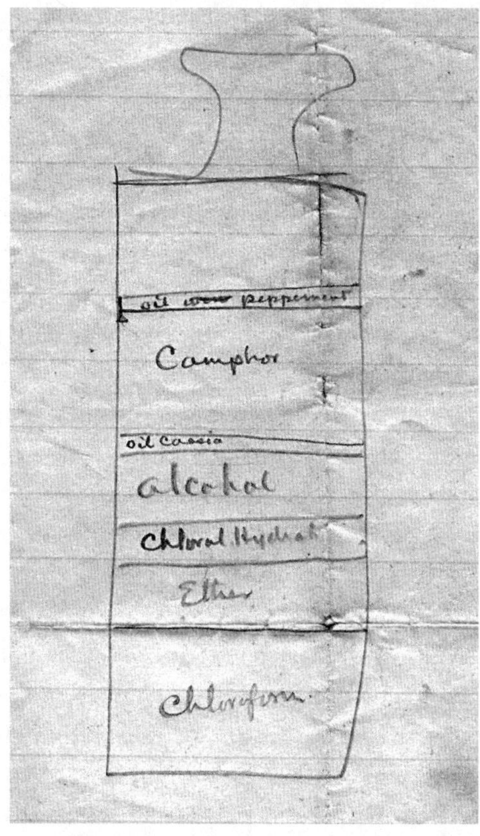

One of the Edison items acquired from Kruesi's descendant, a drawing of one of his many inventions.

My focus was on the letters, which promised to be interesting enough. I didn't spend too much time on the "cable." This is for a few reasons: I didn't yet know the above story, and perhaps most important, I'm always skeptical about claims and begin with the presumption that things are not authentic unless proven otherwise. Whatever this piece of cable was, its significance would for the moment remain a mystery.

But this email began a journey of discovery for me.

The material arrived in a cardboard box, with the letters in a folder and the cable in bubble wrap, with the word FRAGILE on the outside. Inside the bubble wrap, this object was housed in a padded envelope. I opened it, and pieces of what most closely resembled soot fell out. It took me a while to figure out what I was looking at.

What a weird sight this was. The "cable" wasn't really a cable, but a piece of metal encased in a rocklike substance, or so it seemed to me. It was unassuming, rather dirty, with pieces of the rock splitting off and the cable not readily visible without closer inspection. But the man who contacted me had included two other things that made me take a second look. First, the object had a tag attached to it that noted that it was from the first underground cable, and the date it was dug up. The tag and the writing looked age appropriate, which was a positive.

Second, after Edison died, a group of his colleagues and former assistants banded together in a society of Edison devotees to promote his work and preserve his memory. The secretary of that organization: F. A. Wardlaw. This artifact came with a letter to Kruesi from Wardlaw, which read:

> This is a piece of the original underground conductor that fed Edison's home, exactly like that used for yours [Kruesi's home] and [Charles] Batchelor's, at the historic demonstration of the Edison electric light at Menlo Park, N.J. in 1880. It was the first underground cable ever used for this purpose. Taken from the earth by myself Sept. 29, 1933, after having been buried on the east side of Christie Street, just opposite your old home, for fifty-three years.

I found a news source online that confirmed how, in 1933, as new electric cables were being installed along Christie Street, Wardlaw had dug up a few pieces of the copper wire that had been buried more than fifty years earlier. Edison died in 1931.

If this was right, could this be one of those pieces? Or even the only such piece? Establishing authenticity of objects—establishing provenance—requires a great deal of research. I wasn't ready to make a definitive claim yet.

I went to the University of Pennsylvania, to the rare-book library, and pored over old sources, finally stumbling across a passage in an obscure article describing what the original cable leading from Edison's lab to the homes looked like. Conductors, it read, "were composed of No. 10 BWG copper wire. . . . The system was a simple two conductor, multiple circuit. . . . After a few weeks of experiments, the best of the insulating compounds was selected for use. This compound was composed of refined Trinidad asphaltum, mixed with oxidized linseed oil to give it the right consistency, and a little paraffin and beeswax were added to make the material smoother."

While this passage was an exciting find, it seemed to cast doubt on my having something authentic, as I didn't remember the wire having two conductors.

So I went home and, as Karen advised me, took a second look at our object. I took it out of the case, looked closely, and was astonished to see that it *was* a two-conductor circuit. And after some additional research, I determined it was no. 10 copper wire. This matched the description precisely. Far from diminishing the object, the article I'd found had identified and authenticated it. Moreover, what I'd naively dismissed as rock or soot was the asphalt used by Edison.

The puzzle had one more piece. Did it make sense that Wardlaw would have sent artifacts to just one person? No, it didn't. While the seller was a direct descendant of Edison's chief lab aide at the time, Edison had many close colleagues who helped in this project. I wanted proof that Wardlaw had sent other things to other people. That would set a pattern. And I found it, online at the Smithsonian no less, which displayed an artifact with the same provenance: a lamp used to illuminate Menlo Park on December 31, 1879, when Edison introduced his invention to the world. It was in the exhibition *Lighting a Revolution* at the National Museum of American History. It contained the same label as ours, written in the hand of the same man, Wardlaw, gifting it.

So to authenticate this incredible artifact, we'd assembled a battery of evidence: the object was in the hands of the direct descendants of the recipient; they had the letter sending it, along with a tag identifying it; it matched the description of the artifact, which we obtained after great research; and it matched other widely accepted provenance.

So here we had it: the first underground wire in the world, part of that great 1880 test in Menlo Park, used to electrify Edison's and Kruesi's homes.

I felt as if I were on my hands and knees on Christie Street, digging up that piece of history again after nearly a century, sifting through the dirt and exposing the cable and the asphalt. Cutting off pieces with a wire clipper and reliving Edison's experiment and invention all over again.

This memento wouldn't have survived if not for a variety of factors: Wardlaw's work in unearthing and saving the artifacts, the Kruesi family's efforts in safeguarding the piece for generations, and our research to identify it and bring it to the attention of the public. It was one of the most important artifacts relating to electricity and light ever to reach the market.

We bought the artifact, along with a number of Edison's letters to Kruesi, most of which related to the insulation around the wires that lit New York City in 1881. The media widely reported the discovery of the cable, which we priced at $100,000.

It is indeed remarkable: a testament to Edison's practical brilliance. Edison had changed the way we live. This artifact of history reminded me of how sometimes a single idea, a single person, can change the world.

▲ Charles Vaughn Houston with his wife, Sophronia, my ancestors; he went to California in 1849 to find gold.

CHAIRMAN OF THE JOINT CHIEFS OF STAFF
WASHINGTON, D. C. 20318-9999

30 September 1993

Mr. Nathan Raab

Dear Mr. Raab,

Thank you for your letter and kind words. Our brave men and women displayed great courage and made tremendous sacrifices to win the Persian Gulf War. We owe them our deep gratitude.

In answer to your questions, General George C. Marshall had a great influence on my career, but my parents deserve most of the credit for my success. They provided a solid foundation on which to build. I would like to be remembered best for always putting the welfare of my troops first.

I appreciate your taking the time to write. Your self-addressed stamped envelope is enclosed.

With best wishes,

Sincerely,

COLIN L. POWELL
Chairman
of the
Joint Chiefs of Staff

► A letter to me from Colin Powell, one of many I received from notable figures as a child.

STATE OF NEW YORK
Executive Chamber
ALBANY

Jany. 26th, 1900.

Mr. Henry L. Sprague,
Union League Club,
N.Y. City.

Dear Harry:--

Your letter of the 25th really pleased me.Of course, I shall not feel real easy until the vote has actually been taken, but apparently everything is now all right. I have always been fond of the West African proverb: "Speak softly and carry a big stick; you will go far." If I had not carried the big stick the Organization would not have gotten behind me, and if I had yelled and blustered as Parkhurst and the similar dishonest lunatics desired, I would not have had ten votes. But I was entirely good humored, kept perfectly cool and steadfastly refused to listen to anything save that Payn had to go, and that I would take none but a thoroughly upright and capable man in his place. Unless there is some cataclysm , these tactics will be crowned with success. As for the Eveing Post, Parkhurst and Company, they of course did their feeble

best to try to get me to take action which would have ensured Payn's retention and would have resulted therefore in a very imposing triumph for rascality. They have often shown themselves the enemies of good government, but in this case I do not think they are even to be credited with good intentions. They were no more anxious to see dishonesty rebuked than a professional prohibitionist is to see the liquor law decently administered.

With warm regards,

Faithfully yours,

Theodore Roosevelt

◄ Theodore Roosevelt's famous "speak softly" letter, which my father found buried in a dealer catalog.

"I have always been fond of the West African proverb: 'Speak softly and carry a big stick; you will go far.'"

► My father, far left, shows me a regimental flag at a Civil War reenactment in 1983. He is wearing his Union soldier's hat, and I am holding a plastic sword.

► Benjamin Franklin in 1767 in London, where he wrote "B Free Franklin" on the back of our letter.

"I was out all day yesterday at Versailles."

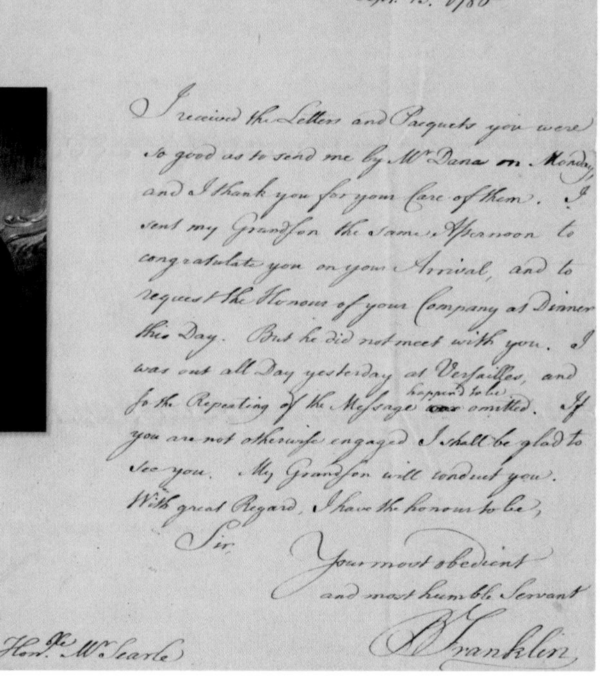

Sir

Passy, Wednesday morning
Sept. 13. 1780

I received the Letters and Pacquets you were so good as to send me by Mr Dana on Monday, and I thank you for your Care of them. I sent my Grandson the same Afternoon to congratulate you on your Arrival, and to request the Honour of your Company at Dinner this Day. But he did not meet with you. I was out all Day yesterday at Versailles, and so the Repeating of the Message happen'd to be omitted. If you are not otherwise engaged I shall be glad to see you. My Grandson will conduct you.

With great Regard, I have the honour to be,
Sir,
Your most obedient
and most humble Servant
B Franklin

Honble. Mr Searle

Believe me, my dear Sir
with sincere admiration
Yours very faithfully
Ch. Darwin

This note requires no answer, so pray do not trouble yourself to acknowledge it.

◄ Charles Darwin recounted his now-famous expedition south on the *Beagle* in an important letter that we found overlooked at a book fair.

"My wife has just finished reading aloud your 'Life with a Black Regiment.' . . . When you were here I did not know of the noble position which you had filled. I had formerly read about the black regiments, but failed to connect your name with your admirable undertaking."

Key West

January 15, 1935

Dear Mr. McConnaughey ;

We always gaff a marlin in the head no matter where he is hooked . Gaffing them there gives you control over the part of the fish that is dangerous ie.his head and bill . Also the head of the fish is what you bring toward you and is what you gaff for .. When you get their head up by the boat the tail may be fourteen feet away if the fish would be big enough . How are you to lead their tail toward you when the hook is in the fishes mouth ? Also the gaff holds best in the fishes head and you can then grab the bill and hang on while you club him across the top of the head between the eyes . A gaff in the head kills the fish too and does not spoil the meat .Unless you gaff through the gills a fish bleeds very little when gaffed in the head .

Some people gaff under the pectoral fin but I think this is messy and besides you cannot lift a big fish that way . Gaffing in the tail I have never heard about until your letter . I have seen one gaffed that way accidentally but had no idea anyone would ever do it on purpose . However there are lots of ways of doing all sorts of things and if Mr. Guild gaffs them that way he must have developed a technique for it.- But everyone in Cuba where I learned to fish for marlin gaffs them in the head and out of about one hundred and twenty that I have caught would say that all but four or five have been gaffed in the head and those were gaffed elsewhere by slips or by accident .

If you write or see Mr. Guild will you tell him this for me and give him my compliments and best wishes .

I can see how technically anybody could make out a case for gaffing in the tail-ie you pull the tail out of water and the fish is helpless etc. But how do you get close to his tail when you bring him in head first ? Also I can assure you I have never lost a marlin gaffed in the head and since the object of gaffing a fish is to make sure of him and to kill him at the same time I can recommend that way of gaffing to you without any reservations .

Thanks for your letter (am sure I'll dream some night now about gaffing some marlin wrong and to ; would be willing to try it if they were plentiful enough) and I hope you'll have a chance to gaff one yourself this season .

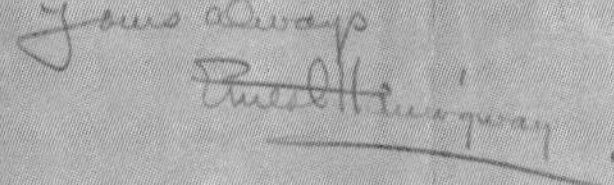

Yours always

Ernest Hemingway

▲ Ernest Hemingway standing alongside a marlin caught using a method described in a letter we found in the collection of a retired professor.

"We always gaff a marlin in the head no matter where he is hooked. Gaffing them there gives you control over the part of the fish that is dangerous, ie his head and bill."

► Key to my understanding of the emotional power of historical documents was an archive of letters between Ronald Reagan and daughter Patti Davis, pictured here before their estrangement.

Dear Patti

I've just gotten an answer off to Dr. C. telling her not to worry, it's par for the course.

Haven't time to write more I'm in between meetings.

Love

Dad

year.—The difference in the quality of them, though there was no perceivable [difference] in the quality of the soil previous to the preceeding crop, was so apparent as to be discerned almost as far as the field could be seen.—Those on the Potatoe ground being so much the most luxuriant.
It would seem from the public gazettes that the minority in your State are preparing for another attack of the -now- adopted Government, how formidable it may be, I know not. But that Providence which has hitherto smiled on the honest endeavours of the well meaning part of the People of this Country will not, I trust, withdraw its support from them at this crisis.—With best respects to Mrs Peters & yourself, in which Mrs Washington joins me, I am—Dear Sir
Your most Obedt
Humble Servant
Go: Washington

Richard Peters Esqr.

▸ George Washington was a land surveyor under the king, and his documents from this era can fetch top dollar, but, as we discovered, they also attract the attention of forgers. This authentic letter relates to his work on the land but also praises God for the progress of the nation.

"That Providence which has hitherto smiled on the honest endeavors of the well meaning part of the People of this Country will not, I trust, withdraw its support from them at this crisis."

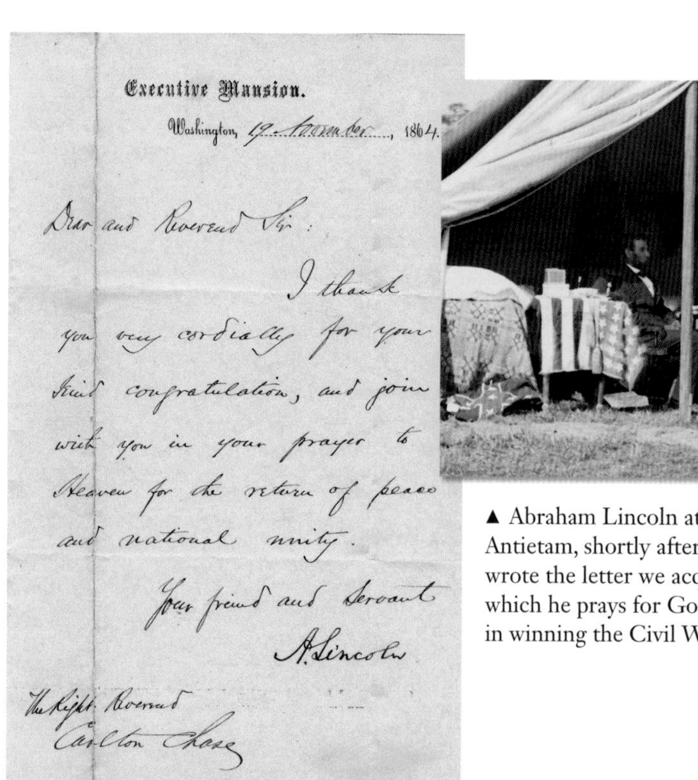

Executive Mansion.

Washington, 19 November, 1864.

Dear and Reverend Sir:

I thank you very cordially for your kind congratulation, and join with you in your prayer to Heaven for the return of peace and national unity.

Your friend and Servant
A. Lincoln

The Right Reverend
Carlton Chase

▲ Abraham Lincoln at Antietam, shortly after he wrote the letter we acquired in which he prays for God's help in winning the Civil War.

► An archive announcing Napoléon's death, which did not appear in the catalog description.

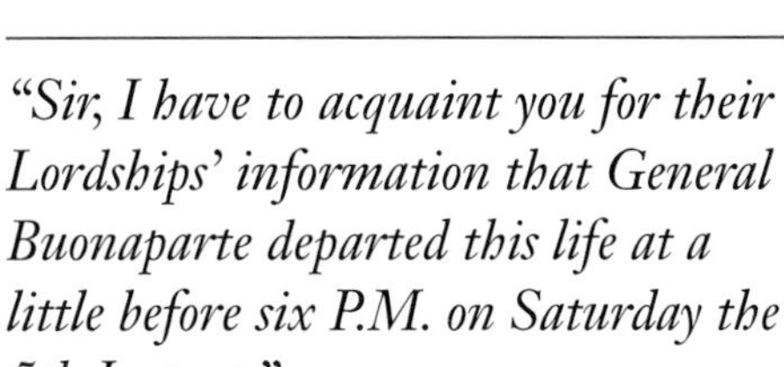

"Sir, I have to acquaint you for their Lordships' information that General Buonaparte departed this life at a little before six P.M. on Saturday the 5th Instant."

▼ Winston Churchill (far right) as a prisoner of war. One of the men in the photo may have been the recipient of the small note he wrote to a captor, which we discovered in South Africa and acquired.

"Mr HG Spaarwater, has been very kind to me and the British officers captured in the Escort armoured train. I shall be personally grateful to anyone who may be able to do him any service should he himself be taken prisoner."

◄ A fragment of the first underground wire used by Thomas Edison to light a home.

"This is a piece of the original underground conductor that fed Edison's home . . . at the historic demonstration of the Edison electric light at Menlo Park, N.J. in 1880. It was the first underground cable ever used for this purpose. Taken from the earth by myself Sept. 29, 1933."

► Susan B. Anthony's letter decrying the treatment of women as "pets," with her underlines for emphasis. Anthony is pictured below (the central figure).

"I know you think women are the pets of society . . . but to be a pet is not to be an equal, and what I want is for women to be equal before the law in every respect."

National American Woman Suffrage Association.

MEMBER NATIONAL COUNCIL OF WOMEN.

Honorary President, Susan B. Anthony, 17 Madison Street, Rochester, N. Y.

President, Rev. Anna Howard Shaw, 7443 Devon Street, Mt. Airy, Philadelphia, Pa.
Vice President at Large, Carrie Chapman Catt, 205 West 57th Street, New York City.
Corresponding Secretary, Kate M. Gordon, 1800 Prytania Street, New Orleans, La.

Recording Secretary, Alice Stone Blackwell, 3 Park Street, Boston, Mass.
Treasurer, Harriet Taylor Upton, Warren, Ohio.
Auditors { Laura Clay, Lexington, Ky. / Cora Smith Eaton, M. D., Masonic Temple, Minneapolis, Minn.
National Press Committee, Elnora M. Babcock, Dunkirk, N. Y.

NATIONAL HEADQUARTERS, WARREN, OHIO.

OFFICE OF HONORARY PRESIDENT, ROCHESTER, N. Y.

February 11,1905.

Heitmuller Art Company,
Washington, D.C.

My dear Sirs--

Your communication of Feb.4th is received. I have no doubt that your autographs are very fine and the portraits of all the distinguished men you mention must be fine also, but I am especially interested in the autograph signatures and the pictures of distinguished women. When you get a collection of autographs and portraits of the distinguished women of the last century,- of Mary Woolstencraft, Frances Wright, Ernestine L. Rose, Elizabeth Cady Stanton, Paulina Wright Davis, Lucy Stone,etc.,etc., I will talk about patronizing you. But while women are by the law excluded from a voice in the government under which they live I can only work for their emancipation. I know you think women are the pets of society. That they may be, but to be a pet is not to be an equal, and what I want is for women to be equal before the law in every respect.

Sincerely yours,

Susan B. Anthony

SEPARATE ENTRY BLANK MUST BE FILLED OUT
FOR EACH SHIP ENTERED

Name of Entrant Amelia Earhart
Address Seymoor Hotel New York
Pilot Amelia Earhart Address as above
Pilot's Dept. of Com. Rating and Number Transport 5716
Pilot's F.A.I. Certificate Number
Pilot's N.A.A. Annual Sporting License Number 226
~~Alternate~~ Pilot Helen Richey Address McKeesport, Penna
Alternate Pilot's Dept. Com. Rating and Number T-15151
Alternate Pilot's F.A.I. Certificate Number 7967
Alternate Pilot's N.A.A. Annual Sporting License Number 25
Make of Airplane Lockheed Electra Dept. of Com. No. R 10620
Type of Airplane Land Monoplane Make and Type of Motors P&W Wasp
Bore 5 3/4 Stroke 5 3/4 Cubic-Inch Displacement 1340

I herewith certify that I have read; that I understand; and that I agree to adhere to the Rules and Regulations [pub]lished in connection with the National Air Races Competitive Events and that the foregoing information is corre[ct to] the best of my knowledge and belief.

Entrant's Signature

Entrant's Address

State of New York
County of Kings
Subscribed and sworn to before me this 3 day of September, 19
by Amelia Earhart the identical person who executed the foregoing statem[ent]
Notary Public Samuel Levy
(SEAL) My commission expires
NOTARY PUBLIC
KINGS COUNTY & QUEENS
Kings Co. Clk's No. 358, Reg. No.
Queens Co. Clk's No. 1145, Reg. No.
Commission expires Mar. 30, 1937

TO BE FILLED OUT BY ENTRANTS IN THE
RUTH CHATTERTON SPORTSMAN PILOTS DERBY

Are you entering the East Wing of the Derby?
(Cleveland to Fort Worth or Dallas)

Are you entering the West Wing of the Derby?
(Fort Worth or Dallas to Los Angeles)

Only Entrants in both Wings of the Derby are eligible for the Ruth Chatterton Trophy.

What cruising speed will you use? (See Rules and Regulations)
Specify actual measured cruising speed in still air

I hereby certify that neither I nor any of my passengers have received compensation either directly or indirectly in any form for piloting an airplane since August 15, 1935.

Entrant's Signature, Ruth Chatterton Trophy

NOTE: *If you do not have F.A.I. Certificate and Annual Sporting License, secure same immediately from the National Aeronautic Association, Dupont Circle, Washington, D.C. Refer to General Rules and Regulations. This information must be given on entry blank. Parachute jumpers must hold Annual Sporting License.*

▼ Amelia Earhart at the 1936 Bendix race. We found her entry form for this race, describing the plane she stands on.

► Thomas Jefferson and Meriwether Lewis. A manuscript we discovered ordering books for the Library of Congress had both their handwriting on the same page. Nothing like it had ever reached the market and that remains true to this day.

TAPE NO. ______ FOR General Clifton HALF TRACK 3 3/4 IPS

Subject	Date	Recording Time
Radio Traffic involving AF-1 in flight from Dallas, Texas to Andrews AFB on November 22, 1963		

Recorded by
White House Communications Agency
THE WHITE HOUSE
Washington 25, D.C.

◄ The box holding the lost JFK Air Force One tape as we first found it.

"Andrews supplying ambulance for body to take to Walter Reed. Repeat please, repeat please. Walter Reed for body, Walter Reed."

► The envelope from Martin Luther King's jailhouse letter to Pauline Jackson.

► Georg Bredig's post-1933 passport, with the "J" of Jew (Juden) written prominently.

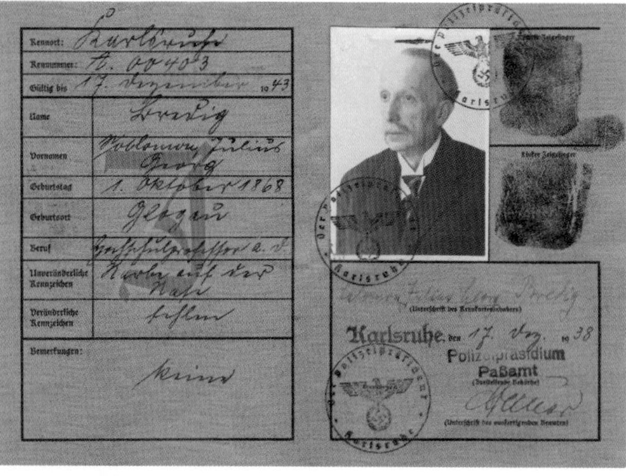

◄ On examining the archive, we found this coded diplomatic communiqué of John Quincy Adams, who uses "666" to refer to the British.

"[While this] crisis may try the temper of our country, if there is a drop of blood flowing in the veins of our country-men that carried their fathers through the Revolutionary War, they will not be intimidated and we will ultimately secure a glorious triumph."

* * *

Emerson, in his book *Representative Men*, praises those who expand our horizons and help us see past our immediate surroundings to something great: "There are persons who, in their character, answer questions which I have not the skill to put."

Like Edison, who changed our world and daily lives, Albert Einstein allowed our minds to venture to concepts and dimensions well beyond our planet. He changed the way we think about the nature of space and time—sometimes to much confusion.

In April of 1945, an American soldier stationed on the island of Luzon, in the Philippines, was puzzling over an article in the magazine *Science Digest*. The soldier, Frank K. Pfleegor, was an engineer and scientifically minded; he figured he should be able to comprehend an article written in a popular-science magazine. But then, this was an article written by the great Albert Einstein himself, and it sounded more like science fiction than science. Indeed, Pfleegor had the impression the physicist had left out some crucial steps in his thinking. After discussing the matter with his tentmates—all of whom were also engineers and equally confused—he decided to write a letter to Einstein. Why not? Maybe he could clear up the confusion. Maybe the physicist would even write back.

The soldiers had been stationed on Luzon since January, and the fighting there was over, leaving time for such leisurely pursuits as discussing the space-time continuum and the theory of relativity. They were members of the Twenty-Sixth Photographic Reconnaissance Squadron, called the Lightning Bugs after the planes they sent to spy on the enemy. They'd supported the successful American island-hopping campaign in the East Indies, then flew missions in support of the 1944–45 Philippines campaign. Soon enough they'd be called upon to help with the assault on Okinawa; the action in the Pacific Theater would close out the war in the coming months.

Einstein had, meanwhile, been working for years on a way of unifying his theory of general relativity, which described the relationships among space, time, and gravity, with theories of electromagnetism and quantum mechanics. A grand, unified theory was the goal—a way of accounting for phenomena from the scale of light-years all the way down to the subatomic level. Einstein had fled Germany in 1933 and was now working at the Institute for Advanced Study at Princeton University; he'd recently been exploring a new mathematical approach to describing the curvature of space, relying on so-called bivectors rather than differential equations. He'd described this work in the article that had so mystified the soldiers in the Philippines. The bivector equations measured the distance between any two points, using four dimensions to describe each one (x, y, z, and t for time). Because of the way he'd explained this rather abstract idea, the article had seemed to imply that he thought there might be eight dimensions (variables) rather than four, a huge set of variables.

Sergeant Pfleegor wrote to Einstein on April 17, 1945:

> In our tent we usually spend our evenings discussing various scientific topics. Tonight we attempted to tackle a problem from the Nov. 1944 issue of Science Digest, entitled "Einstein's At It Again." By your theory, space is composed of two spaces of four dimensions each. Space is composed of the whole extent of the universe. According to the law of impenetrability: two objects cannot occupy the same space at the same time. Can space be divided? The article was not very enlightening. Some of us stick by the single four dimensional space. The rest say it is made up of two spaces of four dimensions. Why not three or four dimensions etc.? We would appreciate an answer.

Pfleegor sent the letter via V-mail (short for "victory mail," a mail system for the armed forces) and addressed it to Albert Einstein, Princeton University.

I was struck by the detail of the soldier's letter but also by his interest. What was this soldier doing, on the other side of the world, writing Albert Einstein and thinking that he'd respond?

But he did. Less than a month later, much to his surprise, Pfleegor received an answer, typed on Einstein's Institute for Advanced Study at the School of Mathematics letterhead, dated May 11, 1945. It explained that though Einstein had looked into the idea of more variables, he would be basing his future work on four.

> Dear Sir: I see from your letter of April 17th that the attempt of my last publication was not reported in an adequate way. I have not questioned there that space should be looked at as a four dimensional continuum. The question is only whether the relevant theoretical concepts describing physical properties of this space can be or will be functions of four variables. If, for instance, the relevant entity is something like the distance of two points which are not infinitesimal near to each other, then such distance has to be a function of the coordinates of two points. This means a function of eight variables. I have investigated possibilities of this kind in the last years, but my respective results seem to me not very encouraging. For the time being I have returned to ordinary differential equations [from general relativity] with dependent variables being simply functions of the four coordinates [space-time]. What the future has in store for us nobody can foretell. It is a question of success.

Chew on that one for a while. I certainly did. The soldiers had written him with a respectful and not unreasonable question about relativity and related science—science beyond many average readers. Einstein had responded with a complex letter, relating to two points measured in four-dimensional space. I had to call my friend whose specialties include this type of science to understand it. But it sure did delight the soldiers and was reported in the military's *Stars and Stripes* newspaper: "Army 'bull-sessions' are usually noteworthy only for the noise that accompanies them, but in the case of Sgt Frank K. Pfleegor of the Lightning Bugs such a session led to correspondence with no less a figure than the great Albert Einstein." It showed Einstein to be a very human and approachable figure, despite his genius.

That's where the story ended, until one of Frank Pfleegor's heirs discovered that his father had kept the letter and the man realized it might be valuable, which it was. He drove a hard bargain and we ended up paying far more than we wanted, but we bought the letter from the family.

We have Einstein collectors all over the world; the challenge here was not selling it, but deciding to whom I should mention it first. We're helping to put together large collections of Einstein-related documents in California, New York, North Carolina, London, and Delhi. The most prized of the great physicist's letters are those that discuss science and especially relativity. We sold this letter for $40,000 to a tech entrepreneur in Colorado, who saw it on cable news. The buyer was touched knowing that the greatest scientist of the twentieth century, the man who changed the way we think about space and time, took the time to write men in harm's way on the other side of the planet.

You can't remove history from its context: Einstein's letter is as much about the soldiers as it is about him.

CHAPTER 13

"I Know You Think Women Are the Pets of Society"

One evening at dinner, talking about business, as we often do, my dad turned to Karen and said, "I see dead people." We laughed. "I'm serious," he explained. "Each time we get a document, I imagine what it was like back then, what they were like." I remember a sign, printed in the old software program Print Shop off our dot-matrix printer, hanging next to his bed. It went up in 1987, and there it remains, hanging from the same piece of tape: NEVER FLINCH, NEVER WEARY, NEVER DESPAIR.

My father drew inspiration from it, from Churchill. It's the same sentiment that led to his desire to collect. He was collecting documents, and he was collecting the character and personality of the figure. That is the essence of the hunt for history.

This was on my mind when I asked myself, *Why is Susan B. Anthony so pissed off?* I suspect no one has asked this question in at least a hundred years. A man on the West Coast had sent us a box of letters. Letters from African American spiritual leader Father Divine and magician Harry Houdini, and some random signatures cut off letters—a standard discovery when dealing with things collected during the Victorian era. More or less junk. But at the bottom of the pile was a scathing letter Anthony had written, complete with exclamation points and underlines.

Anthony was born to a Quaker family in 1820. The Quakers took an early and strong stand against slavery in America, and the idea of equality is central to their religious philosophy. So perhaps not surprisingly she got into it early, at the age of seventeen, handing out antislavery petitions. By age thirty-six, she was the head of the New York chapter of the Anti-Slavery Society. Around this same time—along with her close friend and colleague in the fight for women's suffrage Elizabeth Cady Stanton—Anthony founded a women's temperance society. She'd been involved in the temperance movement of the day, but couldn't speak at forums and rallies because she was a woman. She expanded her fight for equality to the rights of women, in particular the right to vote. She fund-raised relentlessly, walked the halls of Congress drumming up support for her cause, and was arrested for voting in 1872, refusing to pay the fine associated with the arrest. She gave up to a hundred speeches per year. We know of her tireless work, which paved the way for my mother, sister, wife, and daughter (when she's old enough) to vote. But Anthony didn't live to see the Nineteenth Amendment ratified in 1920. Sadly, she herself never got a chance to legally vote in any national election.

On February 4, 1905, a rare-book and autograph dealer in Washington, DC, Anton Heitmuller, sent a letter to Susan B. Anthony, the honorary president of the National American Woman Suffrage Association. Heitmuller offered to sell Anthony a collection of photographs and autographs of notable historical figures of the nineteenth century.

All the notable figures included in the collection were men. Big mistake, it seems.

The most likely explanation is that Heitmuller, who billed himself as "Specializing in Selling Collections of Autographs/Manuscripts, Historical Broadsides and Curios," was insensitive but mainly guilty of overzealous salesmanship. As a fellow dealer of historical documents a hundred years later, and with some benefit of hindsight, I can see his error vividly, but I'm glad he made it. Because the letter he wrote elicited a reaction so uncharacteristically scathing that you can feel Anthony's personality jumping off the page. She replied six days later:

> My Dear Sirs—
>
> Your communication of February 4th is received. I have no doubt that your autographs are very fine and the portraits of all the distinguished men you mentioned must be fine also, but I am especially interested in the autograph signatures and the pictures of distinguished women. When you get a collection of autographs and portraits of the distinguished women of the last century—of Mary Wollstonecraft, Frances Wright, Ernestine L. Rose, Elizabeth Cady Stanton, Paulina Wright Davis, Lucy Stone etc. etc., I will talk about patronizing you. But while women are by the law excluded from a voice in the government under which they live, I can only work for their emancipation. I know you think women are the pets of society. That they may be, but to be a pet is not to be an equal, and what I want is for women to be equal before the law in every respect.
>
> Sincerely yours,
>
> Susan B. Anthony

The letter was typed on Suffrage Association letterhead, and Anthony had gone over the letter with a pen, underlining words for emphasis: "To be a <u>pet</u> is not to be an <u>equal</u>," for example. Her controlled fury was palpable.

Susan B. Anthony wrote many letters and lived a long time, so they're not necessarily all that uncommon. But this was different. I realized the importance of the letter as soon as I read it. It illuminates her larger motivations, her political and emotional essence. Why had she embarked on the struggle for suffrage to begin with? We don't have to speculate. She tells us in this letter, the letter I now found at the bottom of this pile—an outpouring of emotion from this diplomatic figure, who was not known for her hotheadedness.

But the whole exchange highlighted two things that I see now, years later, looking back. First, it was a period when people were beginning to collect these sorts of things. And second, the history that was being collected was entirely male. For Anthony, that was an affront to her life's work. Here she is, eighty-five years old, near the end of her life, and among the revered figures of the previous century—as advertised by Heitmuller—is not a single woman. And that women don't yet have the right to vote is for her very much the reason for this state of affairs. Women aren't respected, aren't yet seen as equal players on the stage of history.

Heitmuller was an autograph dealer, and he was selling an emotional connection to these historical figures. These documents connect you to people who inspire you, people whose lives you admire, people whom you want to emulate. And not a single woman in the bunch? I think Anthony's perspective must have been that after all this time, after all this work, one should be able to find a woman to include—many had made a difference. And she lists them! All the women she notes in her letter to Heitmuller were prominent suffragists and abolitionists, women who'd fought for the rights of themselves and others and made a demonstrable impact on history.

Heitmuller's mistake was that he didn't fully understand the power of the material he was selling. For Anthony, the pieces he offered to her were emotionally hurtful—insulting. She had the option of not writing him back. She could have ignored his letter. But she didn't. And ironically, this angry letter of hers in the present day becomes a valuable letter itself.

In the Victorian era, letters written by prominent women, including Harriet Beecher Stowe, Julia Ward Howe, Abigail Adams, and Mary Todd Lincoln began to be collected. Today, women's autographs are widely sought after—we have clients who collect nothing *but* women's autographs. Documents and artifacts related to first ladies from Martha Washington to Jacqueline Kennedy are quite valuable. Some people are interested in the social messages of Eleanor Roosevelt—she was an early supporter of civil rights. And some in women explorers and adventurers like Amelia Earhart. Not long after Susan B. Anthony was demanding the right to vote, Earhart was defying stereotypes by competing in air races, flying across the Atlantic Ocean, and attempting to circumnavigate the globe.

The man who sold us the Susan B. Anthony letter had bought it from the estate of Anton Heitmuller himself. Meaning that not only did Susan B. Anthony think enough of his initial letter to respond to him, but that Heitmuller thought enough of her response to not sell it—to keep it. He died with this letter in his possession.

History doesn't speak in riddles. It speaks in metaphors. In the accomplishments of others we see possibilities for ourselves. But that is not possible if history is not yours, if you are written out of the books. Many minority groups want to see—and want their children to see—their reflections in the history books.

Every time I look at Anthony's letter, a different part of it pops out at me. It's on display downstairs in my house—Karen made a reproduction and framed it for everyone to see. While it is in a frame, and not hanging from tape like my father's quote of Churchill's, the idea is the same.

Susan B. Anthony changed the world in immeasurable ways. She died in 1906, a year after telling Heitmuller that she would never stop working toward women's emancipation, including the right to vote, full property rights, and dress reform (meaning women should not feel compelled to wear corsets and other restrictive clothing). The world was changing, and she'd helped to change it. Women were riding bicycles and driving cars; they were increasingly freer to travel unaccompanied by men; soon enough, they'd be flying airplanes.

Amelia Earhart grew up in this environment, in Kansas and Iowa, the elder of two daughters. Her father was a lawyer, and her mother had unconventional views about girls and how to raise them; she dressed her daughters in bloomers and let them climb trees and go hunting. Amelia was at times called a tomboy and always aspired to success; she kept a scrapbook of articles written about women who pioneered in fields including the law, advertising, film production, and engineering. She caught the flying bug in 1920; one ten-minute flight at a Long Beach, California, airfield was all it took. She started saving money for lessons, which she took from Neta Snook, herself an aviation pioneer.

This was the beginning of the golden age of aviation: air races caught the public's attention, with records being set and broken all the time. Flying was the new and ultimate adventure. When Charles Lindbergh flew solo from New York to Paris in May 1927, he landed as a global celebrity. A crowd of 150,000 people greeted his plane when he arrived in Paris after the 33.5-hour flight. The astounding attention Lindbergh had garnered for aviation would propel Earhart's career. The following year, she was asked to participate in a transatlantic flight, from Newfoundland to South Wales, one of three people on board and the only woman. Her fame after that was immediate. Earhart wrote a book and embarked on a national lecture tour; she appeared in ads for Lucky Strike cigarettes and promoted commercial air travel for Transcontinental Air Transport (later renamed TWA).

She also competed in various air races and contests. She was the first woman to fly solo across the Atlantic Ocean and back again, and the Raab Collection once had her signed landing certificate. She competed in the Women's Air Derby, a race from Santa Monica to Cleveland in 1929 and came in third. The race was nicknamed the Powder Puff Derby and was one of the National Air Races, a series of competitions started in 1920. As the speed and reliability of aircraft improved during the twenties and thirties, these races were a proving ground for both pilots and aircraft. There were long-distance races, landing competitions, and parachute-jumping contests. High-profile races were added in the 1930s: The Thompson Trophy was a precision race in which pilots steered at low altitude around fifty-foot pylons on a closed course. The Bendix Trophy was a cross-country race; the Shell Trophy was a speed dash.

All the best pilots participated in these events, but women weren't generally invited to compete—aside from in women's-only contests. That would soon change. Amelia Earhart helped to found a group of women aviators called the Ninety-Nines, and they wanted to compete in *all* races, not only among themselves. In 1932, women were allowed to compete in a number of races, though not all. In 1934, women were not allowed to compete with men, and in 1935, women were only allowed to compete using a commercially licensed aircraft with a maximum speed of 150 miles per hour. Amelia Earhart, along with many other women pilots, opposed all these restrictions and demanded to compete head-to-head with the men.

In 1936, they got their wish. The events of the 1936 National Air Races would be open to all, men and women alike.

The races took place in Los Angeles that year—site of all the 1936 precision and speed contests. The premier event was the Bendix, starting at Floyd Bennett Field, in Brooklyn, New York, and ending at Mines Field (now called LAX) in LA. The lineup of pilots included the best talent, all flying the latest planes. Earhart was flying her new Lockheed Electra. It had been built to her specifications and was larger than her previous plane, the famous fire-engine-red Lockheed Vega. The Electra was built for distance because Earhart was already contemplating an around-the-world flight.

Joe Jacobson was flying a Northrop Gamma; Louise Thaden was flying a Beechcraft Staggerwing; Laura Ingalls was flying a Lockheed Orion; and George Pomeroy was flying a DC-2. The previous year's winner, Benny Howard, flew with his wife, Maxine, as copilot.

The race was dangerous. Joe Jacobson's plane exploded in midair above Stafford, Kansas; he managed to parachute to safety. Benny and Maxine Howard crashed their plane in New Mexico and were stranded for hours, trapped beneath the plane's engine, before being saved. Earhart also ran into trouble: the cockpit escape hatch blew open in midflight, almost killing her and her copilot. They managed to close it with a rag until they got to Kansas City for refueling, where they rigged the door shut with wire. This cost them significant time, but Earhart still finished in fifth place. Indeed, the women proved themselves worthy, dominating the race. Louise Thaden won, becoming the first woman awarded the Bendix; Laura Ingalls took second place. So the women had won three of the top five places.

Many years later, I was contacted by a man named Robert Johnston. Way back in 1965 he'd just bought a pickup truck, and a friend of his said he had a job cleaning out an old shack outside Las Vegas. The shack belonged to another friend of theirs. They were free to take whatever they wanted from this shack and would use Johnston's new truck to take everything else to the dump.

Robert was in the aviation business, as was the friend whose shack they were emptying. There was nothing to salvage except for an old .22 rifle, which the two returned to their friend. But on the second trip to the dump, as Johnston was pushing debris out of his tailgate, he saw a stack of blue papers and noticed the name Michel Détroyat, which he recognized. Détroyat was a renowned French pilot in the 1930s. Johnston tossed the paper on the ground and noticed the next page had a different name, one that he also recognized: Jacqueline Cochran, another great aviator from the 1930s—she'd won the Bendix Trophy in 1938 and still lived in Southern California. She was a friend and longtime customer of Johnston's.

He grabbed the stack of blue papers and saved them from the dump, putting them on the passenger seat of his truck. He planned to look at them later, but instead he stuck them at the back of a closet shelf in his house, where they remained for the next fifty years.

What he'd now discovered, cleaning out that closet, was extraordinary: the blue papers were the official entry forms for the 1936 National Air Races. Each form was six pages long, four of which were the printed rules and regulations. The pilots filled out the remaining two pages, including detailed information about their planes, engines, propellers, and servicing, as well as licensing information. The forms were signed by the pilots and notarized.

The collection was a snapshot of the golden age of flight, a time when daredevil adventurers—men and women—were breaking records and changing our perception of speed and travel. Crossing countries and oceans in days and hours rather than weeks would change the world.

Of great interest was the Earhart entry form. She is an icon of American optimism and ambition, an inspiration to many, and she was fearless. She would die only a year later, during her attempt to circumnavigate the world, flying the very plane—the Lockheed Electra—described in detail on her National Air Races form.

She wrote in her own hand that it was a Lockheed, a "land monoplane (bimotored)," that it had flown only fifty hours and was "new." The motor, a Pratt & Whitney, had suffered no accident. Maximum rpm? Twenty-three hundred. She noted she was staying at the Seymoor Hotel and listed her license number and copilot. In short, she was painting a picture of her plane and flying life, as did the other entrants. The man writing us had these remarkable documents. From all the greats of the era.

In attempting to circumnavigate the world, Earhart made it most of the way, crossing South America, the Atlantic, Africa, India, and Southeast Asia, before losing her way in the South Pacific. Her disappearance set off the most extensive search-and-rescue effort ever attempted to that time and included the navy and the coast guard. No sign of Earhart, her copilot, Fred Noonan, or the Electra was ever discovered.

Robert Johnston had salvaged history from the garbage. He'd discovered history he wasn't even looking for. Nearly a half century after the entry forms were saved, they were sitting in front of me, on my desk, being read in full.

Johnston was, by then, very old and had an agent negotiating on his behalf. She was an antiques dealer, and he'd approached her first. Such a thing is not uncommon. Antiques dealers, who usually don't carry historical documents, do occasionally get offered one, and if they look online, they find us. We offered Johnson $12,000. He was a little disappointed and asked for $18,000. We initially declined, but after thinking about it further decided to counter with $16,500, which he accepted. As he wrote in a provenance letter to us, "About fifty years later, Wilma [his wife] died. As I was cleaning out her closet I found the blue papers on the back of her top shelf. So what was trash fifty or more years ago is now valuable artifacts. In retrospect, I have now taken very good care of and protected these documents."

These documents then traveled with me overseas to show to one of our longtime clients. His father had been an aviator for his nation's air force during the early years of the country after independence. This collector is now in the telecom, tech, and investment business, and a billionaire. He loves things that relate to science (he buys many of our Einstein letters) and also space and aviation, the latter interest, I suppose, stemming from memories of his youth and upbringing. He bought the aviation material over breakfast one morning, sorting through that and a selection of a dozen or so other pieces that matched his collecting interests. At that same meeting, he bought Churchill's resignation letter to King George VI in 1945, when Churchill stepped down as prime minister after the war in Europe ended, as well as a letter from inventor Samuel Morse relating to his greatest invention: the telegraph.

CHAPTER 14

Thomas Jefferson's Library

For a few years, more than two hundred years ago, the White House was occupied by the foremost American embodiment of the Enlightenment. President Jefferson hosted grand dinners, inviting senators, congressmen, luminaries, inventors. They ate food and wine imported from Jefferson's favorite vendors in Europe, a list he built in part during his time as ambassador to France. The conversations at that table must have been spectacular, and we gain some insight from contemporary reports of exotic and uncommon dishes being served, the wine flowing, and the president's wide-ranging intellect. His library was filled with books from the Continent that he'd bought and imported, books in English, German, Latin, and French. Jefferson seemed intent on living all of history in the present, or as Frederick Jackson Turner, the author whose name is synonymous with the westward movement of America, wrote, "Each age tries to form its own conception of the past. Each age writes the history of the past anew with reference to the conditions uppermost in its own time." This was not only the mission of Jefferson but the mission of the American founders, who fashioned their vision of America on the great republics of the past. John Adams seemed to internalize the connection between iconic republics of the past with the threats facing America, writing, "When foreign Nations interfere, and by their acts, and agents, excite and foment them into parties and factions; such interference and influence, must be resisted and exterminated or it will end in America, as it did anciently in Greece, and in our own time in Europe, in our total destruction as a republican Government and Independent power."

Jefferson's eyes were pointed to the West, to a new country that would stretch from sea to shining sea. Into Jefferson's orbit came a young officer, an outdoorsman, brought in by Jefferson to serve as his private secretary. His name, now memorialized by history, was Meriwether Lewis. In Jefferson's letter offering Lewis the position as an aide, Jefferson hinted at the treasured experience Lewis would have in this capacity: If you accept, Jefferson explained, it "would make you know & be known to characters of influence in the affairs of our country, and give you the advantage of their wisdom." Jefferson's family and Lewis's were close in Virginia, and Lewis spent countless hours by the fireside of Jefferson both in Washington and at Monticello. Lewis's military experience had given him knowledge of the West, which was Jefferson's primary motive in selecting him. This relationship would turn out to be history making.

More than any other team before them, Lewis and Jefferson would give truth to Turner's perception that "American democracy was born of no theorist's dream; it was not carried in the *Susan Constant* to Virginia, nor in the *Mayflower* to Plymouth. It came stark and strong and full of life out of the American forest, and it gained new strength each time it touched a new frontier."

Henry Remsen Jr. was a financier and banker in New York City. His father had been a patriot during the colonial era and was part of a group of merchants who agitated for freedom from the king, and then for war. His son had taken up the mantle of service and business, serving as chief clerk of the State Department in 1789, then as the first teller of the New York branch of the Bank of the United States. Importantly, he also served as a secretary to President Jefferson.

A few years ago, Henry Remsen's great-great-great-grandson contacted us. He'd inherited a number of colonial-era historical documents, some printed, some manuscript. These items had been in his family's possession since the 1700s. It's quite rare to come across documents held in one family for so long; the Remsens had been a prominent merchant family in the colonial, revolutionary, and federal periods. Along the way, you would expect some relative to have sold the material, donated it, lost it, or tossed it.

My father went to the descendant's home in Maine, not far from our place up there. A pleasant visit and an opportunity to see the originals. Much of what was in the collection were broadside prints—the kinds of things you'd tack up on a building or a church. Some of these beautifully printed artifacts were patriotic broadsides calling the nation to arms; others dealt with candidates for the provincial congress during the American Revolution.

As he was sorting through the materials, my father found a letter signed by Thomas Jefferson, written, as my father told me initially, entirely in Jefferson's hand. This was a long list of books with mostly French titles.

My father called me and mentioned it. We agreed to make an offer to buy the letter, but the seller said he wanted more for it—a lot more. The negotiations ended for the moment, but we made periodic contact with the owner. This was a simmer, not a boil, of a negotiation. He simply wanted a lot of money for the piece, appeared to be in no particular rush, and so things continued this way.

My dad finally came to me and said he thought we should pay what the man wanted. The letter was worth it, my dad was convinced.

I *wasn't* convinced. "Dad," I said, "there are a lot of letters out there relating to Jefferson ordering books—he maintained a large book collection and often wrote ordering this book or that book. And in fact we have two letters like that for sale on our website right now, neither for more than twenty thousand dollars." I didn't see how we were going to make a profit by purchasing this letter at that high price. "I'm just not sure I see it," I said.

But a large part of the hunt is trusting instincts. While we won't buy something if one of us flat out objects, if someone believes strongly in a piece, has that blink moment or a vision of what it is and what it can be, that carries a lot of weight. And the lesson I learned early on echoed in the back of my head: "Don't just assume, look closer," my dad would say. It was his way of saying we needed to dig a little bit below the surface, to sit down and pay close attention. So with these things in my mind, I looked closer, reading the document line by line. Dozens and dozens of books were listed, most part of multivolume sets, and the list was divided into topic areas: History; Law; Laws of Nature and Nations; Maritime Law; Politics; Geography; books by Diderot; and classics in Latin, Spanish, French, and Greek. The titles included numerous dictionaries and reference works: *Dictionnaire historique et bibliographique par l'Avocat*: *Robinet dictionnaire morals, politique et diplomatique*; *Abrege chronologique de l'histoire de France par Hénault*; *Annales Romaines par Macquer*; *Arithmétique linéaire de Playfair (printed in Paris about 1787)*; *The Spanish dictionary of their academy*.

At the end of the three-page list was a note:

> Mr. Duane is employed to purchase the preceding books in Paris under the control and approbation of William Short esq who is desired to pay for them out of the monies remitted to him for that purpose & according to the advice forwarded to him by
>
> Th. Jefferson, Washington, July 19, 1802

This was no small order for books. Jefferson, from his position as president, was authorizing someone to spend a large amount of money on a large quantity of rare books in Paris.

I was intrigued. This letter was indeed different from other Jefferson letters I'd seen regarding his book collection. It was a different format. Something about it that I couldn't quite put my finger on was irregular.

We are always looking for that element of a document that separates it from the rest, calls forth its history into the present in a way that we—and our customers—will love. If we're moved by the action being undertaken through the letter, or the language being used, we figure someone else will be too. We own every document we sell, which means we invest in our own material.

We took the plunge and bought the letter based primarily on my dad's gut instinct, and my sense that this letter "had legs."

When the piece came in, I looked at it closely and immediately realized something was wrong. My father had told me it was written by Jefferson himself, and the signature was certainly his, but I hadn't examined the handwriting of the body of the letter myself closely enough to assess that judgment. The document was worth acquiring regardless. But when it came in, I knew right away it was not Jefferson's handwriting, which I know well. His handwriting has a soft feel to it; it's relatively upright and curved more than angular. It is not overly expressive. I felt keen disappointment as I told my father, "This is signed by Jefferson but most of this letter is not in his hand. Someone else wrote it. I'm one hundred percent sure."

My father said, "Damn."

Then he said, "You know, we should check whether this is in Meriwether Lewis's hand. It's unlikely, but don't forget he was Jefferson's secretary. See if you can figure out if the timing works."

Such a scenario was possible, if unlikely. During Lewis's apprenticeship and residence with Jefferson, Lewis would shuttle back and forth between Congress and the White House, delivering messages of great importance. Some were in his hand and signed by Jefferson, who had mentored him, taught him what to read, and how to properly write. Normally, we wouldn't care about an aide who might have written a letter for his boss to sign. But the Lewis connection is different, and their interactions changed the course of history.

Jefferson had bought Louisiana and all those western points from Napoléon in 1803—the Louisiana Purchase—and shortly after, Jefferson set about exploring it, sending Lewis in May of 1804 to command the expedition. (Although Clark was there too, Lewis was in charge.)

They collected samples of plant and animal life and made contact with Native American tribes. Eventually they found a way to the Pacific Ocean. Lewis realized there was no single waterway there. They'd succeeded in their mission to reach the coast, but they'd also proven that the rivers wouldn't wind easily to that destination. They had to cross a mountain range, which required an experienced Native guide and perfect timing. Too late, and winter would set in upon them. Too early, and the passes wouldn't be clear. Since the elevations were so high, this meant waiting until the summer to even begin, and it meant that returning would have to wait for the next warm season. But they succeeded, opening the mind of the new country to the treasures of the West, and proving that such a journey was possible.

Clark later wrote about that moment of discovery: "Ocean in view! O! the Joy . . . This great Pacific Ocean which we have been so long anxious to see and the roaring or noise made by the waves breaking on the rocky shores."

Lewis and Clark returned to great fanfare; Lewis published his journals, and so began a new era in American exploration, brought about by a man whose name has come to represent our nation's westward push. Lewis's mission may not have opened a direct route, but his act was the face of Helen in ancient Troy, one that launched a thousand ships (or tens of thousands of covered wagons).

Now, as a casual aside, my father had asked me to check if this document was part of that relationship, a connection with the intellectual mentorship of Lewis by Jefferson. If this large order of books had indeed been written up by Lewis and signed by Jefferson, that would make the document vastly more valuable and interesting, tying these two important figures together.

And so I started my investigation. What was this document *exactly*? I had two major questions: Why was Jefferson ordering all these books? And who was this mystery scribe?

Some of the more consequential presidents and other major historical figures have teams of people collecting their correspondence. These, the "papers projects," normally reside at universities.

So the Washington papers project is at UVA; Einstein is split among UCLA, Princeton, and the Hebrew University of Jerusalem; and the Jefferson papers project is at Monticello and Princeton. Many of these also have a hub of cooperation at the Library of Congress, which possesses many of the original materials. I contacted Barbara Oberg, an editor at the Papers of Thomas Jefferson at Princeton University, and Julie Miller, an archivist at the Library of Congress. This outreach would lead me to the answers to both of my questions.

President Adams created the Library of Congress in 1800, and when Jefferson took office in 1801, he learned that of the $5,000 set aside for buying books, only $2,200 had been spent. The library under Adams had been quite rudimentary, a small room with a handful of books, and it hadn't been given a great deal of attention, let alone funding. The modern Library of Congress came into existence under Jefferson. He moved the library to the Capitol and appointed his friend, John Beckley, as the first Librarian of Congress. In April of 1802, Jefferson described his plans for the collection: "I have prepared a catalogue for the Library of Congress. . . . I have confined the catalogue to those branches of science which belong to the deliberations of the members as statesmen and in these have omitted those classical books and modern which gentlemen generally have in their private libraries but which can not properly claim a place in a collection made merely [for] the purpose of reference."

Jefferson created two separate lists of books for purchase, one destined for London and the other for Paris. A political ally named William Duane would be in charge of buying the books. In a letter to Duane, Jefferson wrote, "I now inclose you the catalogues of the books which are to be imported for Congress and which you desired to have placed under your procurement. . . . It is desirable that the books should be received before the meeting of Congress or as soon after as possible."

When I read this, my eyes opened wide. I called my dad: "I know what this is. This list of books was in fact the first major acquisition for the Library of Congress itself."

"Who wrote it?" my dad asked.

"I'm not there yet." But I was narrowing in on the answer.

Could it have been Meriwether Lewis? I had my suspicions. But suspicions don't sell documents, and they don't change history.

Working with the Library of Congress and the Papers of Thomas Jefferson, I sought out examples of Lewis's writing. Then I compared handwriting samples. Lewis's handwriting leans slightly to the right, a common bent, but idiosyncratically. Lewis begins many of his letters with a line leading into it. Imagine if instead of writing a *t* as a downward line, you started it with an upward stroke of the pen before moving down. Many of his letters start that way. His handwriting bears a vague resemblance to Jefferson's script but has a more unrefined, somewhat raw feel to it.

I felt a dawning realization that our letter *was* written by Lewis. A slow process, it wasn't a lightning bolt or an "Oh my God" moment. It happened over two or three days.

Working with the archivists, I examined all of Jefferson's messages to Congress known to be in Lewis's hand, which are not numerous, as well as official messages that Jefferson delivered, his State of the Union messages, copied by Lewis and signed by Jefferson. I was looking for clues, those telltale upticks in the handwriting before each letter, other quirks and flourishes. The Library of Congress had a copy of this same list of books, entirely in Jefferson's hand, evidently Jefferson's original draft of what I had in front of me.

He'd asked his aide to create an official copy, then signed it with the instruction. That aide, I concluded, was Lewis. Which meant this document had traveled by boat to Europe, to the parlors of London and Paris and to the booksellers there, where Duane bought hundreds of rare books to bring back to the Library of Congress.

I got on the phone with Julie Miller, the archivist at the Library of Congress. We looked at three documents on our computer screens: an image of Jefferson's original draft of his list of books; a letter to Congress written by Lewis; and the final draft of the list of books—my document. I said, "This is in Lewis's hand—this is the same person!"

192 — the Spanish Dictionary of their academy.
192 — Diccionario della Crusca.
42 — Dictionnaire Espagn. François, et Latin par Sejournant. 2.v. 4to
42 — Dictionnaire Ital. et François d'alberti 2.v. 4to
3.716 —

Mr. Duane is employed to purchase the preceding books in Paris under the controul and approbation of William Short esq. who is desired to pay for them out of the monies remitted to him for that purpose, & according to the advice forwarded him by

Th: Jefferson

Washington July 19. 1802

An order for books for the Library of Congress, the top half in the hand of Meriwether Lewis and the bottom half written and signed by Thomas Jefferson.

I called my dad to give him the news, in one of those wow moments when you've found something that connects two important people. And the document was significant in so many other ways—as something that launched the Library of Congress's collection, as a signifier of Jefferson's vision and connection to the Enlightenment, as an example of Lewis's working relationship with his mentor, and in the specific content of the list. It's easy to imagine Lewis and Jefferson reading—and discussing with each other—these kinds of books in preparation for the expedition West.

Treasure isn't always hidden away; sometimes it's hiding in plain sight, but seeing it requires a great deal of instinct and experience and knowledge. What if Duane had tossed the letter, rather than, as I suspect, given it back to Lewis on Duane's return? What if Jefferson hadn't kept it when Lewis went West? What if Remsen Jr. hadn't kept it or his heir had tossed it? What if my dad hadn't pressed us to acquire the piece? What if I'd agreed with my father that this was in Jefferson's hand? What if he hadn't suggested I research Lewis? What if I'd just passed this letter off as having been written by a minor aide in Jefferson's office? What if I hadn't looked closer? The survival of such documents requires all these factors, seemingly working toward a common goal, separated by wars, generations, centuries. Moments like this bring into stark relief my feeling—which has grown over time as I've accumulated experience—that history doesn't leave us, but rather becomes part of us, living on in the present.

The discovery of the truth of this document—its significance—was a joint enterprise and demonstrated how skills play off skills, and how my father and I had learned to work together as equal partners. We'd each relied on our instincts, in different ways, and we both turned out to be correct. It was true teamwork.

We gave the Library of Congress the first option to buy the letter, since they'd helped us immensely, and it directly relates to the founding of that institution. We priced this expensive document in the six figures, which is a significant purchase for the Library of Congress or anyone else. It took months of discussions to make it work, but we did. The letter is now with them, where I think it belongs. They have the original draft in Jefferson's hand, and this final version, written by Lewis.

The books purchased in London and Paris were destroyed twelve years later, when the Library of Congress was burned to the ground by the British in 1814, during the War of 1812. After the war, Jefferson, out of office for a few years already, offered to sell his private library to Congress as a replacement for the collection that had burned. His library at Monticello was the largest personal collection in the United States, comprising more than six thousand volumes. In 1815, Congress paid Jefferson $23,950 for his books, more than doubling the size of the collection that had been lost.

CHAPTER 15

The JFK Tapes

One afternoon in November 2011, my phone rang and my father's picture lit up the screen. I knew he was at a small auction house in downtown Philadelphia, sorting through boxes and binders full of JFK material that would be sold the following day. All of it had belonged to General Chester Clifton Jr., the chief military aide to JFK (and de facto chief of staff, since presidents back then didn't have one) and then LBJ until the end of 1965. The cache of JFK items had been boxed in the attic of Clifton's home for forty-five years. Clifton had died in 1991, but not until after his wife died in 2009 did the couple's heirs decide to find out if the material had any value, and if it did, whether a sale could be arranged. They consigned some of the material to an auction house.

My father loved President Kennedy, and I think my dad's clear, high-school-age memory of the devastating assassination has driven much of his interest in history and can still color his collecting passion. Sometimes he wants to buy documents that interest him but have little value to our customers.

But every dealer has his or her personal interests and, once in a while, tilts toward indulging this collector side. Fortunately, my dad and I are there to keep each other honest.

I was definitely interested in *some* of this material: a logbook of the day-to-day presidential schedule, a rare White House guidebook signed by the president and the first lady, a letter authored by JFK proposing to name Polaris submarines after World War II heroes Douglas MacArthur and Chester Nimitz, other letters pertaining to the Medal of Freedom, correspondence relating to the assassination.

"There's some great stuff here," my dad said. His excitement came through loud and clear.

I agreed. Well, maybe not *great*, but good and worth our attention. "And we have good customers for JFK pieces. Let's talk about bids."

The conversation took a weird and unexpected turn. "But the real gem may be something that we normally don't do," my dad said. "There's a box of tapes here, all from the Kennedy and Johnson administrations. Some seem pretty interesting."

Tapes? I thought. *You have to be kidding me.*

These had to be old-time reel-to-reel audio- and videotapes. Some were labeled, my father said: JFK's inauguration, an address by Douglas MacArthur, cellist Pablo Casals's performance at the White House, and more. This wasn't groundbreaking material. I could hear the youthful enthusiasm of a young Kennedy supporter creeping into our conversation, and I rolled my eyes even though we were talking on the phone. The Casals performance has come to exemplify the classy style of the Kennedy White House (thanks to Jackie), but for purposes of our business, so what? We specialize in pen-on-paper historical documents. These tapes seemed tangential. I had no idea how we'd sell any of them. Then he mentioned two audiotapes, both dated November 22, 1963, one labeled "Traffic on Board Air Force-1," the other "Radio Traffic involving AF-1 in flight from Dallas, Texas to Andrews AFB on November 22, 1963." My father was excited about these in particular.

"Okay, but, Dad—what are we going to do with this stuff?" My idea was to quash his excitement before it took on a life of its own. He used to tell us about the three hundred Spartans who took on the Persian army and Xerxes at the Battle of Thermopylae. Like those men, I succeeded only in slowing the inevitable confrontation.

* * *

My father's interest in these AF-1 recordings rested on their early date, before Clifton left the White House. They had to have been created well before the public version was released. That evening, home from his inspection of the various lots, my father read up on the details of the Air Force One recording on the day of the Kennedy assassination. Every word of the conversations that day between the plane, the White House, and Andrews Air Force Base had been captured and recorded. The recording was one of just a handful of real-time resources that document that day, and it was the main source for information about the people on board Air Force One and their decisions about where to take JFK's body, the nature of the autopsy, who'd be involved in what logistical matters. But there was a wrinkle: the only surviving version of the tape, now deposited at the LBJ Library in Austin, was heavily edited and didn't surface until 1968. The plane was in the air for almost four hours. The tape in Austin is only one hour and forty minutes long. No one had any idea who made the extensive edits to the surviving tape, or why. The official story was that the original, unedited version was simply lost. Staffers with the National Archives and even members of Congress had been searching for the original, unedited tape without luck for almost half a century. In 1992, the congressionally mandated Assassination Records Review Board was tasked with searching for, collecting, and reexamining for public release all assassination-related records held by federal agencies. Regarding the Air Force One audiotape, no luck, and I believed it was safe to say that no one was looking for it anymore.

My father surmised (correctly) that Clifton was probably in the motorcade in Dallas and then on board Air Force One. If he'd been on that flight, and he retired in 1965 . . . well, could this tape be the *full unedited tape*? If not, could it be a *different* tape? My father wanted this box of tapes, period. I was skeptical. Surely these two tapes wouldn't be anything more than a copy of the same old tape that had been in the public domain for decades. Besides, tapes aren't generally what we do.

Nevertheless, my father wanted to buy the tapes, and I agreed to give it a shot as long as the price was right. Maybe we could use the audio content to attract visitors to our website. This is how I justified indulging my dad's curiosity. The unspoken budget I had in mind was not particularly high, and I'd handle our bidding by telephone myself.

The next day, bidding was active for most of the lots. The sale had attracted a lot of attention. Many pieces went for tens of thousands of dollars, but the box with the tapes slipped under everyone else's radar, perhaps because it was under-described in the catalog and no one had bothered to look. The bidding on that lot didn't last two minutes, and I purchased the tapes. My dad was pleased and I suppose I was too, simply because his taste had been indulged.

The next day, I drove downtown and picked up the two boxes we'd purchased—the tapes and another box with assorted stuff. My dad agreed that the tapes—now *our* tapes—didn't have much chance of being different, but the odds weren't absolutely nil. I was prepared to satisfy his curiosity, although this was a little easier said than done. This is the twenty-first century, and reel-to-reel tapes aren't easy to play. I'd need to hire a specialist to digitize the tapes, convert them from their old format into a digital file that could be played and embedded online; a few days later I dropped them at FedEx. It would be a while before we got them back from the company in Pittsburgh. I turned my mind to other things and soon forgot about the tapes. Months passed.

My phone rang with a call from the technician at the digitization company in Pittsburgh.

"Your digitization is done and I'm ready to ship the tapes," he told me.

"Ship them back," I said, and gave my address. But then I thought twice. "Can you send me the digital files just for the two tapes marked 'Air Force One'?" Maybe my dad's enthusiasm had seeped through to me.

This he did, and I opened the files on my computer. They loaded up, and I expected to see a play time of around an hour and forty minutes, the length of the old LBJ tape. Instead, the iTunes player on my Mac registered more than two hours in both cases.

This was a moment I'll never forget. My hands tingled.

Looking at my computer, with the tapes still a couple hundred miles away in Pittsburgh, I knew we'd stumbled across something that would change history. Assuming that the additional length wasn't just blank space in the body of the tape, this would be explosive news on a subject of never-ending fascination for conspiracy enthusiasts, serious researchers and historians, and much of the general public. I called the technician back, and we had a rather long conversation about the chances that the tapes could be damaged in transit. I could imagine them getting magnetized inside a mail-sorting machine.

"It's very unlikely," he said.

"How unlikely?"

"Less than one percent," he said, to comfort me, but that was too high for my taste.

"Wait a minute. Hold them, would you?"

Over the next two days I painstakingly compared our two new tapes, listening, pausing, minute by minute, second by second, word by word, annotating, color-coding. The files were identical—and each came in at two hours and twenty-two minutes—forty-two minutes longer than the version in the LBJ Library. I grabbed the phone.

"Dad, I've listened to the Air Force One tapes start to finish."

"Yes?"

"They're identical."

After a few seconds of silence came the key question: "Are they longer?"

"Yes. All the content of the known version and much more apparently."

Now I definitely did not want to entrust the tapes themselves to a shipping service. A few days later I was in my car, driving to the digitization facility in Pittsburgh. Their office was filled with high-tech audio and visual equipment along with a museum of old machines, some almost a century old, and all *worked*. I packed the tapes in the back of my car and drove home.

The next job was to compare the transcript of our two identical new tapes with the transcript of the older, shorter version. Using our new digital audio file and the audio file from the National Archives and the LBJ Library, I made precise transcripts of each version—pausing, rewinding, comparing. I had to be perfect because we knew plenty of zealous researchers would be all over this new evidence. Whatever I did would be second-guessed. Soon enough I saw clearly that the extra forty-two minutes were *new* content.

If my dad hadn't noticed them, the tapes would probably be moldering in some landfill right now—that's how contingent and fragile these fragments of history can be. And if anyone else at the auction had identified the Air Force One tapes and wanted them and engaged in serious bidding, I would probably have dropped out early. And if we hadn't spent the time doing the work to identify differences, no one would have known what we had or how it was significant. This story demonstrates the breadth of the hunt: you have to recognize the possibility, understand the history, acquire the item, do the research, understand its implications. In this meandering, inconsistent process you never know where you'll end up.

We also left behind a challenge to ourselves and to future hunters. Neither of these new, identical Clifton tapes, as they are now called, is the original master tape, which remains lost. Nearly two hours of the original unedited tape are still missing. But the new version does give historians much provocative new information. For decades, people had wondered about the whereabouts that fateful day of General Curtis LeMay. LeMay was the notorious Air Force chief of staff who'd been more than ready to prosecute a war against the Soviet Union less than a decade after the conclusion of World War II, in which the two countries had been allies. LeMay had been dubbed "trigger-happy" by journalists, and in the wake of the Bay of Pigs fiasco and the Cuban Missile Crisis, his contempt for his prudent commander in chief was common knowledge. JFK even worried that his general would contrive to start a war on his own authority. LeMay was just the kind of figure the theorists loved to finger as a likely conspirator in the assassination. For reasons unknown, any reference to LeMay had been excised from the short version of the Air Force One tape, but in our longer version his chief aide tries to contact him with great urgency: "[This is] Colonel Dorman, General LeMay's aide. General LeMay is in a C140. Last three numbers are 497, SAM C140. His code name is Grandson. And I wanna talk to him. . . . If you can't work him now, it's gonna be too late, because he'll be on the ground in a half hour."

"Gonna be too late" for what? In context, the remark doesn't make much sense, but the exchange did clarify that the general was in the air in the immediate aftermath of the assassination, and that his aide urgently wanted to locate and talk to him, even—surprisingly—breaking into presidential Air Force One radio traffic to do so.

Also on the tape is an abundance of new information about the onboard debate concerning the destination, for autopsy purposes, of the slain president's remains. The previous tape omitted that the original destination was Walter Reed Hospital rather than the eventual choice, Bethesda Naval Hospital. The new version filled in additional details for researchers still trying to understand what happened during the autopsy. The tape also includes expanded discussion of what vehicle would transport the president's body and whether Jackie would go along. (She did.) New names, code names, and expanded conversations related to the flight, the arrival, and other logistics also appear. All of this had been deleted before the official version was released in 1968.

For two months we didn't say a word about our discovery to anyone, not even the government. I kept the tapes hidden in a small cabinet in my home, close to where I could check on them. I imagined government agents raiding our offices. Maybe that's crazy, but it speaks to my frame of mind. What had been my father's hunt, my father's kill, had become mine, and I guarded it zealously from other predators.

* * *

The discovery forced us, the Raabs, to grapple with our role as stewards of this new history. It also forcefully separated our roles as businessmen and custodians of history or, rather, forced us to reconcile the two. What was our obligation to alert the public? What if a buyer wanted to purchase the tapes on the condition that the content *not* be released? We'd bought the tape, but what rights, if any, did the government have? What if the eventual buyer *was* the government and its goal was to destroy it? What could our lawyers do to help us navigate this minefield?

Figuring out a price was also equally complicated. A signed portion of JFK's inaugural address had sold for $750,000, and the new tapes seemed infinitely more important, but was that document analogous to our tapes? Not really. What about the other items we researched? Not really. These new tapes were, in a way, priceless. How do you price something where nothing like it has ever been sold? We researched everything, and we argued a bit too, as we often do about price. My father was pushing for a higher price, I was pushing for a lower one. We finally agreed that $500,000 was fair.

Over the following month we created a stand-alone website with images and audio, including short clips of the new material, and prepared to unveil our discovery. Confidentiality would be the key to any publicity we might get. I put on my PR hat and invited Associated Press reporter JoAnn Loviglio—who had written the story about Teddy Roosevelt's note to Quenty-Quee from Yellowstone and had continued to cover our historical discoveries—to join me at a coffee shop off Rittenhouse Square in Philadelphia. After we established that this conversation would be completely off-the-record, I said, "I have something for you, and it's exciting." I began laying out what we had and put the original tape on the table.

"This seems big," she said. "Why did the government not have this?"

"We've been asking ourselves the same question. JoAnn, I'm willing to give you this story exclusively, but no one can know about this outside the AP. I have told no one except you. You cannot publish this until we launch information online, but then you can do it simultaneously. No one else will be notified in the media."

She agreed. But she also needed her editor on board. This was a fair request, but only after a couple of weeks did the reporter, her editor, and I convene clandestinely in our offices. This was four months almost to the day after the purchase of the tape. We sat around our small coffee table and explained our discovery. JoAnn's excitement was seconded by her editor: this was going to be a big story. We agreed that when we sent out our public release to our extensive lists and opened the dedicated website, JoAnn could be first online with the story, complete with quotes from us. Two weeks later, everybody was ready. We made the official announcement. JoAnn's parallel AP story was headlined "Lost JFK Assassination Tapes on Sale."

I expected some immediate response but had nevertheless scheduled a meeting on another matter out of the office. I figured I could break for lunch and return a few calls, if need be. This turned out to be naive. We'd gotten plenty of national and international publicity in the past, but this was different. As I sat in the large, quiet conference room, a dozen voice mails arrived in about that many minutes. CNN, Fox News, the *New York Times*, the BBC, and other outlets placed calls and wanted immediate responses. This wasn't the time or the place to multitask, so I excused myself from the meeting, caught a cab at the curb, and returned to the office, where I remained well into the evening, returning the early calls, fielding new ones. The last one I answered turned out to be the most noteworthy of all—by far.

"Hello, can I speak to someone handling the Kennedy tape sale?"

"I can help you." I introduced myself.

"This is Gary Stern. I'm the general counsel to the National Archives. And that tape belongs to us."

He explained to me in clear (and effective) terms that we (as in my company) had a serious problem. We'd embarrassed some important people. We learned later that members of Congress had called him demanding to know what the hell was going on and why hadn't all the search parties in the 1990s found this tape but now this dealer in Philadelphia had? And now we intended to sell the tape for half a million dollars? His voice was polite but firm, his message chilling, even threatening: the government owned that tape, no equivocation. "You can choose to try to sell this tape, if you want," he warned. "But you should know that we believe this is ours, and we always win."

I didn't know how to respond. After all our preparation, I wasn't ready for *this* demand. I did know that we had no intention of simply surrendering something that had cost us so much time, effort, and, by now, substantial money. I also knew that just saying no wouldn't be the end of the matter. Nor did I feel it was worth getting in a fight with the government.

I took a breath and leaned forward. "I hear what you're saying. We'll call you back."

We did, but it took a few hectic days. Researchers and documentarians were pressing for details. Members of Congress called. I gave fifteen or so interviews. On our new website dedicated to the tapes, traffic skyrocketed, a good deal of it coming from a server labeled Executive Office of the President of the United States.

On the legal front, we started a search the night of Gary Stern's call for the right lawyer and found someone within an hour. He went right to work and called the next day with what I felt was good news. The date of our two recordings preceded the Presidential Records Act and the JFK Records Act of 1992, the former of which provided that records of the Executive Branch belonged to the public. Finally, since the president had at that time the right to dispose of anything he wished, if the material that included the tapes had been a gift by the White House Communications Agency at the behest of the executive to General Clifton, it was his to keep and his descendants' to sell as they saw fit. And: "They can't prove that it wasn't. So they would have a hard time laying claim to this material," the lawyer concluded. But I knew from his tone that this wasn't the end of the story. "But that doesn't mean they couldn't make your life difficult and delay the sale." I pointed out that this whole episode was a PR disaster for the government. We'd found something, hidden in plain sight, that they'd failed to find for decades. Why hadn't the searchers contacted Clifton as a possible source concerning the tape? Or had they searched and just didn't find anything in that attic? What else had they missed?

Doesn't all this help us? Isn't this leverage? "Perhaps," our lawyer said. But the government could still tie up any sale for months or even years and cost us untold money in legal fees.

We turned to another important factor, one that might be the real ace up our sleeve: neither the government nor anyone else (except that digitization technician in Pittsburgh) knew that we had *two* identical original tapes from Clifton.

"You know," I said, "we have two of these."

"They don't care about that. They want the original."

"No, you don't understand. I have two originals. They're identical, created at the same time."

Silence on the other end.

Finally he responded, agreeing that this might be a way to resolve the conflict. Over the next couple of days we hashed out the details.

In the midst of our negotiations with the government, I also had my first-ever live studio interview, with CNN's Piers Morgan, in the company of historian Douglas Brinkley, who has since become a friend. On the broadcast, Morgan said, "It's a piece of history. This is the most infamous moment of America's modern history, and you've got all this stuff that no one has ever heard before." Brinkley added, "You can't write about the Kennedy assassination without grappling with the contents of this tape. This is a very serious find." Wonderful to hear. I rolled my eyes fifteen minutes later when, backstage, I overheard an on-air exchange between Morgan and Howie Mandel, who was on hand for some reason. Morgan asked Mandel if he believed me. Mandel answered with one word: "No." He was, he explained, always skeptical of these "found in a box" stories. I'm sure other people are inclined to be similarly skeptical, but such is the hunt. And treasure *is* buried at the bottom of boxes. But I wasn't at the moment in a position to reflect on the bigger picture. The negotiations with the National Archives had me feeling as if I were balancing on a tightrope.

A few days after the original phone call from the archives' general counsel, our lawyer returned his call, revealed the existence of the identical duplicate tape, and made an offer: we'd donate one tape to the National Archives but retain all ownership rights to the other (including the right to sell it).

Wasn't this pretty close to a win-win? We thought so, and a couple of days later, we drove down to our lawyer's office in Washington. We were at one end of the conference table, I at the time in my early thirties, and at the other end were the general counsel and four other representatives of the National Archives, experts in audiovisual materials and history. We'd hired a company from our area with the required antique audio equipment to set up shop in that conference room, and for over four hours we all listened intently to both tapes from beginning to end, checking the transcripts we'd painstakingly prepared. The friendly mood in the beginning—after all, our offer to donate one copy *did* solve their problem—got even better as we progressed. Letting their hair down, the archivists even told me about the feathers we'd ruffled by finding what no one in the government had been able to. By midafternoon it was clear to all that the tapes were real, and that they were identical. The Raab Collection and the National Archives had a deal. The handshakes were heartfelt for everyone in the room, maybe especially for me. The relief on our side was overwhelming.

The sale had been in limbo, but now was clear. The other tape now resides in the National Archives' Kennedy Assassination Records division, housed at the John F. Kennedy Library in Boston, fulfilling its congressional mandate to collect historically important materials. The tape will likely remain locked away in a temperature-controlled vault never to see the light of day again. However, you can visit the

National Archives website, listen to the entire audio contents, and read a summary that cites our "great service in discovering and donating this important historical audiotape to the National Archives."

The emotional power of history is the only reason an audiotape that cost maybe fifty cents half a century ago is worth half a million dollars today; it's the only reason that the duplicate identical tape has been stored by the government in total security forever. We've watched with delight as references to the tape appear in new books, articles, websites, and other ongoing research about the assassination. And who knows, one day someone may find the original raw, unedited four-hour Air Force One tape. Maybe this ultimate crown jewel of JFK research is waiting at the bottom of a different box in a different attic somewhere. Not impossible.

I draw attention to this episode not only for all the abovementioned reasons—that curiosity pays off, that the seemingly unimportant can be priceless—but for what this episode meant in my own journey. This was the highest-profile discovery we'd made. I'd gone up against the US government in my early thirties and come out the wiser, though slightly aged as a result. But I felt, if only for a few days, the entire country, even the world, joined me on my hunt, with the collective forces of the US government behind us, trying to keep up.

PART III

THE MEANING OF HISTORY

CHAPTER 16

The Legacy of MLK

"I recently learned that Raab sold the MLK/Coca-Cola letter attached. We would be interested to learn the sale price and to see if we could be put in touch with the buyer to explore an acquisition of the document," wrote the archivist of the Coca-Cola Company. Yes, Coca-Cola has an archive, and they're on their own hunt, collecting the history of the company. Hidden in this generations-long story is something few know: Coca-Cola played an important role in the civil rights movement.

When I received this letter, it took me a moment to place the sale it referenced. Then I remembered.

Of all the historical figures whose letters and artifacts we buy and sell, Martin Luther King Jr. is among the people I admire the most. It must have been unfathomably hard to be in his position and preach such a message of hope. To take on a biased system that rejects you and say, *I am part of this, we are all in this together*, is remarkable. It takes a heroic restraint and optimism to be able to do that.

Many don't realize that Dr. King was a young man when he rose to prominence and international fame. The fire of youth burns strong in some people, and so it did in King, who'd been awarded the Nobel Peace Prize in 1964, at the age of thirty-five—becoming at that point the youngest to win the award. Ironically, Thomas Jefferson, who owned slaves, wrote the document guaranteeing universal human rights, the Declaration of Independence, at age thirty-three.

So, you might ask, why would anyone want a letter written by King to the Coca-Cola Company? Why would King have even written the letter?

For King, winning the Nobel Peace Prize was a remarkable culmination of many trials, but also a validation of his moral vision of a country united in peace, his embrace of Gandhi's tactics of nonviolence, and his dream of a better future. He was in bed when he heard the news. He flew to Norway to accept the award, arriving at a jubilant Oslo Festival Hall with his wife. He received the medal and sat at his table, losing himself in the symbolism of the moment, thinking of the suffering of the men and women he'd left behind. "I accept the Nobel Prize for Peace at a moment when twenty-two million Negroes of the United States of America are engaged in a creative battle to end the long night of racial injustice. I accept this award on behalf of a civil rights movement which is moving with determination and a majestic scorn for risk and danger to establish a reign of freedom and a rule of justice," he declared, perhaps thinking of the incredible weight that had been placed on his shoulders at such a young age.

It was King who showed me William Cullen Bryant: "Truth, crushed to earth, shall rise again; The eternal years of God are hers; But Error, wounded, writhes with pain, And dies among his worshippers."

And the applicability of biblical verse: "You shall reap what you sow."

And Thomas Carlyle: "No lie can live forever."

And James Russell Lowell: "Truth forever on the scaffold, Wrong forever on the throne; / Yet that scaffold sways the future, and, behind the dim unknown, / Standeth God within the shadow, keeping watch above his own."

King used the legacy of white, English-speaking America to show that racism is against our values, that the civil rights movement would leave a true legacy.

He explained it vividly, showing how Rip Van Winkle, in the story by Washington Irving, slept through an entire revolution. "All too many people," King said, "find themselves living amid a great period of social change, and yet they fail to develop the new attitudes, the new mental responses, that the new situation demands. They end up sleeping through a revolution."

His return to the States after receiving the Nobel Prize was jubilant. But not celebrated by all.

The mayor of Atlanta, Ivan Allen Jr., wanted to honor his city's hometown hero King with a dinner. Allen was a former segregationist who'd changed his views, ended Jim Crow policies, and supported the Civil Rights Act of 1964—the only elected official in the South to do so.

The mayor soon ran into trouble with the King dinner. To honor King, and the civil rights movement, was controversial in the white community, so Allen enlisted the help of one of the city's eminent businessmen, Robert Woodruff. Woodruff had been the president of the Coca-Cola Company from 1923 until 1954, was a major shareholder, and remained on the board of directors. He was the very definition of Atlanta's civic elite and well understood that the city would be humiliated and embarrassed if the white community boycotted this dinner. He also felt a moral obligation to support the effort. Woodruff asked Paul Austin, then the president of Coca-Cola, to call a meeting of local business leaders to urge their support, which Austin did in the strongest terms: "It is embarrassing for Coca-Cola to be located in a city that refuses to honor its Nobel Prize winner. We are an international business. The Coca-Cola Company does not need Atlanta. You all need to decide whether Atlanta needs the Coca-Cola Company."

The work of organizing this event fell to a Coca-Cola vice president, Edgar Forio. The business community came around fast. Not only was the dinner a great success, it was considered a turning point in race relations in Atlanta—a sign of the city's new cosmopolitanism. The event took place at the Dinkler Plaza Hotel on January 27, 1965, and was itself a high-profile example of desegregation, showing off as it did an integrated audience of civic leaders publicly honoring a black man. Among the fifteen hundred in attendance were Mayor Allen and former mayor William Hartsfield; religious leaders including Catholic archbishop Paul Hallinan and Rabbi Jacob Rothschild; Ralph McGill, editor of the *Atlanta Constitution*; academic leaders including Benjamin Mays, president of Morehouse College; and the city's entire business elite.

There were speeches and a performance of the Morehouse College Choir, and at the end of the evening the entire room broke into song, singing "We Shall Overcome." King gave a rousing speech, saying, "The ultimate test of a man is not where he stands in moments of comfort and moments of convenience, but where he stands in moments of challenge and moments of controversy."

It was a triumphant moment for King, but the battle for civil rights was far from won.

Just five days later, on February 1, King was jailed with more than two hundred others after a voting rights march in Selma, Alabama. The Selma-to-Montgomery marches took place the following month. March 7 saw voting rights marchers being beaten at the Edmund Pettus Bridge, a nationally reported incident that included the arrest of current congressman John Lewis. A few days later, civil rights activist James Reeb died after a beating by white racists. Then, on March 25, the marches concluded with an address by King in Montgomery. Only hours afterward, Klan night riders killed Viola Liuzzo while she transported marchers back to Selma.

One week after the Edmund Pettis Bridge confrontation, on March 15, King sat down to write Coca-Cola vice president Forio. King hadn't forgotten Forio's work in bringing together King's hometown community, and thanked him for sponsoring the dinner. He continued:

> I must confess that few events have warmed my heart as did this occasion. It is a testimonial not only to me but to the greatness of the City of Atlanta, the South, the nation and its ability to rise above the conflict of former generations and really experience that

> beloved community where all differences are reconciled and all hearts in harmony with the great principles of our Democracy and the tenets of our Judeo-Christian heritage.

The warmth and openheartedness of the letter, even as King is contending with racist violence and murder, is powerful.

Many years later, I was contacted by Edgar Forio's grandson, who offered to sell me the letter, along with the formal, printed invitation and program for the dinner. I bought the documents immediately and sold them to a man whose extensive collection focused on items that moved him emotionally and religiously. He eventually stopped collecting, and I forgot about the letter.

Then came Coca-Cola's letter to me, and the whole incident flooded back to mind. The Peace Prize, the dinner, the bloodshed, King's grace. The archivist wanted this piece badly, envisioning it as a "very significant item in our collection." It symbolized the night Atlanta took its place as a leader in the civil rights movement, and it showed Coca-Cola at the forefront.

Coaxing collectors to let go of treasured items isn't part of our game plan. These enthusiasts develop emotional attachments to pieces, and I knew this to be the case with the then owner of the letter. He felt a religious attachment to his material and would often say of his collected items, "They speak to me." A common refrain of his was "I must have that." But he was done collecting and thinking of selling.

I called him and he was stubborn. I explained the history of the piece, and Coca-Cola's desire to acquire the letter for their collection. I reminded him that he'd previously expressed an interest in selling his material as he got older, so it wasn't as if I were introducing this subject to him for the first time. He wanted to make money on the piece (he'd paid $20,000), and the numbers there were right. So I waived my commission on the sale and he agreed.

Now King's letter to Forio was heading home. After all, the company had been instrumental in making the Nobel dinner happen, both politically and financially, and they felt it was a proud part of the Coca-Cola legacy. Indeed, it was the centerpiece of a major conference involving the King family and is featured prominently on the company's website, which notes that "the recognition from Dr. King is a very important conclusion to the story" of King and the company.

Now the letter is in Atlanta, at the Coca-Cola headquarters, presumably never to be sold again. The archivist's hunt had paid off. And it had put me back in contact with the letter, which had meant so much to me, reminding me, as Samuel Taylor Coleridge had instructed generations earlier, to "Seek for a teacher that cannot deceive—the voice of the eternal word within them."

That same Nobel Prize has been the subject of some controversy of late. King's legacy has been in the headlines in recent years because of the actions of his children, who've fought very publicly among themselves over how to handle the estate. Fights over money have raised such questions as "Is it appropriate to sell King's Nobel Peace Prize, or his personal Bible, to the highest bidder?" (The Bible was used in Barack Obama's second inauguration.) The dispute over those items went to court, where the group of children who wanted to sell them won the right to do so. Some years earlier, in 2006, many of King's papers were put up for sale by auction at Sotheby's, until wide condemnation of the sale brought it to a halt, and a group of donors raised the money to buy the papers and donate them all to King's alma mater, Morehouse College, in Atlanta. Such disputes wear away the moral weight of the artifacts and documents. Their essence becomes about ownership and value in the strictest monetary sense.

And King's documents sit at a crossroads of our historical and moral histories. These high-profile sales could have happened to few other than King. He's the embodiment of what we admire most in people, and his legacy is universally claimed and protected.

So what should I do if I find a letter or document that shows a beloved historical figure in a potentially unflattering light? And what if that figure was Martin Luther King? That is more than an abstract problem—I faced it quite specifically and dramatically. The experience brought into focus my thinking about our role at Raab as caretakers of history. It was the most significant moral dilemma I've yet faced.

One day I fielded a call from a man, Derek, who claimed his mother, Pauline, had received a letter from Martin Luther King in 1962, and did I have an interest in buying it? He explained briefly that the letter was handwritten by King, itself a rarity, and that it had been sent from prison and was still in its Albany, Georgia, jail-cell return-address envelope. It's real, he assured me. *I'll be the judge of that*, I thought.

He seemed nice. The conversation was short but frank. I invited him to my office. He and his wife lived nearby, in the Philadelphia area, and they arrived that weekend. They must have just come from church; they were a middle-aged, African American couple, he in a nice suit, she in a dress and hat. My father and I were certainly underdressed for the occasion.

Derek was carrying an old leather briefcase with papers in it, or so it seemed to me. He slowly opened the briefcase. He showed me a color photograph of his mother wearing a rather exotic outfit, a long silk robe, hair done up, and frills everywhere. Nothing scandalous, but I don't have a similar photograph of my mother.

Derek told us that his mother and King had known each other for five years, meeting when King was on the road. Derek showed us a picture of his family with Dr. King and had brought a book inscribed by King to his grandmother. What was striking to me was that this man's primary purpose in visiting us seemed *not* to sell any letter. Indeed, he held forth for thirty minutes before showing us the letter to determine its content and authenticity—which, purportedly, was the intent of his visit. He and his family were proud of their connection to King, and he was there to tell their family story.

In November 1961, the Interstate Commerce Commission banned racial segregation at all interstate bus terminals. Civil rights leaders in Albany, Georgia, set about testing that—trying to determine if what purported on its face to be a win for their movement would yield actual results. At first, students answered the call, and nine took the risk.

None were arrested, but the call had gone out. Soon Albany became a hub of racial protest, using, for the first time, the whole panoply of tools the broader movement was marshaling: mass demonstrations, jail-ins, sit-ins, boycotts, and litigation. By December, hundreds had been arrested. Then Dr. King arrived, bringing with him national attention. He was arrested and jailed, then released, then tried in court for, among other things, parading without a permit and ordered back to jail in mid-July. He was again released and rearrested after more protests. King wanted to remain in jail as a symbol of the spirit and resilience of the movement. He later wrote, "I shall never forget the experience of seeing women over seventy, teenagers, and middle-aged adults—some with professional degrees in medicine, law, and education, some simple housekeepers and laborers—crowding the cells."

King would later describe the conditions of the jail cells in Albany: "The cells are saturated with filth, and what mattresses there are for the bunks are as hard as solid rocks and as nasty as anything that one has ever seen. The companionship of roaches and ants is not at all unusual. In several of the cells there are no mattresses at all. The occupants are compelled to sleep on the bare hard steel."

King wrote in his diary, "Thursday, August 2: I learned about President Kennedy saying that the commissioners of Albany ought to talk to the Negro leaders. I felt this was a very forthright statement and immediately dictated a statement to the President commending him on his action." The next day, King wrote, "Friday, August 3: They recessed the court hearing until Tuesday. I still have the feeling it is too long and drawn out and that the people should keep demonstrating no matter what happens."

Derek, who, along with his wife, had come to our offices that morning, finally made his way to the bottom of his pile of memorabilia, a mix of family photos and books, most of which he had no intention of selling but had brought simply to help us understand the family's history. He was seated across from me and reached over the coffee table to hand me first an envelope and then a letter.

I saw that the letter was undated, but that the stamp on the envelope read August 3, 1962. The return address was "Albany City Jail, Albany Georgia." Without the envelope and what already exists in the historical record about the protests taking place at that time, dating the letter would have been impossible. But with those important clues in mind, I took up the letter. The handwriting was distinctive and clearly written by King. I noted the rightward angular script, the looped initial letters of each word, and the typical blue pen that many of King's written communications feature.

The signature was a little bit scribbled. He didn't sign his full name, he signed his initials, MLK. The letter read, in part:

> Here in this dirty, dingy cell, in the Albany jail, my mind, with a sort of instinctive naturalness, turns to the beautiful, sunlit countenance of my Pauline. I had hoped that you would have written me by now. I have written a million times in my mind, and I regret that I am just getting it on paper.

He goes on to discuss the likelihood of his being released in time for their planned assignation, and concludes: "Be sweet, just for you know who."

I put down the letter and looked the man in the eyes. This was not merely a jailhouse letter but a jailhouse *love* letter. Poetic prose written by a man sacrificing his life and suffering the indignities of jailhouse confinement. It's no secret that Dr. King had affairs. I was discovering one just now. The man sitting across from me smiled. Actually, more than that: he beamed with pride. His mother had received a jailhouse love letter from the great Dr. King, with whom she'd had a relationship. Within this man's family, the relationship wasn't scandalous or embarrassing at all. On the contrary, they felt it connected them to the legacy of King, and they were honored by that connection. It was surprising and touching.

Theirs was the living embodiment of a principle I've come to know well: letters have the potential to give us strength, to refresh our minds and lives with inspiration, and to allow us to, as Thoreau wrote, "stand on the meeting of two eternities, the past and future." Derek's family drew strength from their connection to King, and it contributed to their vision of the future.

My father and I sat with the couple and chatted for an hour, mostly about the life of Derek's mother, and the circumstances in which King had met her, visited her, and written the letter. Derek had tried to sell the letter at an auction, but it had failed to sell. Sometimes an item can get buried in an auction catalog. And sometimes you see something in a document that others might not. Both were the case here. Sometimes words from a third party can bury the essence of the original missive.

I saw this letter for what it was: a deeply personal communiqué from a hero of mine at a dark moment in his life. Sexual morality aside, the letter parted the curtains that had partly concealed a man I admired.

I did a quick search online for the text of the letter, and for mentions of the relationship between King and Pauline, and found nothing. Another realization: this wasn't a known letter or a publicly known relationship.

I thought at the time that I might see more in the letter than others because of my personal connection, but I was willing to take a chance, so we paid Derek $25,000, which ended up being more than he would have gotten at auction. Dr. King's letters tend not to be terribly expensive, and we generally sell them in the range of $7,000 to $15,000. But this was different—in so many ways.

Buying the letter was exhilarating, exciting. But it was only the beginning.

I knew that I'd soon be faced with the question of how to handle its sensitive contents. There was also the legal question of copyright—would the often-litigious King family sue me over the letter? By law, if you send me a letter, then I own the letter and I can do whatever I want with it, but the words in the letter still belong to you, since you wrote it. Otherwise, if Robert Frost wrote a poem for you, you could publish it and get all the royalties. Copyrights last for decades after an author's death, then the material enters the public domain. So this letter was still protected by copyright. I could describe it and quote from it, blur portions of a scan, but it seemed prudent not to publish the entirety of the letter on our website.

Copyright was an interesting legal question but mainly a logistical issue, one that I felt confident we could overcome. The real question was the moral one. What were the implications of a dealer, even one sympathetic to the legacy of Dr. King, breaking news of an illicit affair between the man and a woman, expressed during his captivity in jail? I didn't want to appear to be profiting from the tarnishing of King's reputation.

We employed an outside PR firm at the time, something we no longer do, and we discussed this issue. The publicists were quite vocal: they said, this will get you a lot of press. You should run with this—you can do it in a tasteful way. What would this involve? A press release, active outreach to our network of reporters, possible television appearances.

I believed they were right that it would be a successful public relations campaign, in the sense that our firm's name would appear in print. But I was less sure that we wouldn't ruffle feathers and provoke a backlash. I got the clear sense during our meeting that Derek and his family wouldn't have minded at all. They'd even discussed writing a book or authorizing a movie on the life of their mother and the relationship. But I was thinking of the people who still derive inspiration from King. How would *they* feel?

For a week we debated this issue. At times I leaned toward proceeding. I know Karen and my father were on the fence. The PR team put pressure on us, arguing vociferously in favor. But I kept coming back to them with this thought: "Doesn't it feel wrong?" Then Karen asked me, "Nate, how will *you* feel, fielding press calls on this letter?" "Not great," I responded. She looked at me again, tilting her head slightly as if to imply that we had our answer.

"Listen," the public relations folks argued. "We think you're overthinking this."

I turned to them and said simply, "I'm not doing this. I'm the one who's going to be on the receiving end of questions from reporters, whose name is going to be in the paper and face on TV. And it affects the reputation of our business. I won't do it. I don't want to be accused of denigrating King's legacy. I have too much respect for the man, and no good can come of it. It is simply not worth it."

We never publicized the letter. I had conversations with people I thought might appreciate the history behind it and sold it to someone who did. We bought it because we thought it was important and relevant, and we loved the family's story. It taught me a lot about the emotional impact Martin Luther King had on the African American community back then. That an affair might be looked on with such pride, that the letter became a symbol of that affair, and that the letter was cherished—that spoke volumes about how much the man meant to the people he died for. It allowed them to drink from the cup of history in an environment where many of the historical figures we are taught to revere are white and men. Here, they opened the history books and saw their faces reflected back.

This was the first time I came face-to-face with my role in changing the public perception of a person—where I saw the impact I could have on someone's legacy. While King's private relationships with women are well-known, we choose to elevate his legacy in other areas where his actions impact us all directly.

So why write about it now? Setting aside that I no longer own the letter, and my motives for discussing it are not financial but rather philosophical, I think the incident is instructive. We don't pick and choose the acts that come before us. But we can bring the great acts of great people into our lives. So had Derek's family, who transformed this act into one of deep and daily meaning. The context of King's writing this letter reminded me that history is never simple. Living in history, towing the line between the future and the past, is a complex journey, and on that journey, as Thomas Carlyle wrote, "the man who cannot wonder, who does not habitually wonder, is but a pair of spectacles behind which there is no eye."

CHAPTER 17

Andrew Jackson and the Trail of Tears

In the fall of 1829, a Mississippi military man and mail contractor named Major David Haley traveled across Mississippi and Arkansas to the seat of the Choctaw and Chickasaw Indian nations. He met with tribal leaders and councils, sending an unmistakable message to hundreds of Native Americans gathered to hear his ostensibly friendly words. He was bearing an offer—from the president of the United States, Andrew Jackson.

The offer was stark: If they left their vast swaths of ancestral land behind and moved west of the Mississippi River, they'd be given some compensation for their land and receive land in the new Arkansas Territory. If they *didn't* leave, well, then they'd lose their sovereignty and be subject to the laws of each of the states in which they resided as well as of the United States. Haley's implicit threat was that if they remained, he'd do nothing to ensure their safety.

His message, communicated directly to Choctaw chief David Folsom, was designed to be delivered to the tribal council. The message, Haley explained to Folsom, had been given to Haley personally in a letter by President Jackson, and this message must now be read aloud to the assembled audience. "Say to them as friends and brothers to listen [to] the voice of their father, & friend," Jackson's letter read. His reference to himself as the "father" of the Native Americans was common presidential rhetoric, a custom begun by Thomas Jefferson. The letter continued:

Where they now are, they and my white children are too near each other to live in harmony & peace. Their game is destroyed and many of their people will not work & till the earth. Beyond the great river Mississippi, where a part of their nation has gone, their father has provided a country large enough for them all, and he ad[vises] them to go to it. There, their white . . . will not trouble them, they will have no claim to [the] land, and they & their children can live upon it as long as grass grows or water runs, in peace and plenty. It shall be theirs forever. For the improvements which they have made in the country where they now live, and for the stock which they can not take with them, their father will stipulate, in a treaty to be held with them, to pay them a fair price.

Say to my red Choctaw children, and my Chickasaw children to listen. My white children of Mississippi have extended their laws over their country; and if they remain where they now are . . . must be subject to those laws. If they will remove across the Mississippi, they will be free from those laws, and subject only to their own, and the care of their father the President. Where they now are, say to them, their father the President cannot prevent the operation of the laws of Mississippi. They are within the limits of that state, and I pray you to explain to them, that so far from the United States having a right to question the authority of any State to regulate its affairs within its own limits, they will be obliged to sustain the exercise of this right. Say to the chiefs & warriors that I am their friend, that I wish to act as their friend, but they must, by removing from the limits of the States of Mississippi and Alabama, and by being settled on the lands I offer them, put it in my power to be such.

That the chiefs and warriors may fully understand this talk, you will please go among them and explain it; and tell them it is from my own mouth you have . . . it and that I never speak with a forked tongue.

Whenever they make up their minds to exchange their lands . . . for land west of the river Mississippi, that I will direct a treaty to be held with them, [and assure them, that every] thing just & liberal shall be extended to them in that treaty. Their improvements will be paid for, stock if left will be paid for, and all who wish to remain as citizens shall have reservations laid out to cover their improvements; and the justice due [from a] father to his red children will be awarded to them. Again I beg you, tell them to listen. The plan proposed is the only one by which they can be perpetuated as a nation . . . the only one by which they can expect to preserve their own laws, & be benefitted by the care and humane attention of the United States. I am very respectfully your friend, & the friend of my Choctaw and Chickasaw brethren.

Andrew Jackson

In no other policy area is Jackson's legacy clearer and more controversial than in his relations with Native American tribes. In the 1820s, as he cemented his stature as a national figure and potential president, the issues were at full boil. He'd taken the position that the Native Americans were simply residents of a jurisdiction like everyone else, without preexisting rights of ownership of the land. This translated well into Old Hickory's brand of populism, which placed power and sovereignty in the hands of the local people of a state or territory, and if the people of these states wanted these particular neighbors *out*, then so be it. In the election of 1828, Jackson rode to victory in good measure on this platform.

The political situation in which Folsom delivered Jackson's letter to the Choctaw and Chickasaw Indians was tense. Mississippi had joined the Union in 1817, and Alabama had followed in 1819; both were now increasingly filled with settlers as the nation expanded, and conflicts with the Native American tribes of the Southeast had been brewing for years. Older states such as Georgia were in the same situation. These states didn't recognize the boundaries of the autonomous Indian nations—the so-called Five Civilized Tribes, the Choctaw, Chickasaw, Cherokee, Creek, and Seminole nations. The

Native Americans had rejected previous attempts to remove them, though they'd given up large swaths of land in previous treaties.

But Jackson had some reason to hope that the Choctaw would listen to him since they'd fought alongside him in the War of 1812. Indeed, Folsom himself had served under Jackson and the famous Choctaw chief Pushmataha. Folsom had been born to a Native American mother and a white father and embraced Christianity, allowing missionaries to open schools for Choctaw children in the 1820s.

But Folsom was adamantly opposed to the removal of the tribe from their home in what was now Mississippi. Furthermore, he'd already heard from a friendly missionary that the land the Choctaw had been promised in the Arkansas Territory was already being claimed by white settlers.

A tribal council was convened to consider Jackson's words. The older leaders had grown weary of confrontation and were prepared to accept a fair solution. Folsom, who led the younger contingent, rose up in fury at the council meeting, arguing that they should all stay and fight. This was their land.

Folsom rejected this "offer" from Jackson. "The red people are of the opinion that in a few years the Americans will also wish to possess the land west of the Mississippi," he said. "Should we remove, we should again soon be removed by white men. We have no wish to sell our country. . . . Here is our home, our dwelling places, our fields, and our schools, and all of our friends; and under us are the dust and the bones of our forefathers."

But it was not an offer. It was a command. Jackson was undeterred. His State of the Union address just days later argued that the only solution to this problem was to move the Indian nations west of the Mississippi. He'd set his administration's Indian policy, which was based on the instructions given to his agent David Haley just days earlier.

The following spring, he pushed through Congress and then signed the Indian Removal Act, authorizing the forcible extraction of the Native American tribes of the Southeast to federal territory west of the Mississippi, in the area of present-day Oklahoma. Over the following years, the tribes trekked west, sometimes at gunpoint, in what came to be known as the Trail of Tears.

As for Jackson's original letter to the Choctaw and Chickasaw tribes, it was apparently lost to history.

Every summer Karen and I decamp with our daughter to our family cottage in Bar Harbor, Maine, where we spend as much time as possible enjoying the cooler temperatures by the sea. One year, we had another reason beside the heat wave to get there fast. Waiting for us was an oversize, forty-pound box that had arrived via FedEx the day before. The sender was a descendant of a prominent Civil War commander. He'd been riffling through his family inheritance in his attic and looking through some historical "stuff" in a box he'd had for years: some documents, a piece of a flag. About a week before we left Philadelphia, my father had taken the man's first call. He explained that he possessed some items that had been in his family for generations. His direct ancestor was Thomas Ewing, who'd served as secretary of the treasury under William Henry Harrison and then as the nation's first secretary of the interior under Zachary Taylor. Three of Ewing's sons became Union generals in the Civil War, one earning status as one of William Tecumseh Sherman's most trusted commanders. Sherman, the irascible Northern general who brought the pain of the war to the South with his March to the Sea in Georgia in the waning days of 1864, was also the senior Ewing's son-in-law, having married his daughter in 1850. The Ewings, then, were a prominent family in the nineteenth century.

"I've shown this to an auction company," the Ewing descendant told my father, explaining that the company hadn't seemed hugely interested, but had estimated $5,000 for one letter in bad condition, in pieces, apparently signed by Andrew Jackson. That price is consistent with a minor Jackson letter that says nothing of great interest. My father asked for some scans, and from the image sent it wasn't clear what the Jackson letter was. But the other pieces looked interesting enough and included a piece of the battle flag that flew at Union headquarters when Vicksburg was taken, so we thought the money would work when we took everything into consideration. We made an offer into five figures, far more than the auction company was offering, pending final determination of authenticity. So the man sent everything cross-country from his Arizona home to our Maine cottage.

It's a long day's drive from Philadelphia to Bar Harbor, and my mind was on our pending vacation—my kayak was waiting under the house. While we were en route, my father called. He was already up in Maine, and he'd opened the Ewing box with his usual zeal to see what he'd find. You never know what's at the bottom of a box, and each shipment promises something unexpected. He was moderately excited about the flag; a drawing of the general's headquarters; a map of the Vicksburg campaign; and a letter written by Hugh Ewing to his wife announcing the South's surrender at Vicksburg in July 1863, one of the turning points of the war.

In the bottom of the box, my father had found nine shreds of paper scattered, the largest the size of a grossly misshapen index card. One featured the bold signature and accompanying trademark flourish of Andrew Jackson, so this was presumably the letter the auction house had valued at $5,000. What was all this, and what did it mean? Presumably no one outside the Ewing family had seen any of this material since the Civil War. No one outside that family knew it even existed.

"There are just a bunch of pieces of paper," my father explained. "I can't even tell if they all fit together. We'll look at it when you get here. But I can say from the bits and pieces that this seems promising."

When we arrived at the house the box was waiting. I found the fragments of the mystery letter still in Ziploc-style bags. They were not together—the family hadn't realized that they were part of the same document.

I took them to our study, a salon constructed at the front of our late nineteenth-century home. In this very room, more than a century ago, President Grover Cleveland had chaired a cabinet meeting, and notables of the era had sat for drinks, men such as J. P. Morgan, John Jacob Astor, James Roosevelt (FDR's dad), George Dorr, Oliver Wendell Holmes, and Burton Harrison, who'd been Jefferson Davis's personal aide in the Civil War. Back then, our home wasn't a residence, but a private club—the Mount Desert Reading Room—a hub of intellectual thought in the golden age of Bar Harbor. The heavy maroon drapes keep it on the darker side. My parents had replicated the furniture to be historically appropriate of the late-Victorian era. The wood floor alternates between dark walnut and light oak and is one of the more original aspects of the house. The whole room feels a little like a Gilded Age men's club.

I placed the nine pieces of paper from 1829 spread out in front of me like a puzzle. We were going to have to assemble this puzzle before we could begin to understand what we had. This was a challenge, but when I had them set out in front of me in one place, I noticed that the pieces had the same pen and ink markings, the same strength and tone against the paper. The pieces were all the same darker brown, not faded differently piece by piece. They belonged together. The signature was Jackson's: bold and distinctive, large and confident, often larger than any other writing on the page, which fits his character and historical legacy. I called in my father and we immediately sat down at the table and began putting together the pieces of the puzzle. The signature went at the bottom, the date, October 15, 1829, at the top. Okay, that was a start. For the rest, we weren't totally at sea because the script oriented us east-west, and some edges were straight. This one seemed to go here, this one there . . . it took about forty-five minutes to position the pieces and understand where the holes in the paper were. We seemed to have about three-quarters of the document in front of us, the whole about the size of a legal pad. It was indeed a letter signed by Andrew Jackson, and written in the hand of his nephew/secretary.

the only one by which they can expect to preserve their own laws, and be benefitted by the care and humane attention of the United States.

I am very respectfully,
Yr. friend, & the friend of my
Choctaw & Chickasaw brethren

Andrew Jackson

The first fragment of the Andrew Jackson letter we found in the box.

Old Hickory, as he was called, was a political giant for over a generation, either loved or hated by his contemporaries—a divergent assessment that continues today.

A populist military figure, he took power eight years after the death of Napoléon and engendered in his soldiers and many others the same anti-elite veneration that made him both hero and villain, tyrant and man of the people. He wielded his power and influence like a cudgel and, like Napoléon before, knew that the idea of a man, what he represents, can inspire devotion in others. The two of them are decidedly different people, but give truth to the adage that if you fail to see through the great people of the world to the ideas they represent, you won't understand them.

Many collectors today have a Jackson shelf (President Trump among them, in a way: he moved Old Hickory's portrait into the Oval Office in 2017). Anything signed by the man counts, but the details can move the price a full decimal place or even more, with letters of great content selling for more than $100,000. Jackson's material is most valuable, generally speaking, when it displays his command of the executive branch, shows him as the hero of the Battle of New Orleans during the War of 1812, or relates to Native American affairs. People want to see strength in Jackson. If he wrote a letter apologizing for something, that would not motivate a serious buyer. However, that same letter placing blame on the other party, defying him to challenge him again, that would be a nice letter to have. As an aside, I feel the opposite about a letter from Washington, where I would prefer his typically diffident or philosophical style to a blustering arrogance.

As this new puzzle came together, piece by piece, it began to dawn on us that this was no ordinary letter. Damaged as it was, it felt different and evoked an emotional quality that comes with being in the presence of real history. The experience was heightened by the time-consuming reassembly.

Certain passages rang out loud and clear: Jackson was asking Native American tribes to voluntarily leave their lands in the Southeastern states and resettle west of the Mississippi: "Where they now are, they and my white children are too near each other to live in harmony & peace." This sounded like a promise of war. This is when I first learned the story of David Haley and David Folsom and the convening of the 1829 tribal council. The history came rushing toward us. This was clearly the very letter of instruction given to Haley by President Jackson, carried to the Choctaw nation, and now in tatters at the bottom of a box that hadn't been opened in a generation. The content of this letter has been known since Jackson's day from his retained draft, but any historian or collector who has studied these events and the Jacksonian era would have assumed that the final version was lost. Here it was now, though, worn but still speaking to us today of the many hands it had passed through and the many people who'd heard its message almost two hundred years ago.

So what do you do when a document arrives in pieces? This isn't humpty-dumpty. You put it back together.

I called Frank Mowery, the head of conservation at the great Folger Shakespeare Library and our conservator for many years.

Many documents arrive separated at the folds. This is common. Letters or documents are folded, and from that moment it weakens the rag paper or wood pulp that keeps the piece together. Those can easily be put back together, often with no visible sign to an untrained eye. But this was an extreme case. The letter had obviously been errantly tossed in the box, some pieces had gone missing, and it had been left to its own devices. That the letter had survived at all was remarkable—so much gets destroyed and lost to history. Conservators do remarkable work, piecing everything together, placing the pieces on a foundation with paper that seamlessly replicates the original, removing damaging acid, stabilizing materials—whatever is possible to save as much as possible.

But in this dire case? "Frank," I said, "this one is something special, but it's a mess. Real problems." I described in detail what we'd found and then pieced together, and Frank described a relatively new technique that might just work, leaf-casting, which uses a special paper slurry to fill in gaps. When I sent Frank an image of the pieces, he remained optimistic, so I placed each piece in a separate Mylar sleeve, boxed them securely, and sent them on their way.

Frank floated the pieces of the letter in an aqueous solution and allowed the paper substitute to fill in the gaps. This resulted in a piece that is held together by these interstitial connections and resembles the letter as it was written, with the elements missing appearing as blank in the final.

I waited for Frank's return package with great anticipation, and when the box arrived two weeks later, I approached it carefully, because the contents were fragile. The leaf-casting was a success.

This document is a relic of a complicated and unsettling time in American history, an artifact of white dominion over Native tribes. The westward expansion of the nation in the early nineteenth century caused great pain and dislocation for the Native American tribes, and this letter embodied all of that pain. We felt awestruck.

History is not always pretty, or heartwarming—it doesn't necessarily come with a happy ending. But there is real value in preserving it, in listening to the truths that these documents have to tell us. The Jackson letter to the Choctaw and Chickasaw tribes in 1829 illuminates a moment when two civilizations came into conflict, and the Native Americans were subjugated.

I've never before owned a document of direct communication between leaders of two rival civilizations, not nations but civilizations. I expect this will be my last. I say that because the letters of leaders and monarchs we carry, such as one of the king of England writing his counterpart in France, don't reveal a clash of civilizations, but contentions within civilizations. Yet the result of the Haley-Folsom encounter, as often happens, wasn't great for one of those civilizations. Clashes of civilizations usually end in the absorption or defeat of one. The hunt had yielded us this extraordinary moment in that encounter, and in a small way recovering Jackson's letter had allowed us to participate in and feel the power of that struggle.

Understanding this letter was part of my journey to better understand my own hunt. This was a sheet of paper, yes, but it was symbolic of so much more, not just for one person but for a group of people—one whose residence on this continent even predates my family's early arrival in the 1600s. Their subjugation and replacement differs radically from *my* family's experience, which has been characterized primarily by acceptance and assimilation.

I'm sensitive to the pain of this moment for many. We carried a remarkable Ulysses S. Grant–authored letter written forty years after this one in which he comments on the end of Native American civilization. The lifestyle of the Native, he writes, is nearly dead. This Jackson letter was the point of a spear that prodded that lifestyle out of existence. We heard from many proud representatives of Native American tribes, saying nice things about our discovery. It was their own historical find, their chance to draw attention to their story—to participate in the telling of the American story.

The only person who wasn't pleased was the editor of the Papers of Andrew Jackson, who felt the letter put Jackson in an unnecessarily bad light.

History may repeat itself, but historical acts don't. This was unique, and its importance undeniable. For this reason, the condition of the document, which wasn't great, did not detract from the piece or the price we gave it. Rather, it became part of the journey of the document, from Jackson's pen, to Native tribes of the South, lost for generations and in tatters, to our door, reassembled, to a public, national exhibit.

The piece was sold to a private collector for $100,000 and spent a year on display at the National Constitution Center in Philadelphia.

CHAPTER 18

Smuggled Out of Nazi Germany

"Nate, I spoke to a man on the phone who says he has two letters of Albert Einstein relating to relativity. His ancestor was a scientist in Germany at the same time as Einstein. Can you meet with him next week? He'll be in town." My father, on the phone with me, added as an aside, "He says he has some other family papers as well." I hung up and looked at my email, which contained scans of the documents the man had sent. The Einstein letters appeared to be authentic and were spectacular, touching on his greatest discovery, the theory of relativity. But these two letters were just the first glimmers of a much deeper vein of history. Thus began what was for me a rewarding and painful journey. It started with Einstein, but slowly, inexorably, the story grew, and changed, and darkened. This historical discovery would change me.

Georg Bredig, whose name we hadn't before heard, was a prominent German scientist, one of the inventors of the field of physical chemistry and the father of catalytic chemistry. He studied in Leipzig, Amsterdam, Heidelberg, and Zurich, before returning to his hometown of Karlsruhe. Bredig, whose stay at the ETH university in Zurich would overlap with that of Einstein, was part of a vibrant German ecosystem of great scientific and mathematical thinkers that flourished in northern Europe before World War II. In his travels, Bredig had studied and corresponded with many of these thinkers, including Einstein, Max Planck, Robert Koch, Paul Ehrlich, Fritz Haber, Ernst Cohen, and Walther Nernst. Bredig had worked in Amsterdam under the tutelage of Jacobus van 't Hoff, the first Nobel Prize winner in chemistry. In Leipzig, along with his mentors Nobel Prize winners Wilhelm Ostwald and Svante Arrhenius, Bredig had helped found the first stand-alone physical-chemistry lab in the world. His friendship with Arrhenius was close; Arrhenius was the most prominent Swedish scientist of his day and sat on the Nobel Institute's board of voters. He is considered the father of modern climate science.

In this dynamic age of scientific and mathematical discovery—the early decades of the twentieth century—the boundaries between these fields were blurring. Physics, mathematics, thermodynamics, quantum physics, physical chemistry, relativity—all were interconnected, and the scientists all wrote to one another about their latest theories and developments.

A direct descendant of the prominent German scientist sat on my living room couch next to his wife. He opened a worn black suitcase and pulled out the two Einstein letters. I could immediately see they were authentic. Bredig and Einstein both taught at Zurich, and Einstein received his PhD there; Bredig took a keen interest in his younger colleague's work.

The first letter from Einstein was sent from Zurich and addressed "My dear colleague!" It was a long letter, filling one side of a wide sheet of paper, with punch holes on the left that Bredig used to bind his correspondence and other papers. The date was January 20, 1913: "I am very grateful that you have not resented my ill-mannered silence; I can't bring myself to write, unless I have something substantive to say (personal ossification)."

Einstein had issued his theory of special relativity in 1905, with its famed $E = mc^2$ formulation, equating energy with mass and the speed of light, and positing that the speed of light in a vacuum is always constant, and that time and space are not independent, but rather relative, dependent on your position as observer. Now, eight years later, Einstein was working toward what would be his theory of general relativity, incorporating an understanding of gravity and acceleration into his original theory, a step that would change centuries of thinking on the subject.

Einstein's letter discussed a paper Bredig had sent him by Michael Polanyi on the topic of entropy—or disorder in scientific systems. But Einstein saved the crux of the communication for the end. And as I read this letter, I realized what I know now but he couldn't have known at the time. He was presaging his great discovery:

> Scientifically, I am torturing myself now exclusively with the problems of gravitation, whose treatment unfortunately requires more mathematical skill than I can summon up. But I just can't let the thing go.

In this remarkable Einstein letter we see the dogged determination that made him great as he moved closer to his greatest breakthrough, his second theory of relativity. To me, reading the letter felt akin to being with George Washington crossing the Delaware, or Neil Armstrong taking off for the moon. Within months, Einstein would articulate a new way to think of the gravity that separates apples from tree branches and keeps the moon in orbit around the Earth. No forces pull on these objects, he saw. They're merely responding to a curvature in the fabric of space and time—the visual metaphor for this mathematical reality being a bowling ball pressing down into the fabric of a trampoline, pulling smaller objects toward it. In this same way, for example, our sun curves space, holding Earth and the other planets in its orbit. This shocking and profound theory cemented Einstein's reputation.

I was floored. And that was only the first letter.

I pulled out the second from a manila envelope. Written in 1920, it also concerned Einstein's theory of general relativity, which he'd published in 1915. The topic of this letter was how to prove his revolutionary theory—how to test for the predicted effects of gravity on space-time. According to the theory of general relativity, light leaving the sun ought to be shifted into a higher frequency as it leaves the massive gravitational pull of the sun itself, the so-called redshift. Bredig had written to Einstein asking if such a redshift could be measured on Earth, and the answer was no. "One must operate with a 'real' gravitational field, if one wants to solve the real question," Einstein wrote. "As concerns the astrological validity of the matter, so the answer to the question is rather hopeful, thanks to the discovery of the photosynthetic methods of measuring photographic plates." The letter included mathematical formulas and a discussion of clocks in motion running slower than stationary clocks. I knew this was a valuable document as we again see Einstein at work on relativity—a genius grappling with the most difficult and abstract phenomena imaginable. The "photosynthetic" methods he refers to in the letter did eventually prove his theory to be correct, many decades later.

I turned to Bredig and said, "These are great letters. I'd love to buy them both."

"I'm not sure I am ready to part with the second one," he said.

"These things have emotional meaning to him," his wife explained. "He will sell it. He just needs time."

"Don't sell if you're not ready," I answered. "We will buy one or both whenever the time is right."

"I have a few other things I'd like to show you," Bredig said, as an afterthought.

He reached into a second bag he'd brought, which I'd presumed to be his luggage for the overnight. Instead, he pulled out a photograph of his grandfather, sitting among his fellow scientists at the opening of that first physical-chemistry lab in Leipzig, and a couple of objects, a compass for drawing and a box for holding supplies. Bredig brought out a second photo of the same groundbreaking scientists, dressed in women's clothing, clearly horsing around for the camera. He had a letter from Max Planck and another from the famed first director of the Nobel Institute for Physical Chemistry, Svante Arrhenius.

"There's a lot more of this at our house. You should come see," he said, in understated fashion. I made little of it, so entranced was I with the Einstein letters.

We bought the first letter, which he'd apparently come to sell, and left it at that for the moment. He didn't want to sell the other and we never push.

Time passed, and the collection left my mind. Then, months later, Bredig called again. He was ready to sell the second letter. What would we give him? We made an offer; he wanted $5,000 more, and we obliged. We ended up paying slightly more than $50,000 for the two.

Einstein's lifetime correspondence can be roughly divided into a handful of categories: science, and especially the theory of relativity; philosophy and religion—the nature of life and our role in the universe; nuclear proliferation, warning about the dangers and the risk to humanity; and Judaism. He was a supporter of the state of Israel and raised money for Brandeis, the first Jewish American university. Although not religious in the strict sense of the word, he was deeply involved in helping Jews come over from Europe to escape the Holocaust.

Generally speaking, the most valuable Einstein letters are from the first category. And this man had two of them, never before offered for sale.

"Why don't you come down, get the second letter, and see what else we have?"

Who knows, I thought. *Maybe he has a number of Planck letters.*

The Bredigs now live in the rural South, not far from the Tennessee Oak Ridge nuclear facility where the man's father, Max, had worked—a scientist and chemist just like his father, Georg, all those years ago. He picked up my father and me at our hotel and drove us to the family's single-level ranch-style house, a bit dated and set on a lush, wildly overgrown hill. He and his wife weren't young; she sat in the living room watching a television that, like the rest of the decor, seemed vintage 1970s.

We sat down on lounge chairs, and he brought me the second Einstein letter. Magnificent, just as I remembered it. We'd hopefully get six figures for the two relativity letters. Now we went downstairs to see whatever the "rest" of the material was. We'd come for the Einstein and a glimmer of hope that maybe instead of two Planck letters he had five.

He led us to the basement, down thickly carpeted stairs, and I could feel the dampness in the air. He arrived at the last step, turned right, and pushed open a swinging door to expose a large room with fluorescent lights and two small windows letting in a bit of natural light. The smell of age was strong in the room—an overwhelming odor of old paper, like in a rare-book store.

I walked into the room first, looked around, and my eye settled on table after table of books, letters, photos, and objects, from left to right, and ending with a pile almost as tall as I am. The scope of the thing hit me. *This is no group of letters*, I thought. *It's the older Bredig's entire library.*

Here in a basement was a vast collection: thousands of pages of correspondence, meticulously organized. Hundreds of scientific pamphlets, in a variety of languages, that Bredig had assembled during his career. A collection of Bredig's scientific tools, from his laboratory in Karlsruhe. Hundreds of books that Bredig had used for reference, including first editions of many of the great publications—Einstein's first publication of the theory of relativity, for example, and Marie Curie's work on radiation. And hundreds of pieces of correspondence from the great scientists whom Bredig had known or with whom he'd worked. Unknown and unpublished letters, we were informed to our surprise.

It was a treasure trove, as if the man had moved his entire library, his entire life, intact across the Atlantic and set it up here. We later discovered that was exactly what had happened, though under stunning circumstances.

You never know what you're walking into in these situations—what exactly you're going to find. You have hopes, and you base your decision whether to chase something down—to fly to Tennessee to look at a scientific archive, for example—on trust in the person you're dealing with, and a kind of sixth sense that it might pay to go.

My dad and I immediately went to work sifting through the mass of stuff, so much of it that we feared having to extend our trip by days. Now Bredig's heir was bringing out folder after folder of material, and we started to see names we recognized: Planck, the Nobel Prize–winning physicist and father of quantum mechanics, and Fritz Haber, the Nobel Prize–winning chemist, and so many other important scientists we could barely keep track.

Bredig's correspondence with Svante Arrhenius, the chemist and climate scientist, spanned decades and included discussions of the creation of the Nobel Prize. From 1896:

> The great Nobel fortune will go to a fund; scientific work from the entire world is supposed to be supported from the interest. . . . Only the gods know how things will go with the Nobel legates.

They wrote about their families, their work at their institutes, and they gossiped about fellow scientists, touching on many of the latest scientific developments in the early 1900s. That old rascal Planck, for instance, was always changing his mind about his theories, Arrhenius wrote:

> The theories of energy quanta are extremely appealing, but it is hard to follow along especially since Planck frequently makes changes and expresses his doubts about his earlier views. Before the question has been uniformly worked through, one cannot say how far the current hypotheses are feasible or in need of improvement.

Around 1910, Bredig wrote to Arrhenius stating his belief that they were living in a golden age of math and science. Arrhenius, more the pessimist, wrote back to Bredig:

> As far as the mathematical heyday under Planck, Einstein, and others is concerned, I am adopting a skeptical attitude. Next to Lorentz, Planck is the most sophisticated and I have great respect for his achievements. I can remember quite well the time in which he helped us and where he played a useful role because the opponents superstitiously had the mathematical fetish.

Bredig kept announcements of new scientific theories, both in pamphlet and book form, and corresponded with other scientists about the blossoming field of physical chemistry. The archive included pages and pages of complex equations from the first scientist to win the Nobel in chemistry, Bredig's mentor Jacobus van 't Hoff.

The scientific pamphlets were so numerous that they took up ten banker's boxes (cartons roughly twelve by ten by fifteen inches). The books were scattered around the room in loosely organized fashion on old metal bookcases.

An entire world emerged in that dark basement that day—a lost world of intense debate, camaraderie, and world-changing discovery. Einstein in Zurich, Haber in Karlsruhe, Arrhenius in Stockholm, Ernst Cohen and Van 't Hoff in Amsterdam, Max Planck in Berlin, all writing and publishing and pushing one another forward, even as war and conflict intrude; all with Bredig in the middle.

But one ominous letter from Arrhenius provided the bridge to the next chapter in Bredig's life. Brief and not detailed, the letter proved to be a great understatement.

"I know that things are quite difficult for the sciences and scientists in Germany," Arrhenius wrote in the immediate aftermath of World War I. Germany had no money left for such trivialities as science. And for Bredig and the many of his colleagues who were Jewish, things would only get much, much worse.

* * *

The scientific papers occupied three-quarters of the basement room, but in the corner was a whole group that we came to at the very end. Barely had we absorbed the enormity of the scientific archive when Bredig turned to us and said, understated as always, "I have some immigration-related papers too."

He turned to an old wood-topped dining table. From under it, he pulled out ten banker's boxes labeled with words like IMMIGRATION and VISA. Each box contained about three hundred to four hundred documents. I sighed and looked at my dad.

"This man's whole life is here," I said, and it was true. Georg Bredig and his son had been meticulous hoarders of documents and had ordered and organized them, as if they were keeping them for some unforeseen purpose or were perhaps cognizant of how precious they were and how close they had come to losing them.

In April of 1933, two months after Hitler was appointed chancellor of Germany, the regime passed a law ordering the dismissal of any civil servant—including scientists and professors at all universities—who had one or more Jewish grandparents, or who had publicly opposed the Nazi Party. Some saw the writing on the wall and left. Einstein was among them.

Eighteen hundred German Jewish scholars lost their positions, including Bredig, who was forced into retirement that year. Soon after that, also in 1933, his wife died. It must have been a devastating year. At this point the tone of the archive shifted away from science altogether. Bredig, who'd been on a path to earning his own Nobel Prize for work in physical chemistry, published nothing afterward of any consequence. How could he? He had no access to his lab. And his students would not—or *could* not—work with him; he was now referred to as the "Jewish professor Bredig" and accused of making "very significant statements of an un-German and harmful attitude."

Max, his son, had kept every letter his father had sent him, along with copies of all his letters to his father. There were hundreds, all bound together, in chronological order. The record of the terrible history and personal tragedy of the Jews in Nazi Germany was all here in this room, I realized. Bredig was now pulling folders out of boxes about the events of the late 1930s.

In February 1936, an early reference to the tightening vise: "I am canceling all newspapers and radio subscriptions. All this is hardly bearable for me anymore but I am trying very hard to 'keep my composure despite all the hardships.' " Bredig and his son were scholars, steeped in literature in addition to the sciences. They were proudly German. Georg ends his letter to his son with a note on resistance, quoting the great German writer Goethe, insisting that he intends "to stand one's ground resisting all powers." This quote would be taken up later by the only serious German resistance movement, the White Rose group in Munich in 1942.

In November 1936, Georg wrote his son, underlining a crucial word, that he was "of the urgent opinion that for your generation there is no future here and it would be best to go <u>abroad</u>."

Max began to see the world changing around him. In June of the following year, he wrote to his father:

> This week, HH [they often used code and abbreviations to protect the identities of their friends] told me of a new initiative of a small clique which doesn't even know me personally to make my company Jew-free, in order to earn the designation "exemplary firm" [*Musterbetrieb*, the term for Nazi-approved businesses]. . . . If you know something about the question whether a company has to be free of Jews to be an "exemplary firm," please let me know. HH doesn't believe he can employ me longer than January or April considering the cowardice of the relevant people and his own vulnerability.

For Max, this was the end. He found a family willing to sponsor him in Michigan and left, never to return. But his correspondence with his father continued, and it was all in that basement.

On October 22, 1938, Georg reported that his passport had been confiscated. He'd clipped out newspaper articles—all in the archive—which Jews were told to clip and save. One article read, "All passports of Jews of German citizenship have expired as of October 7, 1938. The passports have to be handed in between the 7th and 21st Oct 1938."

This was the end for Georg, though he did not know it. He clung to his German life and German friends, even if they'd abandoned him. But in November 1938, his life in Germany became unsustainable. One of the worst instances of Kristallnacht on November 10, 1938, took place in Karlsruhe, where Georg still lived. He was arrested, along with his daughter Marianna's husband, Viktor Homburger, who ended up at Dachau. The seventy-year-old Georg was forced to stand for an entire day, head against the wall, in a stable in the Gottesaue barracks.

In the weeks and months that followed, the Nazis made life increasingly unbearable for Jews, imposing more and more indignities and restrictions, and Georg sank into a deep depression.

Max set to work to get his father out of Germany. Then salvation. Max had persuaded Princeton University to employ his father, who had made it to Amsterdam.

Hugh Taylor, in Princeton's Department of Chemistry, wrote Max a letter: "I am happy to say that President Dodds is in process of addressing to your father an invitation to accept the position of research associate at Princeton for the period of two years."

This position saved Georg's life. We found no evidence he ever worked a day at Princeton or set foot on the campus. He received no pay. He immediately cabled to accept the offer.

The man's whole life now stood before us. His studies in Leipzig, scores of pages of scientific notations, his books, his love for his children, for science, and even for Germany. His urgent cables, his visa to the United States, the receipts for all his travels.

But the archive and story didn't end there. Far from it. Georg's daughter, Marianna, her family, and many other scientists and friends were still trapped in Europe, mostly in occupied France. Max, dismissed by his father years earlier as a ne'er-do-well but now having proved himself by saving his father, took it on himself to save his sister and other Jews stranded in Nazi territory. His nature was to shoulder such a burden, though it must have deeply pained him to see such horror, be so distant, and have such responsibility for the lives of others.

As we made our way through the collection, I could feel the weight of it, the tragedy. Marianna's family had been dispersed, like so many others, into internment camps. From Camp de Gurs, in southwest France, the family wrote frantically, frenetically, using coded language to avoid the censors, sending letter after letter to Max, who was trying to arrange safe passage to New York. This wasn't a case of each family looking out for its own; this was an emergency in which numerous groups had formed to help get Jewish refugees out of Europe. Money was needed to buy food and supplies to send into the camps, and also to bribe the officials to secure release.

I read the letters Marianna had sent from the internment camp in southern France in 1941. There were notes of hopefulness, including helping the "less well-off Jewish circles":

> This kind of help is not a question of money, the money is easier to find, but more of taking on the responsibility. It is a question of empathy, of participating in the suffering of your fellow humans in the battle against the apathy of the heart.

There was news of friends and relatives, and suicide:

> I also advise you to write to Mrs. Neuburger to get more news about Aunt Vally. I only know, that at the time of the deportation, she was found unconscious on the floors, since she ingested poison.

> She had called up to us on the third floor. We could not get up since we were being deported. Her friends Bibi and her sister, Laso, and Dr. Neumann all have taken their lives.

I took a step back. The beginning of the archive was all science—letters back and forth between the earliest Nobel Prize winners, correspondence with Einstein and Planck and the others, celebrating breakthroughs and discoveries. The end of the archive was of a scramble to survive. I looked behind me at the smiling photographs of chemists and mathematicians, the scientific equipment, the letters from luminaries in Europe, Jewish and Christian. I saw the tremendous care Bredig had taken in assembling his library. And I looked in front of me at the despair, the loss.

This journey had started with two Einstein letters and ended in the tragedy of the Holocaust, the educated Jewish scientific community fleeing a country they loved. I tried to imagine what Bredig, who died in 1944, just four years after arriving in the United States, would have thought had he known what happened to all the Jews left behind. What had happened, for example, to his friend Ernst Cohen, the great chemist who'd helped get Bredig to the Netherlands and who'd been executed at Auschwitz.

I thought of my cousin Jack, whom I'd visited as a child, and who'd made it through the Holocaust. We used to go to his house for seder, and my father told me many times about Jack's extraordinary survival, and the killing of his wife and children right in front of him. Bredig's story felt personal to me.

A few weeks later, Bredig's grandson loaded the archival material in a car and drove up to Pennsylvania. He parked in front of our office, and we carried twenty-five banker's boxes to the elevators. Georg Bredig had been through hell, seen it all, and remarkably the whole archive had been kept together.

Now began the painstaking organization and understanding of the material. We divided the archive in two—a scientific collection and a Jewish Holocaust collection. The scientific material was fascinating, but I couldn't turn away from the Holocaust story, which drew me in deeper and deeper.

One story particularly haunts me.

Eva and Alfred Schnell were friends of the Bredigs'—Alfred was a young chemist. Max received a series of handwritten notes from the Schnells, sent through the Red Cross. They were in hiding on a farm in the Netherlands and used fake last names to conceal their identities. They wrote in vague language since the censors could read the notes, and they were barred by the Red Cross from making political statements of any kind:

> September 30, 1942. Unfortunately still without news for you all. Mom is in a nursing home in Amsterdam. . . . Still clinging to hope.
>
> August 11, 1943. Hope you, Max alright. Although without any news from you. Living in small village to avoid difficulties, helped by friends. Signed Alfred and Eva Escaper
>
> September 22, 1943. Being fairly well, although suffering from submergeritis, recovering slowly, life danger presumably excluded. Maintaining patience notwithstanding another winter before us. Signed Alfred and Eva Kwik

Max worked feverishly to get them out, but fruitlessly. Alfred and Eva were killed in November 1944. Alfred was forty-three, Eva was thirty. According to eyewitnesses, they'd been discovered by Dutch soldiers loyal to the Nazis. They'd been living in a small room under the haystack. Alfred was forced to dig his wife's grave, then his grave, then watched his wife being shot before he too was gunned down.

Less than a year later, Alfred's brother Federico received a letter from a young man who'd been in hiding with Alfred and Eva at the end of their lives. A copy of the letter had been sent to Max and I was looking at it:

August 5, 1945. It is a difficult task to write you this letter. But I feel it not only as necessary to express my feelings of sympathy with you in the loss of your brother Alfred and his wife, but also as a duty of honor to them, whom I have had the privilege to reckon among my best friends, to tell you about them in the time that I lived in close fellowship with them. You will have heard from another friend of Fred's and Eva's, Miss Anny van der Sluys from the Hague, about the horrible circumstances under which their life came to an end, where they were found and where they are buried.

I am a 24 year old student in Theology at the University of Utrecht. On the 5th May, 1943 the Germans ordered all Dutch males who had refused to sign a declaration of loyalty to the Nazi regime to go to Germany for slave labor by the 6th of May. Out of 16,000 students, 11,000 did not go but hid themselves (dived as we call it). On May 21st, 1943, I arrived at my final hiding place, a farm in the village of Oldebrooke, about 15 kilometers south of Zwolle. After a few weeks my boss came home one evening from a visit to his neighbor, an old widow and said to me: "There are a couple of Jewish people living with Mrs. Blaaw and they ask you to visit them some time. They would like to talk to a student."

It was the beginning of a friendship which I shall never forget. They introduced themselves by their Christian names, as they were not anxious to let their family names be known. We got on very well together, we talked and laughed and smoked cigarettes rolled from clandestine Belgian shag.

I see again how we used to sit in the room where Eva and Fred lived. It was about six meters long and five or six meters wide, and had whitewashed walls. It had one window which gave a view on a cornfield. We used to sit at the table, Eva and Fred opposite to each other and facing the window. And so we could sit there together and talk and laugh for hours and forget all about the war and the dangers. They were not at all sentimental in their love, but they could cast a glance at one another in a way which made you feel something of the perfect unity in which they lived

> together. Their greatest fear is that they ever be separated. That has not happened.
>
> I always came from them with new courage. Often we imagined how we should visit one another and stay with each other when peace and normal life, for which they were longing so much, should have returned. Our dreams will never come true. Often I ask myself why they had to die. The only thing I know from experience is that God loves me even when he seems to be chastising me. I pray that you find consolation in this great loss. But you may rest assured that Eva and Fred will live forever not only in the memory but also in that of several of the boys who experienced their friendship and love.

I cried when I read this letter, devastated at the pain of this one family's loss, the brutality, the evil. Just one story among many, in letters no one had read since they were sent, stored in boxes in a basement in Tennessee. I was determined to tell these stories, regardless of the cost. They were stories of bravery, of pain, of hope. I wondered how all this material had survived. How had a Jewish scientist managed to secret his entire library out of Nazi Germany? Georg himself answered the question.

In 1939, before he left Germany, Georg asked his son Max, now in America, for help safeguarding Georg's life's work. He couldn't leave his library in Germany, he said, since it would be destroyed, and he couldn't sell much of it there, either. Could a buyer be found in the States? Perhaps a book dealer would pay for the freight to bring the material over? No such dealer was found. Fortunately, Georg's colleagues at the offices of his old friend the Dutch chemist Jacobus van 't Hoff offered to help: he would store all the material in his laboratory in Utrecht.

When Bredig left the Netherlands for New York, his library stayed behind, surviving the war in Nazi-occupied territory. The family sent for the collection after the war, and it came over on a boat, intact. Now, many decades later, here it was, in my office.

Telling these stories was the largest logistical undertaking of my career. Translating hundreds of letters, in modern and old German, understanding the science and organizing the voluminous correspondence; we employed two scientists and three translators in this process. Georg and Max Bredig had given me a job: to preserve this history, to tell their stories, and to tell the stories of the others. Georg feared that his archive would be destroyed, that his life's work would be lost to history. We sold the archive—the *entire* archive—to the Science History Institute, an international organization devoted to the study of science. Now the stories of the Schnells, the Homburgers, and the Bredigs will be told and not forgotten.

CHAPTER 19

Vein of Gold

I breathed deeply, waiting for Bill Crawford to unlock and open the cabinet. Crawford's great-great-great-great-grandfather was the American statesman William H. Crawford, today largely forgotten but in his time a political figure very much at the center of things.

Bill claimed to have an astounding collection of important documents, so we'd traveled through heat and storm to see it.

I looked at Karen and my father, sitting across the table from me. We were in the Deep South, and Bill was about to answer the question we all had: Was he really in possession of a vast archive and historical treasure—the deepest of all possible veins of gold—or had we wasted a weekend and learned a hard lesson?

The door swung open, slowly, to reveal dozens of black binders, labeled with numbers that corresponded to a list we had in front of us. I opened the first portfolio to see a sheaf of large Mylar sleeves, two letters per sleeve, facing opposite directions, separated by black liners. In a pocket on the inside cover of the binder, Bill had listed each piece and identified it if he was able to, which was far from always. It was a careful and handsome presentation. I removed the first letter from its sleeve, ran my finger over it, held it up to the light, and just took it all in—the blink test, the moment of truth.

* * *

The War of 1812 was the first war declared by the United States, which was then only twenty-three years old. The war was part of a larger conflict—the Napoleonic Wars—taking place in Europe, between France and its allies, and a coalition of nations arrayed against them. America's entry into the war came after a protracted series of blockades and restrictive trade laws imposed by the English and the French, who sought to choke each other commercially. The English seized American sailors and "impressed" them, forcing them into the service of the king. Napoléon hinted he would drop his trade restrictions against America, and that—combined with Britain's continuing maritime hostility and its provocation of Native Americans against the American settlers in the West—pushed President James Madison over the edge. In 1812, he declared war on England.

Many called it the second war of independence against the British; it was accompanied by a resurgence of nationalism and unity and further spurred the movement west. This period saw the emergence of a number of key figures in American history: future president James Monroe would serve as secretary of state and war simultaneously; future president John Quincy Adams came to the fore as a peace negotiator; future presidents Andrew Jackson, Zachary Taylor, and William Henry Harrison rose to prominence with their wartime military leadership, as did Winfield Scott. And the great negotiator Henry Clay would make his first major appearance in international diplomacy.

At the epicenter of the action, stationed in Napoléon's court and receiving briefs from all sides, was William H. Crawford. When John Quincy Adams and Henry Clay met in Belgium to end the war in the waning months of 1814—by negotiating the Treaty of Ghent with the British—they sent their updates to Crawford.

I looked at the letter in my hands, which was from the Duke of Wellington. Wellington, who signed only his last name, was no marginal figure in this war. Along with Harrison, Taylor, and Jackson,

Wellington made his name in this period, defeating Napoléon in 1815 at perhaps the most famous battle in world history, the Battle of Waterloo. This defeat ended the Napoleonic Empire and changed Europe forever. Wellington went on to serve twice as prime minister of England and was a close adviser years later to Queen Victoria.

Wellington's handwriting is difficult to read. So was this letter. His words jumble from one to another with little regard to form. If you look at any single letter alone, you'll find it hard to decipher. But familiar with his handwriting, I managed to read aloud the letter, which Wellington wrote in the third person. In December of 1814, he was Great Britain's ambassador to France at the same time Crawford was there:

> The Duke of Wellington presents his compliments to Mr. Crawford and has the pleasure to inform him that he has just received a dispatch from his Majesty's Plenipotentiaries at Ghent in which they have informed the Duke that they had on the 24th latest signed a Treaty of Peace and Amity with the plenipotentiaries of the United States.

I was thunderstruck at what this letter signified. It announced the signing of the treaty that ended the War of 1812, America's first treaty with a European nation under the US Constitution. The duke continued by stating that the two nations should never have been at war in the first place, that they should have been friends. A wonderful, important letter, with deep insight into the perspective of the British military about the American venture.

Was it authentic? I held it up to the light, looking for ink depth, show-through to the opposite side, watermarks, and evidence that we were dealing with period ink and paper, all skills I'd honed over the previous decade. I looked at the handwriting, which was frustratingly familiar in its scribble. I recognized it from countless other Wellington letters I'd seen.

"This looks good to me," I pronounced.

I turned to Bill and Jane and asked, "Did you know you have an important letter from the Duke of Wellington?"

Bill nodded. The moment was a deep pleasure for both of them. They'd never engaged an official appraisal, but neither had they ever doubted what they had in their possession. I passed the letter to Karen and my father and could see their unspoken excitement.

I pulled out the next document, a letter from Thomas Jefferson describing his first reaction to the end of the war—a letter Bill had told me he particularly liked. Jefferson wrote that in the War of 1812, as in the Revolutionary War,

> [British] conquests were never more than of the spot on which their army stood, never extended beyond the range of their cannon shot. . . . If England is now wise or just enough to settle peaceably the question of impressment, the late treaty may become one of peace, and of long peace. We owe to their past follies and wrongs the incalculable advantage of being made independent of them.

But there was another Jefferson letter that Bill hadn't mentioned. In it, Jefferson gave his vision for the country America should be and attacked the opposing vision and its principal advocate: Alexander Hamilton. Sounding like future president Lincoln, he wrote strikingly that government for the people, rather than central, federal power, would lead to peace and prosperity:

> A government regulating itself by what is wise and just for the many, uninfluenced by the local and selfish views of the few who direct their affairs, has not been seen, perhaps, on earth. Or if it existed, for a moment, at the birth of ours, it would not be easy to fix the term of its continuance. Still, I believe it does exist here in a greater degree than anywhere else.

Jefferson painted the picture of a rural country and wrote that Hamilton was

> a man whose mind was really powerful, but chained by native partialities to every thing English; who had formed exaggerated ideas of the superior perfection of the English constitution, the superior wisdom of their government, and sincerely believed it for the good of this country to make them their model in every thing; without considering that what might be wise and good for a nation essentially commercial, and entangled in complicated intercourse with numerous and powerful neighbors, might not be so for one essentially agricultural, and insulated by nature from the abusive governments of the old world.

This was perhaps the best Thomas Jefferson letter I'd ever seen. The four long pages of perfect Jeffersonian script, in his tight, easily legible handwriting, culminated in his signature, resting thrice the size of the script under the final line.

The next letter: Henry Clay, who'd pushed for war, wrote to Crawford telling him of the burning of Washington: "What does wound me to the very soul is that a set of pirates and incendiaries should have been permitted to pollute our soil, conflagrate our Capital, and return unpunished to their ships!"

John Marshall, America's first great chief justice, had issued an important opinion on the early banking system in the United States and had sent it to then secretary of the treasury Crawford. In this opinion, the only such communication from a chief justice to a cabinet member I'd ever seen, Marshall held that the governmentally chartered Bank of the United States, which issued stock that was sold to investors, could only sell a certain amount of stock each year, and that the government itself could buy that stock. The bank had hoped to inflate the value of the stock and sell it privately, but the government stepped in to buy at the earlier fixed rate. This was during the first major economic crisis in the United States.

I kept sorting, jumping from one binder to the next. There were letters from the Marquis de Lafayette decrying the American practice of slavery, written to Crawford, himself a Southern slave owner; Crawford's signed appointments as secretary of war and the treasury were still with the family, signed by James Madison and James Monroe; the negotiators of the Treaty of Ghent, including John Quincy Adams, had sent Crawford final versions of that treaty, the only such documents, as far as I know, outside the American and British national archives. And there were letters in code, sent from the negotiators in Ghent. John Quincy Adams sent news of British intransigence and gave confidential news on the diplomatic instructions being sent from Washington by President Madison. The code, or number-based cipher, he used for the British: 666. When I pulled the letters out, my hands shook.

Each document was examined and read by each of us, more than three hundred in all. We were in that room for seven hours. We had in our hands nothing less than an entire museum of important pieces, one hidden from the view of scholars (and collectors) for the better part of two centuries—six generations of Bill's family. The content of some of the letters was known, though no one knew where to find the originals. Others were completely unpublished. They'd effectively been lost to history.

As the scope of what we were witnessing sunk in, I casually asked Bill where he'd been keeping all these pieces.

"Oh, they were in a box in my mother's house, and a few years back I put them into binders. I hope you like them." A typical note of self-effacement from Bill.

We offered nearly a million dollars for the collection—every dollar a purely speculative investment, with no guarantee that we could sell enough of the material to recoup the costs. Bill asked for $100,000 more than we'd originally offered. We thought long and hard, knowing that this would be a historically large expenditure for material bought on spec, not on behalf of a customer.

"If we don't buy this material, what are we doing in this business?" I said to my dad.

He approved, but made sure: "Are you comfortable with this level of exposure on this material? If not, we can say no."

Karen was on board.

It fell to me to make the final call: "I want this stuff. I don't want to let this material go."

We met Bill's number and shook hands. I believed in the material and was motivated by it. I felt we had struck a deep vein—a mother lode—and the treasures would both inspire us and prove inspirational to buyers.

Once the deal was done, Bill drove the letters to Philadelphia, where they were immediately deposited in the big safe in our office. There was too much to bring home on the plane.

Now came the heavy lifting. We had to sort through the documents, transcribe and describe each one for our catalog and website. We wouldn't sell these en masse, so what would each be worth on the market? This was a big deal for us, testing our knowledge, experience, connections, connoisseurship—not to mention capital funds. I believed it was win-win all around. Bill and Jane are enjoying their retirement, and we've been proud to have the collection.

We found good new homes for much of the archive. The Newberry Library in Chicago acquired a large collection of correspondence to Crawford relating to negotiating with Native Americans in the South. The College of William & Mary bought forty-five letters of James Monroe as president to his secretary of the treasury, Crawford. Lafayette College bought the Lafayette letters. And to private collectors we sold documents at prices from $10,000 (the Wellington letter) to $325,000 (the Jefferson letter on the War of 1812). We have long since made back our money from the group.

This archive encompassed thirty years of Crawford's life and involved many of the people we consider today to be America's Founding Fathers. It was the white whale, the deepest possible vein of gold stretching below the American landscape. When I picked up those pieces then, and when I think of them today, I feel the pulse of America in them, and I bear witness to the remarkable devotion of these public servants to our country.

With such a large collection, rather than capture a moment in time, you see history play out *over* time. You get depth, personality, tragedy, victory, and extensive context—just as we had in the Bredig archive. But where the latter had been a story that culminated in tragedy, one in which I saw my family's history embodied, this was the story of the American journey, of which my family had equally been a part. I have family who fled the Nazis, and ancestors who fought in the American Revolution. One of my ancestor C. V. Houston's relatives, and therefore mine, fought in the War of 1812. These men and women had died long ago and could no longer speak. But I could give them a voice. My obligation was to understand and tell the stories of the people involved, an obligation I've embraced.

"I have no expectation," Emerson wrote of history, "that any man will read history aright who thinks that what was done in a remote age, by men whose names have resounded far, has any deeper sense than what he is doing today." My journey had begun with a capricious decision to join the business my father started. It had taken me to see framed documents and collections in sleeves. My journey had dropped me with Georg Bredig on a boat escaping from Nazi Germany and being greeted by Lady Liberty holding her torch high and welcoming us into the safety of New York's harbor. My journey had sat me next to Jefferson at Monticello, where I read volume after volume from his great library and debated the vision of what America should be. And it placed me in the Oval Office at the dawn of Camelot with John in his rocking chair and Bobby brainstorming by his side, full of youthful energy, ideals, and glamour and—*snap*—just like that, there I was, aboard AF-1 as I listened, in real time, to the frantic and tragic ending of it all.

My journey had set me at the crossroads of eternity, stretching back into the past and forward into the future, and given me the vantage point of the present, into which it all dissolved. The hunt had gained a depth I could not otherwise have imagined, and a perspective on my own life that only a true understanding of the complexities of the historical human experience can offer. The letters and objects had become a window through which I took my own personal inventory.

Epilogue

I have included in this book a number of references, and not by chance, to great writers of the nineteenth century, from Germany and England but mainly from the United States, during which time a uniquely American literature flourished for the first time. There is energy and insight in youth—the youth of a person, the youth of nations—and the writers of this period capture so much in so few words.

I have a small collection of documents and artifacts from these men, such as Emerson and Thoreau, which aren't for sale, which mirror my enthusiasm and which I cherish without having to fend off others in the commercial marketplace. One such piece is the first edition of Thoreau's first book, *A Week on the Concord and the Merrimack Rivers*, and inside is a quotation handwritten by the author, and beneath it his autograph. Thoreau's autograph is rare, and I have never seen another signed quotation of the author of *Walden*.

Thoreau's poem conjures the past as a vehicle for living in the present and invokes the stones of Carnac, an ancient set of structures in Brittany that was a source of inspiration in the nineteenth-century Age of Romanticism. He writes, in part:

> Where is the spirit of that time but in
> This present day, perchance the present line?
> Three thousand years ago are not a-gone,
> They are still lingering in this summer morn.

The poem ends with the quotation inscribed in my book: "If Carnac's columns still stand on the plain, / To enjoy our opportunities they remain."

Writers in that era were intent on melding the past with the living present, collapsing the two ages. In a sense, though we might frame it otherwise, we're all doing the same thing—we have no choice. We can no more live the past than the future. Rather, ours and others' experiences in the past burn like a fire in the present, or, as Emerson wrote, one aims to "live all history in his own person." To have the past alive within you, but to make your life in the present.

History was all around me from the start, before I was even old enough to absorb it. It thrilled me as a boy when I picked up a bullet from the battlefield at Gettysburg, and when I heard my father tell his stories about the great figures of the past. History began to settle on me in junior high school when I wrote notables for autographs, picked up when I thought I'd give the family business a try, and deepened as I gained knowledge and came into my own. The more I saw and learned, the more momentum I picked up, the more history meant to me.

But I've come to realize that the work I do is not merely a meaningful adventure and is not simply about finding one gem here or there. It's much more than that—it is important. The hunt for history is a journey of discovery, a search for further meaning. Jefferson's pen writes the story of our own lives. Lincoln's wisdom lights our own path. Churchill's courage gives us strength. Einstein's vision compels us to aspire. We live their stories in our own lives.

Owning these documents, these artifacts, touching them, makes history's power vivid, and each discovery allows our hearts and minds to bathe yet again in its light. I am hunting for history, but I am also hunting for myself, and if you have read this book and care about these stories, so are you.

There is so much left to explore. Hidden in attics and basements, hanging on walls, filed away in cabinets of people of all walks of life, all over the world, are treasures we have yet to find. Each day brings new discovery, each email is a call to the hunt, none of them the same: Winston Churchill, Susan B. Anthony, Napoléon, George Washington. As long as we continue to draw inspiration from the great men and women of the past, the hunt will continue, and we will be there.

Acknowledgments

I want to thank the many archivists and scholars who have helped me in my work, in particular Diana Buchwald at the Albert Einstein Papers Project; Thomas Jefferson Looney at the Papers of Thomas Jefferson at Monticello; Barbara Oberg, Linny Schenck, James McClure, and Thomas Downey at the Papers of Thomas Jefferson at Princeton University; Benjamin Huggins at the Papers of George Washington at UVA; David Miller at the Smithsonian National Museum of American History; Brenda Lawson and Sara Georgini at the Massachusetts Historical Society; Gerald Gaidmore at the College of William & Mary; Daniel Preston at the Papers of James Monroe; Douglas Mayo at the Colonial Williamsburg Foundation; Julie Miller, Barbara Bair, Michelle Krowl, and Nathan Dorn at the Library of Congress; Michele Lee Silverman, now at the Folger Shakespeare Library; Lee Arnold at the Historical Society of Pennsylvania; and Robb Haberman and Brant Vogel at the John Jay Papers at Columbia University.

I'm grateful to Janet Benton, who helped me shape the first inklings of the idea of the book you are now holding. For her patience, guidance, and belief in the potential of my story, I thank my agent, Jane von Mehren, and the team at Aevitas Creative Management. Thanks are due to my editor, the brilliant Rick Horgan, whose enthusiasm for this project and wisdom have been critical, as well as to the team at Scribner, including Colin Harrison, Rosaleen Mahorter,

Brian Belfiglio, Ashley Gilliam, Beckett Rueda, and Emily Greenwald, who have helped make this book all it can be. Thanks also to Luke Barr, a great writer, who played an indispensable role in crafting this book and whose advice I've valued throughout the process.

I'm grateful to my grandfather Kenneth Sheppard and my uncle Saul Leibowitz, whose examples of humility and selflessness have set a moral tone that I try to bring to life and business.

I want to thank Neale Lanigan, an expert in autographs and now a minister, who advised my father early in his career, teaching him many of the same lessons my father later taught me, and that I've described in this book.

Thanks to Hadar McNeill, whose work with our firm has allowed me to devote my time and energy to this important project.

My hunt for history wouldn't have been possible without the hard work of my parents, who founded Steven S. Raab Autographs thirty years ago at our dining room table and later welcomed me and gave me their confidence to take the reins of the business. While my father has surely gifted me with more knowledge of history and the hunt than anyone, my mother merits equal thanks for passing along the most important piece of advice I've ever received: take one step at a time and do the job in front of you. It's an approach I've applied numerous times during this project and many others.

And, finally, thanks to my home team: my wife and business partner, Karen, without whom none of this would be possible, and my inspiring daughter, Elizabeth, who I hope will, like Thoreau, work to solve the problems of the surveyor but whose true aim will be the deeper insights in life.

Index

Page numbers in *italics* refer to illustrations.

INDEX

INDEX